Marcus Berkmann has spent in front of various television sc England batsmen. In his leisure time he has written columns on sport for *Punch*, the *Independent on Sunday* and the *Daily Express*. He is a regular contributor to *Private Eye* and is a regular contestant on Round Britain Quiz on Radio 4, and writes book reviews for the *Daily Mail*. His books include *Rain Men: The Madness of Cricket*, *Zimmer Men: The Trials and Tribulations of the Ageing Cricketer*, *A Shed of One's Own* and *Berkmann's Pop Miscellany*.

'There are riches on every page ... go and buy this magical book. It's almost as much fun as scoring a century. Almost.' *Daily Mail*

'This is charming stuff from a writer who has not lost a certain boyish delight in the game or its myths and legends.' *The Times*

'Anyone with the slightest knowledge of the game is likely to find *Berkmann's Cricketing Miscellany* extremely funny.' *Country Life*

'The essential Christmas gift for all cricket lovers.' *Spectator*

'A delightful assemblage of pearls of wisdom and trivia.' *Sunday Times*

'Fantastic stories.' *Radio Times*

'An alternative Wisden, and the perfect thing to have in your kit bag for when rain stops play.' *The Bookseller*

ALSO BY MARCUS BERKMANN

Rain Men: The Madness of Cricket

A Matter of Facts: The Insider's Guide to Quizzing

Fatherhood: The Truth

Zimmer Men: The Trials and Tribulations
of the Ageing Cricketer

A Shed of One's Own: Midlife Without the Crisis

The Prince of Wales (Highgate) Quiz Book (ed.)

Ashes to Ashes: 35 Years of Humiliation (and About 20
Minutes of Ecstasy) Watching England v Australia

Set Phasers to Stun: 50 Years of *Star Trek*

The *Spectator* Book of Wit, Humour and Mischief (ed.)

Berkmann's Cricketing Miscellany

Marcus Berkmann

ABACUS

ABACUS

First published in Great Britain in 2019 by Little, Brown
This paperback edition published in 2022 by Abacus

1 3 5 7 9 10 8 6 4 2

A CIP catalogue record for this book
is available from the British Library.

ISBN 978-0-349-14512-9

Typeset in Times by M Rules
Printed and bound in Great Britain by
Clays Ltd, Elcograf S.p.A

Papers used by Abacus are from well-managed forests
and other responsible sources.

Abacus
An imprint of
Little, Brown Book Group
Carmelite House
50 Victoria Embankment
London EC4Y 0DZ

An Hachette UK Company
www.hachette.co.uk

www.littlebrown.co.uk

To Julian, Richard, Mitch and Steven,
my fellow trufflers

Contents

Introduction

The genesis of this book was an essay I wrote for that splendid cricket periodical *The Nightwatchman*, and that piece arose from a short holiday I took with my friend Julian, who lives in Lincolnshire. Julian used to be a senior civil servant, and he has a mind like a stiletto. We were watching the semi-final of the Champions League on Sky Sports. Pakistan's exciting new fast bowler Rumman Raees came on to bowl.

I looked at Julian. I said the word 'Raees' and then raised my eyebrow, as though to say, 'What other cricketing relevance does that name have?'

It took him, at most, a second and a half to respond.

'The only Mohammad brother not to play Test cricket,' he said. I congratulated him.

'Do you know anybody else who would have got that?' asked Julian, with a big beaming grin.

I thought a moment. 'Only two people. Steven Lynch of ESPNcricinfo, and my friend Richard, who lives in Hampshire.'

Later on, I emailed Richard to tell him of this conversation. He too used to be a senior civil servant, and he has a mind like a sabre. The following day he replied.

'By an astonishing coincidence,' he wrote, 'I was looking at the Mohammad family (which also includes Shoaib, the nephew of the five brothers) yesterday morning just before the start of the game. I'd searched "Raees" on Cricinfo to find out more about Rumman Raees and of course one thing led to another. When I found a Mohammad Raees, who played a single first-class match in the early 1970s for Pakistan International Airlines, I got to wondering whether I could think of any other pairs of cricketers who shared their names in reverse. Unfortunately I didn't get very far because I was forced to start doing some work.'

I'm imagining him in his huge office, drinking incredibly strong coffee and asking his secretary to take dictation, while actually trying to think of cricketers who share their names in reverse. His email continued:

'At a birthday lunch last Sunday, I profoundly impressed an Australian woman by knowing that Wally Grout's full name was Arthur Theodore Wallace Grout. I promise you, it just came up in conversation.'

I have some very strange friends indeed.

Richard has sent me some wonderful emails over the years. He specialises in putting together cricket teams of players of the past with particular characteristics: all called Herbert, maybe, or Test players with fathers who were vicars, or, if he's really in the mood, Test players whose fathers were vicars called Herbert. When he was working at the Home Office in the early 2000s, they moved to a vast and splendid new building in Marsham Street, Westminster. To be precise, it is three connected buildings. The Home Secretary of the time, David Blunkett, decided to run a competition to name the building. Richard suggested they should be called Hobbs, Hammond and Hutton. As he recounts, 'One of the most serious mistakes Mr Blunkett made in his time as Home Secretary was to reject my suggestion and instead to name the buildings Peel, Fry and Seacole after some "social reformers".'

Julian, meanwhile, specialises in sending me fiendish quiz questions, which he has put together while pottering around on Cricket

Archive when he really should be finishing his forthcoming paper on early Windsor armchairs. 'Which England fast bowler in the twenty-first century took ten wickets in an Ashes Test match and was never picked again? Only one man has carried his bat three times in three completed innings in Tests. Who?' Sometimes he gives me the answer before I start gnawing off the handle of my umbrella, and sometimes he doesn't. (The answers are Andrew Caddick and Desmond Haynes.) Here he is on August 5 2016: 'What do Shane Warne, Darren Gough, Harbhajan Singh, Nuwan Zoysa, Stuart Broad and Rangana Herath have in common? Answer: each has taken a hat-trick as a bowler in Tests and also been one of the batsmen dismissed in another Test hat-trick: Warne by Harbhajan, Gough by Warne, Harbhajan by Broad, Zoysa by Mohammed Sami, Broad by Peter Siddle and Herath by Abdul Razzaq.' I'm guessing that a lot of important work went undone on that day as well.

Psychiatrists might wonder why intelligent men waste their valuable time on such rot, but I don't. Julian and Richard are, in their different ways, two of the happiest men I know. I occasionally wonder whether I should introduce them, but I worry that their meeting would cause a vast rip in the space–time continuum, and bring the end of the universe as we know it. The risks wouldn't just be to me and my friendship with them both, but to all humankind.

I had fun writing this up for *The Nightwatchman*: the piece essentially wrote itself. A few days later I got a call from Chris Lane, the man in charge at *Wisden*, who had an idea for a *Cricket Miscellany*, a little like Ben Schott's famous volumes of nonsense but aimed squarely at the crazed cricket fan. He thought I was the man to compile it, and I have to admit, I agreed with him. This book, then, is the result, of decades of enthusiasm, years of reading and months of serious scribbling. I enjoyed compiling it so much that I actually finished it and submitted it a full month before deadline: an unprecedented and almost certainly unrepeatable event.

And it would not have existed without Chris's conceptual powers or his immense generosity, for which I'm very grateful.

Berkmann's Cricketing Miscellany is split into twelve chapters, starting with January and ending, as these things do, with December. This is an entirely arbitrary structure, but it works as well as any. Most of the features I have included have no chronological content at all, and are just thrown in willy-nilly. But some do, as you will find out. The only element that needs a little explanation is my selection of twelve favourite Test matches, for which I give the scorecard and a brief match report. The original idea was to have one a month: the best Test ever played in January, for example, followed by the best ever played by February. But this quickly foundered. There have been no interesting Test matches ever played in May, and I know, because I have checked. And there were four wonderful games played in December. I thought it would be possible to write about some slightly obscure matches in an entertaining manner, but why include some boring match everyone has forgotten and have to leave out Edgbaston 2005? Bonkers. So I abandoned that idea and have just included twelve matches I really wanted to write about, for various reasons, with a maximum of two matches per calendar month. (The two December games that don't make it are the 1982–83 Ashes game, when Allan Border and Jeff Thomson put on eighty-odd for the last wicket and we won by three runs; and the victory in the dark in 2000–01, when England beat Pakistan virtually in the middle of the night, thanks to Graham Thorpe, Nasser Hussain and Steve Bucknor, who refused to take the players off. Maybe next time.)

The book naturally reflects my own preferences and prejudices. It's strongly Anglocentric, because so am I. T20 cricket barely features in it at all, and even one-day internationals are given short shrift. This isn't through snobbery or more generalised disdain, but a feeling that these matches don't last in the way that Tests and first-class cricket do. They are cricket retooled for instant gratification, and thus almost instantly forgettable. (That's not to say I am entirely indifferent to their pleasures. I rather like T20 and have found, to my surprise, that going along to watch a match is much more fun than watching it on TV. A huge six is best seen in the flesh, especially if it's accompanied by fireworks. The opposite is true of ODIs, which are better viewed from the comfort of one's sofa than on a plastic chair surrounded by drunken men dressed as nuns.)

The strongest sense I have had while putting this book together is that I am only scratching the surface of cricket trivia. Every book I have read has unearthed unimaginable joys, and there are many more books to read. I have also been helped immeasurably by the assistance of four of my friends, who have come up with some extraordinary facts, stories, stats and assorted drivel. They are Julian Parker and Richard Corden, as described above; the legendary Steven Lynch from ESPNcricinfo; and the indefatigable trivia hound Mitchell Symons, with whom I have been exchanging daft facts and quiz questions for nearly thirty years. The book would have been appreciably shorter and duller without their contributions.

Julian, for instance, has recently made the acquaintance of Ms Fiona Crampin, granddaughter of Herbert Crampin, once a Grimsby trawler magnate and a keen cricket fan. All the Crampin Steam Fishing Company vessels, he has discovered, were named after cricketers with seven letters in their surnames. Over twenty-five years, from the 1930s to the late 1950s, the Crampin trawlers were as follows:

Pataudi, Bradman, Compton, Hammond, Statham, Trueman, Larwood, Jardine, Yardley, Barnett, Wellard, Padgett, Paynter, Leyland, Hendren, Gregory, Hassett, Pollard.

'A catholic selection, if a trifle odd,' he tells me, 'caused by the requirement for seven-letteredness, the reason for which I have never deduced. Ms Crampin, though a splendid woman in so many

ways, knows little of her grandfather's trawler-naming criteria.'
Richard theorised that maybe Crampin preferred seven-lettered
names because both of his own names had seven letters. All I
know is that I'd rather talk about rubbish like this than do almost
anything else.

Julian actually went a bit further in his researches. He established that both *Hammond* and *Larwood* were sunk by aircraft off
the coast of Norway while in Admiralty Service in April 1940;
and that each were salvaged by the Germans and relaunched under
new German non-cricketing identities. The shame of it! Here's a
photograph of HMT *Hammond* sinking.

And here's one of the *Larwood*'s (British) crew:

If the ships had been named after footballers, would we care? We would not.

I hope, therefore, that you enjoy the following, and if any of it reminds you of some piece of cricketing trivia you feel has been unfairly excluded, please email me at marcusberkmann@macace. net. I have tried to exclude stories I myself have heard too many times before, which may explain some obvious omissions. And I have tried to verify all the stories told, although one or two are simply too good to be left out, whether they are true or not. Do I believe the Jack Crapp/hotel receptionist story, for instance? Not for a moment, but it's a corker.

January

January Birthdays

 3: Arthur Mailey (1886), Alex Hales (1989)
 5: Nawab of Pataudi, Jr (1941), Bob Cunis (1941),
    Marlon Samuels (1981)
 6: Kapil Dev (1959)
 8: Lawrence Rowe (1949)
11: Rahul Dravid (1973)
12: Richie Richardson (1962)
13: Mitchell Starc (1990)
14: Ken Higgs (1937), Martin Bicknell (1969)
15: Ryan Sidebottom (1978)
16: Wayne Daniel (1956)
17: Sir Clyde Walcott (1926)
20: Christopher Martin-Jenkins (1945)
21: Andy Ganteaume (1921), Simon Taufel (1971)
22: Lord Byron (1788)
23: Adam Parore (1971)
26: Kim Hughes (1954)
27: Dean Headley (1970), Chaminda Vaas (1974),
    Daniel Vettori (1979)
28: David 'Syd' Lawrence (1964)
29: Andy Roberts (1951)
31: Brian Bolus (1934), John Inverarity (1944)

Arthur Mailey *(January 3)*

Australian leg-spinner and, according to Neville Cardus, 'incorrigible romantic' who took ninety-nine wickets in twenty-one Tests in the 1920s, including thirty-six in the 1920–21 Ashes series. He also holds the record for the most expensive bowling analysis in first-class cricket. Playing for New South Wales at Melbourne in 1926–27 as Victoria compiled a first innings of 1107 (still a record), Mailey bowled sixty-four eight-ball overs, didn't manage a maiden, and took 4 for 362. He said afterwards that his figures would have been rather better had not three sitters been dropped off his bowling – 'two by a man in the pavilion wearing a bowler hat', and one by an unfortunate team-mate, whom he consoled with the words 'I'm expecting to take a wicket any day now.' R. C. Robertson-Glasgow was an unabashed fan. 'He has always, I fancy, regarded batting as a necessary but inferior part of cricket . . . He is so different from the typical Aussie player of games or runner of races. In Mailey, humour ranks higher than success, kindness above personal triumph.' When he was a young man, he once took the wicket of his hero, Victor Trumper. As he wrote in his autobiography, 'There was no triumph in me as I watched the receding figure. I felt like a boy who had killed a dove.'

Mailey began his working life as a labourer, but later became a writer on cricket, a cartoonist and a painter in watercolours and oils. In London, he had a private exhibition of his paintings, and Queen Mary came to visit. In the main she was gracious and approving, but in front of one work of his she paused.

'Mr Mailey, I don't think you have painted the sun quite convincingly in this picture,' she said.

'Perhaps not,' said Arthur. 'You see, your Majesty, in this country I have to paint the sun from memory.'

Alex Hales *(January 3)*

In 2005 *The Times* reported that Alex Hales, aged sixteen, had scored 52 in an over during a Twenty20 competition on the Lord's Nursery pitch organised by the London County Cricket Club. He had hit eight sixes, three of them off no-balls, and a four.

Bob Cunis *(January 5)*

A New Zealand all-rounder who appeared in twenty Tests between 1965 and 1972. On *Test Match Special*, Alan Gibson once said, 'This is Cunis at the Vauxhall End. Cunis, a funny sort of name. Neither one thing nor the other.' You wouldn't get away with that nowadays.

Kapil Dev *(January 6)*

'An all-round cricketer of charismatic brilliance' was Christopher Martin-Jenkins's pithy assessment. Kapil Dev was the first man to score five thousand runs and take four hundred wickets in Tests. Not so long ago, filmmakers were shooting a film in Hindi about Kapil's finest hour, the 1983 World Cup win. The actor playing Kapil was born in 1985.

Lawrence Rowe *(January 8)*

Elegant West Indian batsman who scored 214 and 100 not out on debut against New Zealand in 1972, and 302 against England a couple of years later. Michael Holding said he was 'the best batsman I ever saw'. But it didn't quite work out for Rowe. In 1974 he played for Derbyshire and suffered crippling headaches and hay fever. The following winter the West Indies sent him home from their tour of India after problems with his eyesight. Finally the problem was resolved: he was diagnosed with a severe allergy to grass. By any standards that's bad luck for a cricketer – it's like a restaurateur having a severe allergy to food.

Rahul Dravid *(January 11)*

Until 2003, India hadn't won a Test in Australia for twenty-three years. But at Adelaide that year Australia were beaten by four wickets, despite scoring 556 in the first innings. This was mainly due to Rahul Dravid, who made 233 and 72 not out, batting for nearly fourteen hours in all. In his autobiography, Steve Waugh describes the innings as 'poetic, with flowing follow-throughs ... His head was like the statue of David, allowing for perfect balance and easy hand-eye co-ordination.' Which is rather more lyrical than we are used to from the old bastard, but as Rob Smyth explains, 'the historian in Waugh recognised that beautiful moment when a player moves from very good to great, and knew it should be marked accordingly'. Maybe he's not such an old bastard after all.

Richie Richardson *(January 12)*

Often wore a watch while batting. But oddly enough, never looked at it. I think it was his way of telling fast bowlers that he was better than them, that they weren't going to hit him, and that, on the contrary, he was going to hit them, all around the ground. The maroon sunhat he wore in preference to a helmet may have enhanced this impression. As he scored 5949 runs in eighty-six Tests at 44.39, and is now Sir Richie Richardson, it all seems to have worked rather well.

Christopher Martin-Jenkins *(January 20)*

In *Wisden* 2013, Mike Selvey wrote an appreciation. 'Only once did I see him flummoxed. Like many cricketers, I used rhyming slang by habit, so if I were to say that someone was having treatment on their Vanburn, you might surmise Holder, or shoulder. During one commentary stint, he thought he would have a stab. "I've been having some trouble with the old Conrad," he said. At first it stunned me, and then I corpsed – so badly I had to leave the commentary box. He meant Conrad Black. I am sorry to say my only thought was of a former West Indian opener by a different surname.'

Andy Ganteaume *(January 21)*

Slow-scoring West Indian batsman – a beautiful rarity in itself – who has one of the strangest Test records of them all. In 1947–48, England came on tour. Ganteaume played for Trinidad and scored 101 and 47 not out, but was criticised by observers for scoring too slowly in decent batting conditions. In a second match against the tourists, he scored 5 and 90 but was not selected for the Test match that followed. Ganteaume claimed that his non-selection was a result of his underprivileged background, and not his inability to get the ball off the square. But Jeff Stollmeyer was injured and Ganteaume was brought in to replace him at the last moment. He opened the batting and scored 112 in his only innings. But again he was criticised for slow scoring, was dropped for the next Test and never played again. His only innings of 112 thus gives him the highest average in Test history.

Lord Byron *(January 22)*

Romantic poet with a club foot who, despite his infirmity, batted at number seven for Harrow in the very first Eton vs Harrow match, at Lord's in 1805. Possibly because he was a peer, he was allowed a runner. According to F. S. Ashley-Cooper, 'Harrow men object strongly to this match being counted as one of the regular series of games between the two sides. It was, in all probability, a holiday fixture arranged between Lord Byron, acting for Harrow, and Kaye, for Eton.' According to the Harrow captain John Arthur Lloyd, 'Byron played in that match, and very badly too. He should never have been in the eleven, if my counsel had been taken.' Harrow scored 55 and 65 to Eton's 122 and lost by an innings and 2 runs. Byron would later write, 'We have played the Eton and were most confoundedly beat; however it was some comfort to me that I got 11 notches the 1st Innings and 7 the 2nd, which was more than any of our side except Brockman & Ipswich could contrive to hit.' The scorecard has him making 7 and 2. There was no further match between the schools until 1818, when the (still extant) annual fixture began.

Kim Hughes *(January 26)*

Captain of Australia for twenty-eight of the seventy Tests he played, Kim Hughes played two glimmeringly good innings (117 and 78) at the 1980 Centenary Test at Lord's, but is now mainly remembered for bursting into tears during the press conference at which he resigned as captain. Hughes was much mocked for his lachrymosity, which was considered unmanly and not strictly Australian. How things have changed in the intervening years. Nowadays it is almost compulsory for Australian captains and coaches to blub as they hand in their resignations. Hughes's only sin was to lose a few Test matches. Pioneers so often find themselves unfairly scorned.

Chaminda Vaas *(January 27)*

Sri Lanka's best-ever opening bowler was born Warnakulasuriya Patabendige Ushantha Joseph Chaminda Vaas, and as such is the only Test cricketer in all history to have more initials than letters in his surname. (Unless you know better, of course.)

Nicknames

Cricket has a long and honourable tradition of giving daft nicknames to its more able practitioners. Many, of course, are either very obvious or slightly more obvious than that. Allan Lamb, for instance, spent years being addressed as Legga. Countless others have just had the letter Y appended to their surnames. Andrew Strauss was known to many as Straussy, while Dominic Cork was widely addressed as Corky. Sometimes this formula produced less than comfortable results, such as Ian Bell's nickname, Belly. And Kevin Pietersen was always going to be KP after someone tried Pieterseny and decided it wasn't quite the thing.

Here, then, are some of the more inventive nicknames cricketers have been given, with explanations where they are available. Some are so brilliant (see Z) that no explanation is required. My favourite nickname of those I have heard on the field of play was given to a guy with the surname Vickery, who played for a team called the Weekenders. He was universally known as 'Morty'. (More tea, Vickery?)

Shahid Afridi: *Boom Boom*
Hit the ball very hard indeed. The Duckworth Lewis Method recorded a song called 'Boom Boom Afridi'.

Jonathan Agnew: *Spiro*
After the 39th Vice-President of the United States. (Who may have taken the 'vice' part of his job title too literally.)

Shoaib Akhtar: *The Rawalpindi Express*
Because he's very fast and he comes from Rawalpindi. My friend Chris Douglas, who also played for the Weekenders, used to be known as the Islington Express for similar, if slightly more satirical, reasons.

James Anderson: *The Burnley Lara*
Because, despite being so hopeless with the bat, he avoided being out for 0 in each of his first fifty-three Test innings. (He has made up for it since.)

Warwick Armstrong: *Big Ship*
The Australian captain for the 1920–21 and 1921 Ashes was 6 foot 3 inches tall and weighed over twenty-one stone.

Michael Atherton: *FEC, Cockroach*
FEC is an acronym, reportedly written on his locker, that stands either for 'Future England Captain' or 'Fucking Educated C***'. The Australians, less bothered by class, called him Cockroach for his durability as a batsman.

Trevor Bailey: *The Boil, Barnacle*
Barnacle because of his dedication to the forward defensive. The Boil because of the way supporters from the East End of London are supposed to have pronounced his name. 'Come on, Boiley!' they would shout, flinging their non-existent flat caps into the air.

David Bairstow: *Bluey*
Because he had red hair. Do keep up at the back.

Gareth Batty: *Nora*
After the character in *Last of the Summer Wine*, which all cricketers watch religiously.

Ian Bell: *The Shermanator, The Sledgehammer of Eternal*
Justice, The Duke of Bellington.
Shane Warne called him The Shermanator after a red-haired geeky
character in the film *American Pie*. The Sledgehammer of Eternal
Justice, by contrast, is the greatest nickname ever given to anyone
in the history of the world.

Ian Botham: *Beefy, Guy the Gorilla*
See Warwick Armstrong. When he was younger his friends had
another nickname for him: Bungalow, a reference to the fact that
he had nothing upstairs.

Geoffrey Boycott: *Fiery*
According to one of his many autobiographies, he's Fiery because
Fred Trueman was 'Fiery Fred' to most fans and all headline
writers. And since Boycott also came from Yorkshire, he must be
GeofFiery. Which was shortened to Fiery after Trueman's retire-
ment. If you believe that, you'll believe anything.

Stuart Broad: *Westlife*
He was so good-looking, he had to be a boyband singer. 'Come
on, Westlife,' shouted Matt Prior, 'give us a ballad!' You probably
had to be there.

Andrew Caddick: *Shack*
From Caddy, to Caddyshack (a film about golf starring Bill
Murray), to Shack.

Michael Clarke: *Pup*
Because when he joined it, he was the youngest player in the Australian team. He was still called Pup when he was the oldest player in the team.

John Crawley: *Creepy*

Graham Dilley: *Picca*

Allan Donald: *White Lightning*
Partly because of his exceptional pace, but also his predilection for smearing white zinc cream on his nose and cheeks.

J. W. H. T. Douglas: *Johnny Won't Hit Today*
Nicknamed by Australian hecklers infuriated by his glacial progress at the crease.

Rahul Dravid: *The Wall*
In his own (slightly boring) words: 'I can't remember exactly the first time but I know where it sort of came out from, where it originated. I think, it probably came out after one of my long, typically maybe boring innings; when I saw the headline, [it read] "The Wall".'

Phil Edmonds: *Goat*
Suggests an overwhelming fondness for the ladies. But our lawyers inform us that this was not so. The very thought. (Could it, instead, be an acronym: Greatest Of All Time?)

Steven Finn: *The Watford Wall*
For his resolute defensive batting as a nightwatchman in a Test in New Zealand.

Andrew Flintoff: *Freddie*
After Fred Flintstone, the first cartoon character ever to share a
bed with his wife on American television.

Joel Garner: *Big Bird*
Not, as it has been widely assumed, named after the character in
Sesame Street, but after Jamaica's national bird, the Doctor Bird,
which is known for its stilt-like legs.

Sunil Gavaskar: *Swoop*
So named by Ian Botham when playing for Somerset in 1980, for
his stark refusal to dive in the field under any circumstances.

Chris Gayle: *World Boss, Universe Boss*
Rare among these nicknames in that Gayle gave them to him
himself. Universe Boss is a recent upgrade from World Boss.
'Who wouldn't want to be me?' he asked in his autobiography,
Six Machine.

Ashley Giles: *The King of Spain*
Giles ordered some mugs to be made for his benefit year, with the
words King of Spin printed on them. The printer made a mistake.
Juan Carlos I was said to be less than impressed.

Jason Gillespie: *Dizzy*

John Gleeson: *CHO*
An acronym for Cricket Hours Only, as that was the only time you
ever saw him.

David Gower: *Lubo, Stoat, Dregsy*
Lubo is after his favourite steak bar in Adelaide. Stoats are reputed
to be randy little buggers (*see also* Phil Edmonds). Dregsy, though,

is the best. It was given him by his friend Gary Lineker, who noticed his tendency, after a big dinner, to go round all the tables after everyone had left and drink all the wine people hadn't finished. Does he still do this? I do hope so.

Umar Gul: *Guldozer*

Michael Holding: *Whispering Death*
Because you couldn't hear him as he ran up to bowl. Unusually, he was given this nickname by umpires, who are The Men Who Know.

Merv Hughes: *Fruitfly*
The biggest Australian pest.

Michael Hussey: *Mr Cricket*
Because of his encyclopaedic knowledge of the sport. He is said to dislike the nickname, finding it 'a bit embarrassing'.

Anil Kumble: *Jumbo*
Coined by Navjot Singh Sidhu. One of Kumble's balls really took off, and Sidhu (at mid-on) shouted, 'Jumbo Jet!' The 'jet' fell away, the Jumbo remained.

Gavin Larsen: *The Postman*
He always delivered.

Darren Lehmann: *Boof*
In Australian slang, boof means head, and is typically used to refer to someone with a big head. Lehmann himself says that as a twelve-year-old he had a huge bouffant hairdo, and the name stuck.

Dennis Lillee: *FOT*
When he'd just started playing for Western Australia, his captain Tony Lock called him over and said, 'Dennis, you're bowling like a flippin' old tart.' Do we believe he said flippin'?

Clive Lloyd: *Super Cat*
Long arms, sinuous demeanour, fielded like a panther. *See also* Phil Tufnell.

David Lloyd: *Bumble*
Because of an apparent similarity between his facial profile and those of the Bumblies, characters in an ancient kid's TV show created by Michael Bentine.

Glenn McGrath: *Pigeon*
His New South Wales teammate Brad McNamara, on seeing his skinny pins, said, 'You've stolen a pigeon's legs, McGrath.'

Ken Mackay: *Slasher*
An extraordinarily obdurate defensive batsman. Such a perfect nickname, no one ever called him anything else.

Ashley Mallett: *Rowdy*
In his own words: 'When I first came to Adelaide from Perth in 1967, I was 12th man for the first match. Not a word did I utter unless I was answering a question from one of the players. After pouring the drinks at the close of play on day three, the keeper, Barry Jarman, walked past me, stopped abruptly, turned and yelled: "Shut up, you rowdy bugger!" The nickname stuck.' Chris Tavaré was also nicknamed Rowdy, for similar reasons.

Vic Marks: *Skid*
Not one to think about too closely, this one.

Mitchell Marsh: *Bison*
Someone on a tour game glued his head on a picture of a bison and it fitted perfectly. (The nickname Swampy had already been taken, by his father Geoff.)

Rodney Marsh: *Bacchus*
Tragically, not because he likes a drop, but because there's a place called Bacchus Marsh in Australia.* As Frank Keating once commented, '"Romney" might have been slightly more original.'

Christopher Martin-Jenkins: *The Major*
Mike Selvey: 'There was nothing secret to it, nothing to do with a military bearing, or clipped diction and moustache to match. One day he blustered his way into the press box. "Hampshire won," he announced to nobody in particular. "Did it, Major?" we chorused, echoing Basil Fawlty. And so The Major he became.'

Glenn Maxwell: *Big Show*
Apparently he hates this nickname, which is presumably why he was given it.

Keith Miller: *Nugget*
Constantly described by journalists as 'the golden boy' for the way he lit up cricket in the immediate post-war years. Hence Nugget.

Don Mosey: *The Alderman*
So named by fellow *TMS* commentator Brian Johnston, in recognition of his rather mayoral demeanour in the box.

---

* The parents of double Booker Prize-winner Peter Carey ran a motor business in Bacchus Marsh.

Tim Murtagh: *Dial M*

Phil Mustard: *The Colonel*

Paul Nixon: *Badger*
'Sometimes they call me The Badger, because I'm mad for it,' said Nixon. Andy Bull called him 'the most abrasive and irritating cricketer to play for England since Dominic Cork'.

Chris Old: *Chilly.*
From 'C. Old', i.e. cold.

Ricky Ponting: *Punter*
Likes a bet on the horses.

Matt Prior: *The Cheese, The Big Cheese*
According to Kevin Pietersen, Prior used to refer to himself in the third person as The Cheese or The Big Cheese. In KP's autobiography, he dedicated an entire chapter to ridiculing Prior's nickname. It was entitled 'Le Grand Fromage'.

Derek Randall: *Arkle*
After the prominent racehorse, as a tribute to his skill and agility in the field. Randall called himself Rags, which had been his childhood nickname (for ragamuffin). He would talk to himself while batting. 'Come on, Rags. Get stuck in. Don't take any chances. Take your time, slow and easy. You idiot, Rags. Come on, come on. Come on, England.' Drove the opposition round the bend.

Barry Richards: *Glue*
Acquired for standing his ground after being apparently caught at the wicket during Australia's 1966–67 tour of South Africa.

Greg Ritchie: *Fat Cat*
Not a slender man, our Greg. *See also* Ian Botham.

Paul Romaines: *Human*

Harbhajan Singh: *The Turbanator*

Robin Smith: *Judge*
His crinkly hair looks a little like a judge's wig.

Andrew Strauss: *Levi, Johann, Muppet, Lord Brocket*
The first two are appalling puns on his surname. Muppet was simply an insult, and Lord Brocket came about because he was posh. (Brocket was on a TV reality show, and Marcus Trescothick saw a slight resemblance.)

Mark Taylor: *Tubby, Tubs*
See also Greg Ritchie.

Jeff Thomson: *Two-Up*
From a famous gambling haunt in Sydney, Thommo's Two-Up School.

Marcus Trescothick: *Banger*
Trescothick is famously keen on bangers and mash for his lunch. 'Sausages were my favourite,' he wrote in his autobiography. As a schoolboy he ate 'sausages, chips, sausages, toast, sausages, baked beans, sausages, cheese, sausages, eggs, sausages and the occasional sausage thrown in, topped off with a sprinkling of sausage'. (*The Trescothick Diet* is available from all good bookshops, price £9.99.)

Phil Tufnell: *The Cat*
Because he slept all day and went out all night. *See also* Clive Lloyd.

Michael Vaughan: *Virgil*
Because (it is said) he resembled the similarly named *Thunderbirds* puppet. Oddly enough, anyone who has seen any of his numerous TV appearances might have gained the distinct impression that Vaughan is held up by strings.

Max Walker: *Tangles*
From his strange, wrong-footed bowling action.

Mark Waugh: *Junior, Afghan, Audi*
Junior because he's a few minutes younger than his brother Steve. Afghan because he didn't get into the Australian side for many years despite scoring mountains of runs: hence the forgotten Waugh. Audi, after the car-maker with the four-circle logo, because in 1992–93 he was out for four ducks in a row. (If he'd been out for a fifth, his team-mates told him they would have called him Olympic.)

Steve Waugh: *Tugga*
Also, at Somerset in the 1980s, dubbed Melon, because of his habit of encouraging the team's fast bowlers with the phrase 'Come on, hit him on the melon.'

Monde Zondeki: *All Hands*

(N.B. In real life Danish Kaneria only had one underwhelming nickname, Nani-Danny. In our house, however, he was always known as Pastria. I'll get my coat.)

Julian's XIs

My friend Julian is a clever man and a master of procrastination. He knows he should be working, and indeed, most of his friends he calls up and chats to for half an hour know he should be working too. Like most experts in his field, he finds distractions: things to do that feel a bit like work, and aren't. For one joyous month as I was starting this book, his distraction took the form of creating cricket elevens out of real cricketers, some of whom lived a long time ago, and all of whom had odd names. It started with his Freshwater Fish XI, and went on from there. This is research at its most abstruse and its most abstract, done for its own sake and also for the sake of not doing something else more urgent. Here's the first:

Freshwater Fish

1	B. Zander	(Stoke d'Abernon)
2	A. Tench	(Nairobi Club)
3	A. B. Shad	(Whittingham and Goosnargh Second XI)
4	Rudd	(Royal Military Academy Sandhurst)
5	A. Roach	(Botany Bay Second XI)
6	Perch	(West Kent Wanderers)
7	Pike	(Dorsetshire and Devonshire Regiment Colonel's XI)
8	E. Guppy	(Bootle Nomads)
9	G. W. A. Chubb	(Border, South Africa, Transvaal)
10	W. Gudgeon	(Stoke d'Abernon)
11	H. Grayling	(Wokingham Oaks and Acorns, Wokingham Third XI)
12th man	J. W. Bream	(Leicestershire Second XI)

The Village Year

Summer starts early in village cricket. By January, we have most of the following season's fixtures wrapped up and tied with a bow. Some fixtures secretaries like to have all theirs done by October, which is a little too keen for me. My preferred technique is laissez-faire. I do nothing until people contact me, most of them by email, although a handful of ancients still use the wind-up telephone. We like to play once a weekend every weekend between the end of April and the end of September, which means twenty-three or possibly even twenty-four games in all. Some fixtures have the exactly the same weekend every year; others move around the schedule like wills-o'-the-wisp. A new fixture, I find, needs about three years to bed in properly. The first year is a blind date: you're both trying to see whether you have anything in common at all, and probably attempting to seem nicer than you really are. The second is the difficult second date. Fundamental differences in the way you both play will start to emerge. The third year is the decider. Is there a long-term relationship to be considered, or are you merely two ships passing in the night?

Most years, though, putting together a fixture list is a little like knitting with spaghetti. Some sides have strict hierarchies of teams they want to play. If they like you they'll give you a plum July or August fixture. If they've gone a little cold, you'll play them in freezing late April or soggy September. (If you're only offered April 15, you know you're in Last Chance Saloon.) Other teams give you the same weekend every year, which is great, but every six years or so will want to shift the game forward a week to bring their calendar back into line. Which is fine, but every team has a different year for shifting forward a week. The fixture secretary's problem is best summed up thus: how many teams have you arranged to play on the first Sunday in July? If it's one, or even two, there's room for manoeuvre. If it's seven you might be in trouble.

February

February Birthdays

1: Graeme Smith (1981)

2: James Joyce (1882)

3: Lord Harris (1851), Bill Alley (1919), Bobby Simpson (1936)

5: E. H. 'Patsy' Hendren (1889), Brian Luckhurst (1939),
   Darren Lehmann (1970)

6: Albert Trott (1873), Fred Trueman (1931)

8: Mohammad Azharuddin (1963)

9: Jim Laker (1922), Glenn McGrath (1970)

10: John Hampshire (1941), Michael Kasprowicz (1972)

11: George Deyes (1879), E. W. Swanton (1907), Bill Lawry (1937)

12: Gundappa Viswanath (1949)

13: Ted Pooley (1842), Len Pascoe (1950)

14: Chris Lewis (1968)

15: Desmond Haynes (1956)

16: Michael Holding (1954)

17: AB de Villiers (1984)

18: Phillip DeFreitas (1966)

20: Eddie Hemmings (1949)

21: Michael Slater (1970)

22: Devon Malcolm (1963)

23: Harry Pilling (1943), Herschelle Gibbs (1974)

24: Brian Close (1931), John Lever (1949), Derek Randall (1951)

25: John Arlott (1914), Farokh Engineer (1938), Stuart MacGill (1971)

26: Sir Everton Weekes (1925), Matt Prior (1982)

27: Graeme Pollock (1944)

28: Tim Bresnan (1985)

29: Alf Gover (1908)

James Joyce *(February 2)*

Cricket obsessive (in his youth) who managed to squeeze the names of thirty-one famous cricketers, and many cricketing terms, into a single page of his modernist masterpiece *Finnegans Wake* (1939). 'She had to spofforth, she had to kicker, too thick of the wick of her pixy's loomph, wide lickering jessup the smooky shiminey.' There are two in there. Later on: 'Goeasyosey, for the grace of the fields, or hooley pooley, cuppy, we'll both be bye and by caught in the slips for fear he'd tyre and burst his dunlops and waken her bornybarnies making his boobybabies.' And two more in there. (For the second, see February 13.)

Bill Alley *(February 3)*

Substantial Australian all-rounder who had flourished for many years in the Lancashire Leagues before signing for Somerset in 1957, aged thirty-eight. In 1961 he scored 3019 runs – he will be for ever the last man to score three thousand runs in an English summer – and took sixty-two wickets. 'On and off the pitch,' his *Telegraph* obituary told us, 'Alley was a tough, highly talkative competitor, very much in the Australian mould.' He found a worthy opponent in Fred Trueman. One time he drove Trueman's first ball and hooked his second, both for four. It was, said Alley, 'a gesture tantamount to tickling a bush snake. Fred reacted with two bumpers, the crowd booed, and at the end of the over I set them off again by striding down the pitch with bat raised. Fred played along by striding out to meet me halfway. Suddenly the fans grew very quiet as they saw Fred push his face into mine. And out of the corner of his mouth came the promise, "First pint's on me tonight, Bill".'

E. H. 'Patsy' Hendren *(February 5)*

Only one batsman, Jack Hobbs, hit more centuries than Hendren's 170. Only two, Hobbs and Frank Woolley, scored more runs than Hendren's 57,610. Hobbs said he was 'as good a player as anyone'. Hendren shares the record (with John Wright of New Zealand) for the most runs ever hit off a single ball in Tests – eight. He hit the ball towards the boundary and was coming back to complete an all-run four when the Australians tried to run him out. The ball missed, and whizzed off to the boundary for four overthrows.

Sir John Betjeman once rhymed his surname with 'rhododendron'.

Albert Trott *(February 6)*

Dual international for Australia and England, who is believed to be the only person ever to hit the ball over the Lord's pavilion, on July 31 1899. Some 119 years later, I was at Lord's with some friends when this fact came up in conversation, and we agreed that knowing this distinguished the true cricket tragics from the half-interested, the uncommitted, the johnny-come-latelies. Trott was the pre-eminent all-rounder of his age, and in his benefit match in 1907 took two hat-tricks in the same innings. Unfortunately, this remarkable feat (which only one other person has managed since) shortened the match, and Trott didn't make as much money from it as he had hoped. Later he said he had bowled himself 'into the workhouse'. In 1914 he wrote his will on the back of a laundry ticket, leaving four pounds and his wardrobe to his landlady. Then he shot himself.

Jonathan Trott claims to be a distant relation of Albert Trott, as would we all if we were given the chance.

Fred Trueman *(February 6)*

In the words of John Arlott, 'He argued with authority. He used a vivid vocabulary. He could be harsh and gentle; witty and crude; unbelievably funny and very boring; selfish and wonderfully kind. And he was, when the fire burned, as fine a fast bowler as any.' In his own words, 'To be a great fast bowler, you need a big heart and a big bottom.'

Trueman played his first Test match against India at Headingley in 1952, and opened the bowling with Alec Bedser. When England took the field, Trueman strode up to Bedser, who was playing his 39th Test and had carried England's pace attack since the war. 'If you keep them quiet at one end,' he said, 'I'll get the bastards out.'

In 2005 Trueman's biographer Chris Waters attended a summit meeting in a pub of the Four Greatest Living Yorkshiremen, Brian Close, Ray Illingworth, Geoffrey Boycott and Trueman. 'To say that it was one of the most bizarre experiences of my journalistic career is an understatement,' wrote Waters in *The Nightwatchman*. 'I tell you what,' said Trueman, hungrily devouring a plate of steak pie. 'I'd like to see Steve Harmison or any of that England lot bowling on the f***ing flat pitches of the West Indies in the 1950s.' Says Waters, 'I could have used any number of conversational examples from that day, but the gist of his gab was that everything to do with modern cricket was crap and that he and the old days were the best things since sliced bread ... Most bizarre of all was when the conversation turned to the comedians Ant and Dec, who were given even shorter shrift than Twenty20 cricket. "Ant and Dec? Ant and f***ing Dec?" expostulated Trueman, nearly bringing up his steak pie in the process. "They're not fit to lick the boots of Morecambe and Wise."'

At birth, Fred Trueman weighed 14lb 1oz.

Jim Laker *(February 9)*

According to Amol Rajan in *Twirlymen*, 'Laker's best attribute as a bowler was ferocious, devilish, air-munching spin. It was said that even in Test matches, with packed crowds, you could hear from the boundary the rip he gave the ball.' 'A craftsman in a great tradition,' wrote Neville Cardus. 'Laker goes down in the history of cricket as a classic exponent of off-spin – the most classic of all kinds of bowling.'

The evening after he had taken nineteen wickets in a Test at Old Trafford, Laker drove away from the ground and headed for London. He stopped off at a pub in Lichfield for a pint. All around him, the pub was abuzz with chatter about the Test result. And yet, sitting there sipping his beer and eating a cheese sandwich, hours after producing the greatest bowling performance of all time, he wasn't recognised by a single person.

Glenn McGrath *(February 9)*

Before the 2005 Ashes series, McGrath was asked what he thought the result would be. 'I think I was saying 3–0 or 4–0 about 12 months ago, thinking there might be a bit of rain around,' he replied. 'But with the weather as it is at the moment I have to say 5–0.'

George Deyes *(February 11)*

Right-arm fast bowler who played seventeen matches for Yorkshire between 1905 and 1907. He may not have been the most accomplished batsman in the county's history: in 1907 he recorded the following sequence of scores: 0, 0, 0 not out, 1, 1 not out, 0, 0, 0, 0, 1 not out, 0, 0, 0 and 0.

E. W. Swanton *(February 11)*

'The doyen of English cricket writers,' wrote Scyld Berry in a magnificently waspish obituary for the *Daily Telegraph* in 2000. Berry mixed extravagant praise with more coded messages about the old thug and bully. 'He was High Church and, occasionally, high-handed. When he was at the peak of his powers, he would deliver a close-of-play summary on *Test Match Special* which was as lucid and authoritative as his prose.' Before he delivered it, he needed a whisky on the rocks to lubricate his throat. 'Woe betide the cricket ground which did not have any ice.'

He didn't go to Australia in 1932–33, but if he had been there, he said that Bodyline simply wouldn't have happened. Instead his reading public had to rely on 'lesser mortals who could not report the game to readers in England with his lucidity and authority'.

And: 'When he travelled to the West Indies ... he alone of the cricket correspondents had to have a bunk bed on the flight to North America. Pakistan and India were not countries he toured: when England went there, the late Michael Melford of the *Sunday Telegraph* had to cover for him.'

I may just have been too young to appreciate him fully. But in the early 1990s, when he was in his eighties, he continued to write a weekly column for the Telegraph that was unequalled in its blistering pomposity and, often, complete wrongheadedness. To the end he remained obsessed with where players had gone to school. I'm sure he was delightful in person and never less than kind to small furry animals, but I suspect that no cricket writer before or since has done so much with so very little.

Bill Lawry *(February 11)*

Defensive opening batsman and Australian captain of the 1960s, who somehow mutated into the most excitable and sometimes deranged commentators of the modern age. Of many memorable commentary moments, my favourite came when England were touring and Phil Tufnell, not celebrated for the excellence of his fielding, was stationed at fine leg. The batsman hit a high one straight at him. If he was going to move at all, it would only be to get out of the way. Lawry had only four words to say:

'Tufnell!' (As he realised that Tufnell was underneath the catch.)

'TUFNELL!' (As he realised that Tufnell was more likely to spontaneously combust than take the catch cleanly.)

'YEAH! TUFNELL!' (As Tufnell took the catch.)

You don't get better than that. Well, you do, but not often. (See October 6.)

Ted Pooley *(February 13)*

Surrey and Middlesex wicketkeeper of the 1860s and 1870s who gained something of a reputation as a trickster. F. B. Wilson, in *Sporting Pie* (1922), wrote thus: 'Pooley would take a ball on the leg side and turn round as if he had missed it altogether: off would go short leg and short slip running hell-for-leather to save the four byes. The batsman would look round, see them tearing after the ball and run. Pooley, with eyes at the back of his head and the ball in his hand, would swing round and stump him. He got quite a lot of wickets that way.'

Pooley should have been England's first-ever wicketkeeper, but for an unfortunate incident. In 1877 England were undertaking their first tour of Australia, but first they went to New Zealand, where they were to play Eighteen of Canterbury. The night before the match, the teams met in the hotel bar. Pooley offered to take one pound to a shilling that he could name the individual score of every member of the local team. As Alfred Shaw writes, 'It is a trick familiar to cricketers, and in the old days of matches against local eighteens and twenty-twos it was not infrequently worked off against the unwary.' In this case a local cricketer called Ralph Donkin took him up on the bet. Pooley then said that everyone on the local team would make 0. He would receive a pound for everyone who did and pay out a shilling for everyone who didn't. The match featured eleven scores of 0 – not unassisted, one would guess, by Pooley himself, who was injured and therefore umpired. After the match Pooley claimed £9 15s (a substantial sum) from Donkin, who refused to pay, as he felt he had been cheated. A fracas ensued. It was Pooley's alleged assault on Donkin that led to his arrest in Otago, and although he was eventually found not guilty and freed, by then the England team had gone to Australia to play the first Test match. Pooley never played for them again.

Michael Holding *(February 16)*

In 1976, Bob Woolmer faced Michael Holding at the Oval on the flattest of flat wickets, just after Viv Richards had scored 291. 'Holding's feet hardly touched the ground as he ran in. He moved in silkily and his body swayed like a cobra's: it would have been magnificent had I been watching from the outside ...

'He bowled, and I moved back and across. I saw that the ball was pitched up, so I moved forward, feet first, and then into the shot.

'Before I knew it, the ball had smashed into my pad. Even though I was wearing state-of-the-art buckskin pads, the pain was so incredible that I thought I had been shot.' Dickie Bird was a not-outer as an umpire, but this ball would have knocked middle stump out of the ground. The finger went up.

Five years later, in the third Test on England's tour of the West Indies, Holding bowled one of the most ferocious opening overs anyone had ever seen. Geoffrey Boycott was the lucky recipient:

'The first delivery was short of a length and gloved me, bouncing well in front of the slips. The second was short and I played and missed as it bounced. The third nipped back and hit me on the inside of the left thigh. The fourth bounced and I played it down in front of gully. The fifth was an action replay of the fourth. The sixth plucked my off-stump crazily out of the ground.'

In his diary that night, Boycott wrote, 'For the first time in my life, I can look at a scoreboard with a duck against my name and not feel a profound sense of failure.'

AB de Villiers *(February 17)*

'He is the most complete batsman of the modern era,' Simon Hughes wrote in *The Cricketer* on AB's retirement from international cricket in 2018. 'He is a player for all seasons and formats. He can adapt his game to any requirements. As a result of his diverse sporting background he is completely ambidextrous and has total 360-degree range.

'This is the guy who has the fastest one-day international fifty (16 balls) and fastest one-day hundred (31 balls) and yet also is capable of stonewalling for four hours for 33 runs (and no boundaries) to save a Test match against Australia . . .

'Furthermore, he is devoted to the team.' And everyone around the world gnashes their teeth and thinks, shame it's not our team.

Harry Pilling *(February 23)*

A sound, nudging-and-nurdling number three batsman for Lancashire who played 323 first-class games between 1962 and 1980, Harry Pilling was always known as 'Little 'arry Pillin'' to the TV commentator and former spin bowler Jim Laker. In the *John Player League* Annual for 1973, there exists a photograph of Clive Lloyd (6 foot 4 inches) standing with and towering over Pilling (5 foot 3 inches). The caption reads 'The long and short of Lancashire cricket.'

Brian Close *(February 24)*

Maybe Yorkshire's greatest-ever captain – a judgement he would be unlikely to dispute – Close first played a Test match in 1949 at the age of eighteen years and 149 days and remains England's youngest-ever Test player. Then, in 1976, he was recalled to face the ferocious speed of the West Indies at the age of forty-five, and remains England's oldest Test player since the 1940s. The interval between his first and his last Tests, twenty-seven years, is the second-longest of all time, after Wilfred Rhodes.

In all that time, though, he played just twenty-two Tests, never scored more than 70 and averaged 25.34 with the bat. He captained England seven times in the late 1960s, won six of them and drew the other, and was then fired for time-wasting in county cricket. (The MCC pompously said that his 'temperament had been shown lacking'.) He was renowned as a gambler on the field, and a hard man, often fielding at short leg, shoving his immense bald head right under the batman's nose. 'A cricket ball can't hurt you,' he once said. 'It's only on you a second.' Mike Brearley also played in those West Indies Tests of 1976: 'Fielding in direct line of fire at short square leg, he whispered to me at backward short leg: "He'll have a lap [sweep] in a minute. I'll get in t'road, and you catch t'rebound." And he meant it.'

Brian Close always ate fish and chips on Friday, and is believed to have smoked two million cigarettes in his lifetime: roughly sixty-eight a day for seventy years.

Derek Randall *(February 24)*

My favourite cricketer of all time. In 1976–77, on tour in India, he ate caviar for the first time. 'Hey, Greigy!' he announced. 'This champagne is all right, but the blackcurrant jam tastes of fish.'

Mike Brearley's nickname for him was 'Twazzock'.

For his 174 in the Centenary Test in Melbourne in 1977, Randall became the first person ever to win the Man of the Match award in a Test match.

John Arlott *(February 25)*

Former Hampshire policeman – he rose to the rank of sergeant – who resigned in order to take a job at the BBC as an overseas literary producer, taking over a desk vacated by George Orwell. When Bradman played his final Test at the Oval in 1948 and was out second ball for 0, Arlott, then aged 34, was commentating. These were his words:

'I wonder if you see a ball very clearly in your last Test in England, on a ground where you've played some of the biggest cricket in your life, and where the opposing side has just stood round you and given you three cheers, and the crowd has clapped you all the way to the wicket. I wonder if you really see the ball at all.'

As Simon Barnes wrote, 'To catch a great sporting moment with such perfection, and to do it in the very instant of its passing, is genius, nothing less.'

In 1958 Arlott was looking to expand his horizons and write about football too. He asked the *Guardian* if he could cover Manchester United's European Cup quarter-final against Red Star Belgrade. The *Guardian*'s football correspondent Don Davies was having none of it and made sure he went instead. He died in the Munich air disaster, along with half the Manchester United team.

When Arlott was retired and Ian Botham lived near him on Alderney, Arlott would ring him up and say, 'Come round. And bring your thirst.'

Farokh Engineer *(February 25)*

My friend Richard, a Lancashire fan, grew up in the 1970s and was obsessed with Clive Lloyd and their Indian wicketkeeper, Farokh Engineer. His father was a senior bank official in Singapore at the time and commissioned a boat to be built, and named *Marianne* after his wife, Richard's mother. He was less than impressed when he discovered that Richard had secretly written to the boatbuilder and instructed him to rename it *Farokh Engineer*.

In 2017 rumours of Farokh's death began to circulate on social media. The rumours were incorrect. 'Friends, I am alive and kicking,' said Farokh. 'I am very well and let me tell you, I don't even need Viagra at 78.'

Everton Weekes *(February 26)*

Here's Harry Pearson, one of my favourite comic writers, from his book about the Northern leagues, *Slipless in Settle*:

'Weekes spent seven seasons at Bacup in the fifties, scoring 9069 runs for them at an average of 91.61, and including twenty-five centuries. He wore an Army and Navy greatcoat even on what the locals considered the hottest summer days and lodged in Gordon Street, where the landlady, Mrs Sharrold, fed him up on meat-and-potato pies. Weekes got his Christian name because his father supported Everton. When the West Indian told Shipley-born Jim Laker this, the off-spinner replied that it was just as well his dad hadn't been a fan of West Bromwich Albion.'

While Weekes was playing for Bacup, Frank Worrell was at nearby Radcliffe and Clyde Walcott was at Enfield. Every Saturday night the three of them would meet up at a chip shop in Clayton-le-Moores, which was owned by Jack Simmons's Aunty Bertha.

Tim Bresnan *(February 28)*

Writing about him in *Wisden* 2012, when he was one of the Five Cricketers of the Year, Tanya Aldred called him 'a novelist's fast bowler: straight-talking, uncomplicated, northern, broad ... And though there's not much spare on him now, he still has the air of a man with an emergency cheese sandwich in his back pocket.'

Uncorked!

In 1921 the Australian leg-spinner Arthur Mailey took all ten Gloucestershire wickets for 66 runs, including that of a boy called Walter Hammond. A mere thirty-seven years later he published his autobiography, which he entitled *10 for 66 and All That*. Was this the ur-pun, the first piece of appalling wordplay that changed cricketing publishing for ever? I doubt it. I suspect that since the first Grace brothers crawled out of the primeval ooze, cricketers have been writing and publishing memoirs with disastrous puns in their titles. Not that I am entirely innocent of this myself. In 2009 I wrote a book about the Ashes, which I called *Ashes to Ashes*. It sold about as many as the 7458 books called *Ashes to Ashes* previously published, and the 2396 books called *Ashes to Ashes* published since.

Other sports have not been unaffected. In 1978 the diminutive footballer Alan Ball published a memoir called It's *All About a Ball*. All about A. Ball. Geddit?

Curtly Ambrose: *Time to Talk*
From a bowler who rarely said anything.

Michael Atherton: *Opening Up*
Which he doesn't, really.

Richie Benaud: *My Spin on Cricket*
Stares out of the cover with a twinkle in his eye as though to say,
I know this is a terrible pun, and I don't care.

Henry Blofeld: *Cakes and Bails*
Literally beyond a joke, situated in that far-off land where humour
goes to die.

Henry Blofeld: *Squeezing the Orange*
What on earth does this mean? (*See* Derek Underwood.)

Henry Blofeld: *Over and Out*
On his retirement from *Test Match Special*.

Geoffrey Boycott: *Opening Up*
He did it before Atherton.

Geoffrey Boycott: *Put to the Test*
Testing times (geddit?) in Australia in 1979–80.

Geoffrey Boycott: *In the Fast Lane*
Tour book of the West Indies in 1980–81.

Dominic Cork: *Uncorked!*
Exclamation mark suggests slight desperation of premature
autobiography.

Chris Cowdrey: *Good Enough?*
No.

Basil D'Oliveira: *Time to Declare*
The most aggressive thing about this book was its title.

Godfrey Evans: *The Gloves are Off*
They have been on for so long, you probably don't want to be in the same room as them.

Graeme Fowler: *Fox on the Run*
Nickname was Foxy.

Graeme Fowler: *Absolutely Foxed*
Nickname still Foxy.

Sunil Gavaskar: *Sunny Days*
Nickname Sunny. Personality less than sunny.

Chris Gayle: *Six Machine*
The nearest thing to a double entendre in the entire book. Gayle is more of a single-entendre man.

Brad Haddin: *My Family's Keeper*
The wicketkeepers' titles are definitely the worst ones here.

Matthew Hayden: *Standing My Ground*
He wasn't out, whatever anyone might say.

Ian Healy: *Hands & Heals*
Sorry, what? (*See* Brad Haddin.)

Michael Holding: *No Holding Back*
It was either that or 'The Bowler's Holding . . . '

Alan Knott: *It's Knott Cricket*
Wrong again. (*See* Brad Haddin.)

Brian Lara: *Beating the Field*
See Derek Underwood.

Darren Lehmann: *Worth the Wait*
It wasn't.

Vic Marks: *Marks Out of XI*
A tour book of the 1984–85 winter, during which Vic didn't play much. Almost too clever for its own good.

Javed Miandad: *Cutting Edge*
Also quite clever, and probably chosen for its cleverness rather than its appropriateness.

Paul Nixon: *Keeping Quiet*
Couldn't.

Matt Prior: *The Gloves Are Off*
Same as Godfrey Evans! (*See* Brad Haddin.)

Yuvraj Singh: *The Test of My Life*
Had nasty cancer. Happily, got over it.

Paul Smith: *Wasted?*
Yes.

Malcolm Speed: *Sticky Wicket*
Administrator finally talks. Sadly, no one reads.

David Steele: *Come in Number 3*
Your time is up.

Alec Stewart: *Playing for Keeps*
Dear God. (*See* Brad Haddin.)

Andrew Strauss: *Driving Ambition*
Probably better than Nibbling Ambition or Nurdling Ambition.

Graeme Swann: *The Breaks are Off*
Both ingenious and, somehow, pitiful at the same time.

James Taylor: *Cut Short*
Career cut short. Also, was short batsman who liked the cut. You're doubled over with uproarious laughter, aren't you?

Mark Taylor: *Time to Declare*
D'Oliveira got there first. (But at least Taylor was a captain, so he did declare from time to time.)

Sachin Tendulkar: *Playing It My Way*
If the book is anything to go by, that's the blandest, most uncontroversial way possible.

Jonathan Trott: *Unguarded*
Took about twenty minutes to take his guard before every ball. Book a bit like that too.

Fred Trueman: *Ball of Fire*
Wouldn't Great Balls of Fire have been better? Actually, probably not.

Shaun Udal: *My Turn to Spin*
Two puns in four words: pretty impressive.

Derek Underwood: *Beating the Bat*

I can't entirely rid myself of the suspicion that, somewhere in the English-speaking world, this is a teenage euphemism for masturbation.

Favourite Tests

Dunedin, February 8, 9, 10, 12, 13 1980

NEW ZEALAND vs WEST INDIES: First Test

West Indies

C G Greenidge	c Cairns b Hadlee	2	—	lbw b Hadlee	3
D L Haynes	c & b Cairns	55	—	c Webb b Troup	105
L G Rowe	lbw b Hadlee	1	—	lbw b Hadlee	12
A I Kallicharran	lbw b Hadlee	0	—	c Cairns b Troup	0
*C H Lloyd	lbw b Hadlee	24	—	c Lees b Hadlee	5
C L King	c Coney b Troup	14	—	c Boock b Cairns	41
†D L Murray	c Edgar b Troup	6	—	lbw b Hadlee	30
D R Parry	b Boock	17	—	c & b Hadlee	1
J Garner	c Howarth b Cairns	0	—	b Hadlee	2
M A Holding	lbw b Hadlee	4	—	c Cairns b Troup	3
C E H Croft	not out	0	—	not out	1
	lb 8, nb 9	17		lb 4, nb 5	9
		140			**212**

1–3, 2–4, 3–4, 4–72, 5–91, 6–105, 7–124, 8–125, 9–136, 10–140

1–4, 2–21, 3–24, 4–29, 5–117, 6–180, 7–186, 8–188, 9–209, 10–212

Hadlee	20–9–34–5		Hadlee	36–13–68–6
Troup	17–6–26–2		Troup	36.4–13–57–3
Cairns	19.5–4–32–2		Cairns	25–10–63–1
Boock	13–3–31–1		Boock	11–4–15–0

New Zealand

J G Wright	b Holding	21	—	b Holding	11
B A Edgar	lbw b Parry	65	—	c Greenidge b Holding	6
* G P Howarth	c Murray b Croft	33	—	c Greenidge b Croft	11
J M Parker	b Croft	0	—	c Murray b Garner	5
P N Webb	lbw b Parry	5	—	(6) lbw b Garner	5
J V Coney	b Holding	8	—	(5) lbw b Croft	2
†W K Lees	run out	18	—	lbw b Garner	0
R J Hadlee	c Lloyd b Garner	51	—	b Garner	17
B L Cairns	b Croft	30	—	c Murray b Holding	19
G B Troup	c Greenidge b Croft	0	—	not out	7
S L Boock	not out	0	—	not out	2
	b 5, lb 2, nb 11	18	—	b 7, lb 5, nb 7	19
		249		**(9 wkts)**	**104**

1–42, 2–109, 3–110, 4–133, 5–145,
6–159, 7–168, 8–232, 9–236, 10–249

1–15, 2–28, 3–40, 4–44,
5–44, 6–44, 7–54, 8–73,
9–100

Holding	22–5–50–2
Croft	25–3–64–4
Garner	25.5–8–51–1
King	1–0–3–0
Parry	22–6–63–2

Holding	16–7–24–3
Croft	11–2–25–2
Garner	23–6–36–4

Umpires: F R Goodall (NZ) and J B R Hastie (NZ)

I have long been fascinated by this Test, indeed this whole series, which yielded such a bizarre result: the apparently effortless, snarling excellence of the West Indies humbled by modest, unconsidered New Zealand. As people always say when you have just been given out lbw to a ball that pitched outside leg stump and hit the centre of your bat, 'It's in the scorebook.' One-nil. It can't be erased. In the event, the Windies would not lose another series, either home or away, for more than fifteen years.

To place it all in context, the visitors arrived after a long and gruelling tour of Australia, where they had won 2–0 in the Tests and played several hundred one-day internationals. Viv Richards had gone home with a strained back, but Gordon Greenidge and Desmond Haynes were still at the top of the order, followed by Alvin Kallicharran and Clive Lloyd. And the four fast bowlers were Andy Roberts, Michael Holding, Joel Garner and Colin Croft. This was, simply, one of the best sides cricket had ever seen.

For once, though, they may have been too arrogant for their own good. At Dunedin, they were fooled by the pitch into selecting a spinner and batting first, when the ball was keeping low and seaming around all over the place. Four West Indies batsmen were given out lbw, all to Richard Hadlee. Only Desmond Haynes saw the need to grit it out, play on the front foot and cut out extravagant back-foot shots. When they came to bowl, the West Indies bowled too short. The New Zealand batsmen took a fearful hammering, but they grafted for their runs as the West Indies hadn't and built up a crucial first innings lead of 109. Bruce Edgar was in for almost five hours for his 65, and will have slept very well that night.

The third day was almost completely rained off, but on the fourth Hadlee again bowled with metronomic spite to reduce the West Indies to 29 for 4. Haynes and Collis King added 87, Haynes and Deryck Murray a further 64, but the West Indian tail folded at some speed and New Zealand needed only 104 to win. The West Indians, however, felt aggrieved. The umpiring had not exactly favoured them. Whenever the ball hit their pad, it seemed, they were out lbw, but when they got someone out caught behind the umpire was fiddling with his white stick or the battery in his hearing aid had run out. According to NZ skipper Geoff Howarth, 'They couldn't complain. If you walk in front of your stumps at Dunedin, you'll get given out.' According to Arunabha Sengupta, writing on the Cricket Country website, 'Clive Lloyd admits now that the West Indies team was jaded and the atrocious umpiring was too much to withstand on the back of a hard tour of Australia.'

The flashpoint occurred when New Zealand were 29 for 2, just before lunch on the last day. John Parker, on 0, appeared to glove the ball to the wicketkeeper, but the umpire, John Hastie, gave it not out. Holding walked over to the striker's end and let forth a mighty kick, knocking two stumps out of the ground. It's one of the most memorable photographs in cricket.

Soon after lunch, though, the New Zealand middle order started to disintegrate and, at 54 for 7, they were heading for defeat. Look at the bowling figures: terrifying. As in the first innings, though, their lower order pulled them out of trouble. When Lance Cairns was out caught behind, New Zealand were 100 for 9, still four short, with only eleven balls left. Stephen Boock, whose highest Test score was 8, saw out the rest of Holding's over and Garner bowled the last. The first ball went for a bye and Boock was nearly run out trying to come back for the second. Three to win. Second ball hit his pads: not out. Third ball, dot ball. Fourth ball, dot ball. Fifth ball, Boock squeezed two runs down to backward point to level the scores. Sixth ball hit his pads, went to backward square leg, and the batsmen ran a leg-bye. New Zealand had won off the last ball by the narrowest of margins. Meanwhile, that photograph was being beamed around the world, to appear in every cricket-loving newspaper known to mankind.

Julian's XIs

Fruit Loaf

1	A. B. Raisin	(Wanganui)
2	M. Sultana	(Hyderabad Women)
3	A. Date	(London University)
4	F. W. Barberry	(Birmingham Union)
5	T. Currant	(North Queensland Under-17s)
6	A. Egg	(Babraham, Coggeshall Town)
7	Butter	(Nottinghamshire Club and Ground)
8	S. Sugar	(Monmouth School)
9	G. W. Custard	(Gentlemen of Somerset)
10	T. Pie	(Headley)
11	A. Tart	(Goodwood)

The Village Year

As snowdrops bloom and daffodils burst into life, so the village cricketer goes indoors and avoids nature altogether. It's time for the annual round of nets, conducted as always in a large shed smelling of liniment, sweat and old plimsolls. Real cricketers have spent months preparing for this moment, keeping fit, doing hours of stretches and press-ups every day, and toning their muscles until they can pick up a cup of tea using only their pectorals. Village cricketers have been sitting in the pub since September. Simply tying their shoelaces exhausts them. Most of them use nets not for practice but as a way of trying to resuscitate their ruined bodies in time for the season proper. The fixtures secretary, being a sadist, has booked two-hour nets with this in mind.

For the first net almost everyone turns up, full of enthusiasm and, in many cases, pies. The effort of batting and, worse, bowling for all that time has several knock-on effects, such as killing enthusiasm completely. For week two, three people will turn up, being the only ones who can still walk. But no one is surprised. As all village cricketers know, the wrong number of people always turns up at nets. People who said they weren't coming come. People who said they were definitely coming don't come. One week, no one will remember to bring any balls, or pads. At least one horrible injury will be sustained every week. It's all utterly pointless.

I myself always struggled with nets, and I worked out that, because of the neon lights, I found it much harder to see the ball than I do out in daylight. Also, because I run the team, everyone bowled much more quickly and accurately than they did in real life, which was flattering, I suppose, but not much fun. One year, though, the nets really worked for me. I started to hit the ball cleanly and fluently, and for the first time I could see that cricket was, at heart, a simple game. Then our fastest bowler sent down a wicked yorker that broke several bones in my left foot. I didn't play until July. By which time, of course, cricket was once again the most complicated game in the world.

Alex
PEATTIE + TAYLOR

TYPICAL OF THE BOSS... HE MAKES SURE HE'S GOT A T.V. IN HIS OFFICE FOR THE CRICKET...

AND OF COURSE HE INSISTS ON HAVING THE LATEST BIG SCREEN DIGITAL INTERACTIVE MODEL WITH THE RED BUTTON THAT ENABLES YOU TO CHOOSE WHICH CAMERA YOU WATCH THE ACTION FROM...

YES

NO WAY WOULD ANY OF US GET A T.V. SET LIKE THAT PAID FOR BY THE BANK...

EXACTLY. HOW ON EARTH CAN RUPERT CLAIM IT'S A NECESSARY TOOL FOR HIM DOING HIS JOB?

MELANIE, TAKE A LOOK FROM THE CAMERA BEHIND THE BOWLER'S ARM... THAT'S DEFINITELY HAWKINS IN THE CROWD...

OH YES... AND HE PHONED IN SICK THIS MORNING...

REMIND ME TO SACK HIM TOMORROW.

March

March Birthdays

 1: Shahid Afridi (1980)
 2: Andrew Strauss (1977)
 3: Bill Frindall (1939), Inzamam-ul-Haq (1970)
 4: Daryll Cullinan (1967), Cathryn Fitzpatrick (1968)
 5: Percy Jeeves (1888), Rodney Hogg (1951), Eddo Brandes (1963)
 7: Henry Mayers Hyndman (1842), Sir Viv Richards (1952)
 8: Phil Edmonds (1951), Ross Taylor (1984)
13: The Hon Ivo Bligh (1859)
15: Colin Croft (1953), Mohsin Khan (1955)
16: Heath Streak (1974)
17: Willie Quaife (1872)
18: David 'Bumble' Lloyd (1947), E. D. Solkar (1948)
19: Ashley Giles (1973), Rangana Herath (1978)
21: Alvin Kallicharran (1949)
23: Wasim Bari (1948), Mike Atherton (1968)
24: Dean Jones (1961), Graeme Swann (1979)
26: Bill Edrich (1916), Rudi Koertzen (1949)
28: Chris Barrie (1960), Nasser Hussain (1968)
30: Wally Grout (1927), Norman Gifford (1940)
31: Hashim Amla (1983)

Shahid Afridi *(March 1)*

On February 19 2017, he retired for the fifth and possibly final time.

Bill Frindall *(March 3)*

The Bearded Wonder and legendary statistician of *Test Match Special* – and there aren't too many sentences where you will see the words 'legendary' and 'statistician' in close proximity. I shared a stage with him once at a literary festival, and we sat together afterwards signing books. My queue was modest, and quickly dealt with; his stretched into a separate postal district. Frindall used to run a touring team called the Malta Maniacs, who had a tie with the Maltese Cross on it. Among those who played for them were the Duchess of York's father, Major Ronald Ferguson.

Inzamam-ul-Haq *(March 3)*

Once took so long to walk off after being given out lbw that the game had already restarted before he had crossed the boundary line.

Percy Jeeves *(March 5)*

In the late summer of 1910, Rowland Ryder's father, then Warwickshire secretary, was on a walking holiday in Yorkshire and stayed the night in the village of Hawes. In the morning he cut himself shaving rather nastily and the doctor, having dealt with the cut, prescribed an afternoon watching cricket. 'Here, on the lovely ground at Hawes,' write Ryder, 'my father saw a young cricketer whose effortless grace as a bowler told something of his potential.' At the end of the innings he went up to him and said, 'How would you like to play for Warwickshire?'

Percy Jeeves (for it was he) said yes and spent the next two years qualifying for his new county. In 1913, opening the bowling for the first time at Edgbaston against Leicestershire, Jeeves took 3 for 24 and 5 for 37. This early season promise was fulfilled. 'His fast-medium deliveries, with their lightning speed off the pitch, yielded a rich harvest: 106 batsmen, including J. B. Hobbs, were victims to his flowering genius.' His wickets cost twenty runs apiece. In 1914 he took 4 for 44 for the Players against the Gentlemen. Ryder says 'it was expected that he would develop into a bowler of world class'.

Jeeves became engaged to Annie Austin, younger sister of the Warwickshire scorer. When the Great War broke out, Jeeves joined the Warwickshire Regiment and was killed at the Battle of the Somme in July 1916.

Half a century later Ryder was adapting *The Code of the Woosters* for the stage and wondered whether its author, P. G. Wodehouse, had chosen the surname of his legendary valet after seeing Percy Jeeves playing cricket. So he wrote to him and asked. 'Back came the reply from Remsenburg, Long Island, almost in less time than it takes to say "How's that?"'

'Yes, you are quite right,' wrote Wodehouse. 'It must have been in 1913 that I paid a visit to my parents in Cheltenham and went to see Warwickshire play Gloucestershire in the Cheltenham College Ground. I suppose Jeeves's bowling must have impressed me, for I remembered him in 1916 when I was in New York and starting the Jeeves and Bertie saga, and it was just the name I wanted.'

If you put all this in a novel, no one would believe it.

Henry Mayers Hyndman *(March 7)*

The first British populariser of Karl Marx's ideas, who was reputed to have turned to left-wing politics in anger at his exclusion from a Cambridge XI in the 1860s.

Phil Edmonds *(March 8)*

Left-arm spinner who, in the 1980s, shared a useful partnership with off-spinner John Emburey, both for Middlesex and England. His wife Frances says, 'He's got a reputation for being awkward and arrogant, probably because he is awkward and arrogant.'

In 1986 England were playing India in a Test match at Edgbaston, when a couple of spectators hopped over the advertising boards and invaded the field of play. The man held up a placard protesting about something or other, while the woman popped the bails down her trousers. The police came on and arrested the pair, the bails were put back on the stumps and play was ready to resume. At which moment Phil Edmonds casually strolled up to the wicket, bent over the bails and gave them a huge sniff.

Willie Quaife *(March 17)*

The only England Test cricketer who was smaller than Little Harry Pilling – some observers put him at 5ft 2in – Quaife batted for Warwickshire for thirty years in the early twentieth century and scored 36,012 first-class runs, most of them in singles. His dogged, almost stroke-free batting saved his county on many occasions, but he often drove opposing crowds to the brink of mental collapse. In 1913, against Surrey at the Oval, he crawled to 50 in four hours and then, according to the Warwickshire cricket writer Brian Halford, 'became introspective'. The historian Robert Brooke has suggested that, so rarely did the little man deal in boundaries, he probably ran more runs than anyone else in first-class cricket. He was, in effect, the ur-Boycott.

And in more ways than one. As Halford says, 'In 1893 his career began amid argy-bargy. In 1928 it ended after some argy-bargy. Most of the intervening years brought some argy or a quantity of bargy – sometimes both.' In 1926, aged fifty-four, he had his best season with the ball, taking seventy-eight Championship wickets at 25.89 with teasing leg-spin. At the end of the 1927 season, Warwickshire, with whom he had been arguing about money for a quarter of a century, announced that he had retired. This was news to Quaife. He issued a robust denial, saying that having just taken a second benefit (from which he received £917), to retire straight after would be 'very ungracious'. Quaife's supporters thronged Warwickshire's AGM and, in the resulting compromise, it was decided that Quaife could play a single farewell match in 1928. He chose the Derbyshire match in early August and scored 115, thus becoming the oldest player (fifty-six years and 140 days) to score a first-class century.

But if he had done nothing else, Quaife would still be remembered for taking part in a unique statistical oddity, also against Derbyshire, in 1922. For four overs, Willie was batting with his son Bernard, and they were facing the bowling of Bill Bestwick and his son Robert. In other words, this is the only time in first-class cricket that father and son faced the bowling of father of son. No doubt Willie blocked them out for a few maidens.

Mike Atherton *(March 23)*

Here's Simon Barnes, in his splendid book *Epic*:

> It was Sunday evening and teatime when Mike Atherton gloved a ball from Allan Donald of South Africa to the wicketkeeper, Mark Boucher. Atherton stood there without moving, his face poker-player blank. It was the fourth Test match between England and South Africa at Trent Bridge, and South Africa were 1–0 up ... Atherton was given not out, and Donald responded with a spell of violent short-pitched bowling from around the wicket ...
>
> Donald was all aggression and hard words; Atherton

responded with a level stare, the same unmoved expression. Once he gave a small nod, to acknowledge Donald's brilliance – brilliance that was still not enough to get him out. The response was passive-aggressive: my cold to your hot. The facial expressions, invisible to those at the ground, told the true story to the rest of the nation, who watched from afar [i.e. on television] and so were much closer.

One thing became very clear as the contest developed, reached its peak and at last ended, with Atherton not out at the close of play. It was that Atherton loved every second of it ... This brutal examination of his sporting and moral hardness was something that stimulated him to the very core of his being.

England won the Test by eight wickets; Atherton ended on 98 not out. When the match finished, Donald knocked on the door of the England dressing room, came in and sat down next to Atherton, and opened a beer. Nasser Hussain was there too. 'The two of them sat there chatting and laughing about it,' he said later. 'That speaks volumes for both men.'

Bill Edrich *(March 26)*

William John Edrich played thirty-nine Tests, averaged exactly 40 and formed a powerful middle-order partnership for both Middlesex and England with Denis Compton. He was also a RAF pilot, who won the DFC for taking part in a daylight attack on Cologne in 1941. He claimed to have flown two bombing missions over occupied Europe, scored a century for Norfolk and made love to a local lass, all within one forty-eight-hour period, although the latter is unconfirmed. Edrich holds the Test record for the most wives (five) jointly with Hugh Tayfield. He died on the same day, April 24 1986, as Wallis Simpson.

Chris Barrie *(March 28)*

Comic actor and impressionist with no known link to cricket, except for a stand-up piece he once performed on a TV show called *Saturday Live*. I think it's one of the funniest things I have ever seen.

Richie Benaud is auditioning to be the new James Bond. The producers ask him to say a couple of lines in his best James Bond voice. The lines are 'The name's Bond, James Bond. Vodka martini, shaken not stirred.'

Benaud has a go. 'Morning everyone,' he says. 'The name's Bond, James Bond. Vodka martini, shaken not stirred.'

Yes, it's not bad, say the producers. Could you have another go, only this time without the 'Morning everyone'?

Richie takes a deep breath. 'The name's Bond, James Bond,' he says. 'Morning everyone. Vodka martini, shaken not stirred.'

Yes, we're moving in the right direction, say the producers. Maybe without the 'Morning everyone' entirely?

Benaud concentrates. He does facial exercises. He takes another deep breath.

'The name's Bond, James Bond. Vodka martini, shaken not stirred.'

Long, long pause.

'Morning everyone.'

Nasser Hussain *(March 28)*

You didn't want to be near Nasser when things went wrong. As Jon Hotten wrote, 'To compound all his other frustrations, he had the unlucky knack of being on the wrong end of some terrible umpiring decisions in a pre-DRS age.' After being given out lbw to Wasim Akram in Rawalpindi, he smashed up a fridge. Given out caught behind to Shane Warne when he wasn't, he broke a crutch belonging to injured fast bowler Alex Tudor. Given out lbw to Carl Hooper when one leapt cruelly low, he went into the dressing room, punched a locker with wooden slats, then couldn't get his hand out. In Hotten's memorable words, 'all of his intensity and insecurity and ambition roiled inside him, the lava in the volcano'.

Quiz 1

I compile and present a quiz for *The Nightwatchman* magazine every three months, which is held in the Long Room at the Oval, under the worst portrait of Alec Stewart anyone has ever seen. In amongst forty or so general knowledge questions can be found seven or eight cricket questions, some of them very easy, some of them tough, one or two utterly impossible. Those questions are distributed throughout this book in the form of four ten-question rounds. This, the first, is the easiest. They get harder. The last one is brutal, and is best approached with what David Gower would call a glass of something agreeable.

1. In 2017, who became the first double-barrelled cricketer to play for England since Norman 'Mandy' Mitchell-Innes in 1935?
2. Who was the first professional cricketer to be knighted?
3. In 1900, while playing for the MCC against London County, this man, more famous in another field, took his first and only first-class wicket. It just happened to be W. G. Grace. Who was this bowler?
4. In February 2013, who became the first cricketer to lead his country in a hundred Test matches? He also has the most victories as captain, with fifty-one.
5. Shoaib Akhtar was the bowler, Nick Knight was the batsman, and he clipped the ball to square leg for no run.

This was during the 2003 World Cup in South Africa. What wider significance in cricket history did this ball have?

6. Don Bradman is the only Australian batsman to score a hundred centuries in first-class cricket. Viv Richards is the only West Indian. Who is the only Pakistani?

7. In 2005, who became the first cricketer to win *Strictly Come Dancing*?

8. Which county cricket ground was elevated to Test status for the first Ashes Test of 2009?

9. On September 12 2005, England won the Ashes for the first time in eighteen years. On September 13 2005, who was awarded British citizenship on the personal intervention of the then Home Secretary, Charles Clarke?

10. In February 2019, Chris Gayle hit his 477th six in international cricket, a new record, beating the 476 sixes hit by whom?

Answers next month.

Favourite Tests

Kolkata, March 11, 12, 13, 14, 15 2001

INDIA vs AUSTRALIA: Second Test

Australia

M J Slater	c Mongia b Zaheer Khan	42	—	(2) c Ganguly b Harbhajan	43
M L Hayden	c sub b Harbhajan	97	—	(1) lbw b Tendulkar	67
J L Langer	c Mongia b Zaheer Khan	58	—	c Ramesh b Harbhajan	28
M E Waugh	c Mongia b Harbhajan	22	—	lbw b Raju	0
*S R Waugh	lbw b Harbhajan	110	—	c sub b Harbhajan	24
R T Ponting	lbw b Harbhajan	6	—	c Das b Harbhajan	0
†A C Gilchrist	lbw b Harbhajan	0	—	lbw b Tendulkar	0
S K Warne	c Ramesh b Harbhajan	0	—	(9) lbw b Tendulkar	0
M S Kasprowicz	lbw b Ganguly	7	—	(10) not out	13
J N Gillespie	c Ramesh b Harbhajan	46	—	(8) c Das b Harbhajan	6
G D McGrath	not out	21	—	lbw b Harbhajan	12
	b 19, lb 10, nb 7	36		b 6, nb 8, p 5	19
		445			212

1–103 (1), 2–193 (2), 3–214 (3), 4–236 (4), 5–252 (6), 6–252 (7), 7–252 (8), 8–269 (9), 9–402 (10), 10–445 (5)

1–74 (2), 2–106 (3), 3–116 (4), 4–166 (5), 5–166 (6), 6–167 (7), 7–173 (1), 8–174 (9), 9–191 (8), 10–212 (11)

Zaheer Khan	28.4–6–89–2		Zaheer Khan	8–4–30–0
Prasad	30–5–95–0		Prasad	3–1–7–0
Ganguly	13.2–3–44–1		Harbhajan Singh	30.3–8–73–6
Raju	20–2–58–0		Raju	15–3–58–1

| Harbhajan Singh | 37.5–7–123–7 |
| Tendulkar | 2–0–7–0 |

| Tendulkar | 11–3–31–3 |
| Ganguly | 1–0–2–0 |

India

S S Das	c Gilchrist b McGrath	20	—	hit wkt b Gillespie	39
S Ramesh	c Ponting b Gillespie	0	—	c M E Waugh b Warne	30
R Dravid	b Warne	25	—	(6) run out	180
S R Tendulkar	lbw b McGrath	10	—	c Gilchrist b Gillespie	10
*S C Ganguly	c S R Waugh b Kasprowicz	23	—	c Gilchrist b McGrath	48
V V S Laxman	c Hayden b Warner	59	—	(3) c Ponting b McGrath	281
†N R Mongia	c Gilchrist b Kasprowicz	2	—	b McGrath	4
Harbhajan Singh	c Ponting b Gillespie	4	—	(9) not out	8
Zaheer Khan	b McGrath	3	—	(8) not out	23
S L V Raju	lbw b McGrath	4	—		
B K V Prasad	not out	7	—		
	lb 2, nb 12	14		b 6, lb 12, w 2, nb 14	34
		171		(7 wkts dec)	657

1–0 (2), 2–34 (1), 3–48 (4), 4–88 (3), 5–88 (5), 6–92 (7), 7–97 (8), 8–113 (9), 9–129 (10), 10–171 (6)

1–52 (2), 2–97 (1), 3–115 (4), 4–232 (5), 5–608 (3), 6–624 (7), 7–629 (6)

McGrath	14–8–18–4
Gillespie	11–0–47–2
Kasprowicz	13–2–39–2
Warne	20.1–3–65–2

McGrath	39–12–103–3
Gillespie	31–6–115–2
Warne	34–3–152–1
M E Waugh	18–1–58–0
Kasprowicz	35–6–139–0
Ponting	12–1–41–0
Hayden	6–0–24–0
Slater	2–1–4–0
Langer	1–0–3–0

Umpires: P Willey (E) and S K Bansal (I)
Third umpire: S N Bandekar (I)
Referee: C W Smith (WI)

Winning in India: everyone finds it difficult, except for India. Australia began this tour as clearly the best team in the world, and one of the best of all time, with fifteen consecutive victories under gum-chewing hyper-bastard skipper Steve Waugh, who probably didn't even smile at his children. But it had been thirty-one years (and four tours) since Australia had beaten India in their own territory. Even England had done better than that.

The first Test at Mumbai was the Australians' sixteenth victory in a row, executed in three days by ten wickets. Easy. At Kolkata they won a vital toss and batted again, and at 193 for 1, with Matthew Hayden in prime biffing form, long-term dislikers of Australia were sighing into their teacups. But Hayden just missed his century, and the middle order vanished, assisted by a hat-trick, India's first in Tests, by turbanned twenty-year-old off-spinner Harbhajan Singh. At 269 for 8, Australia's goose was slowly browning in the oven at gas mark 4. Or at least it would have been had Steve Waugh not still been there. With Jason Gillespie in support, Waugh put on 133 for the ninth wicket, and reached his twenty-fifth Test century after five hours of brow-knitting concentration. Australia were all out for a comparatively fearsome 445.

As Dicky Rutnagur pointed out in *Wisden*, the fact that Australia's last two batted for 222 minutes between them was proof that the pitch was playing easily. So how exactly did India get all out for 171? Glenn McGrath and Shane Warne, of course, were old hands at getting wickets out of nothing, squeezed out of lifeless pitches with sheer personality, but Gillespie and Michael Kasprowicz bowled equally compellingly. Only V. V. S. Laxman's swashbuckling 59 from 83 balls provided any light in a display of otherwise ceaseless shade. India followed on 274 runs behind.

Second time round India batted slightly more effectively, but the game seemed to be going only one way until Laxman and Rahul Dravid came together. Dravid wasn't quite yet The Wall, the batsman of extraordinary will and concentration who would later play

Graeme Swann at Lord's so late that the crowd kept gasping at his confidence and skill. V. V. S. we knew as an exceptionally elegant batsman who never made quite as many runs as he looked likely to. They batted together for 104 overs, including the whole of the fourth day, during which they scored 335 runs in ninety overs. Oh to have been there, and seen this great bowling attack transformed into hapless trundlers! Their eventual stand of 376 broke every record imaginable. As Rutnagur said, 'Their efforts not only dispelled India's troubles, but opened up an avenue to a momentous victory.' As we all know, there's no team weaker than a team that thinks it's heading for an easy victory and now has to contemplate defeat. Especially when that team is Australia.

Sourav Ganguly was able to declare with a lead of 383, and Australia had seventy-five overs to survive, on a pitch that was beginning to turn but not horribly. Despite Hayden's second muscular fifty of the match, they never really looked like doing it. Harbhajan, later to become incomparably Sky Sports' most boring commentator, took six more wickets, to bring his match total to thirteen. In the next match he would take fifteen, India would win by two wickets, and Australia's losing streak in India would continue. Flags and bunting were raised in every cricketing nation but one; in my house we contemplated holding a street party. We would have been the only ones to have gone, but it would have been worth it.

Favourite Tests

Melbourne, March 12, 13, 14, 16, 17 1977

AUSTRALIA vs ENGLAND: The Centenary Test

Australia

I C Davis	lbw b Lever	5	—	c Knott b Greig	68
R B McCosker	b Willis	4	—	(10) c Greig b Old	25
G J Cosier	c Fletcher b Lever	10	—	(4) c Knott b Lever	4
*G S Chappell	b Underwood	40	—	(3) b Old	2
D W Hookes	c Greig b Old	17	—	(6) c Fletcher b Underwood	56
K D Walters	c Greig b Willis	4	—	(5) c Knott b Greig	66
†R W Marsh	c Knott b Old	28	—	not out	110
G J Gilmour	c Greig b Old	4	—	b Lever	16
K J O'Keeffe	c Brearley b Underwood	0	—	(2) c Willis b Old	14
D K Lillee	not out	10	—	(9) c Amiss b Old	25
M H N Walker	b Underwood	2	—	not out	8
	b 4, lb 2, nb 8	14		lb 10, nb 15	25
		138			419

1–11, 2–13, 3–23, 4–45, 5–51, 6–102, 7–114, 8–117, 9–136, 10–138

1–33, 2–40, 3–53, 4–132, 5–187, 6–244, 7–277, 8–353, 9–407

Lever	12–1–36–2
Willis	8–0–33–2
Old	12–4–39–3
Underwood	11.6–2–16–3*

Lever	21–1–95–2
Willis	22–0–91–0
Old	27.6–2–104–4
Greig	14–3–66–2
Underwood	12–2–38–1

---

* Eight-ball overs.

England

R A Woolmer	c Chappell b Lillee	9	—	lbw b Walker	12
J M Brearley	c Hookes b Lillee	12	—	lbw b Lillee	43
D L Underwood	c Chappell b Walker	7	—	(10) b Lillee	7
D W Randall	c Marsh b Lillee	4	—	(3) c Cosier b O'Keeffe	174
D L Amiss	c O'Keeffe b Walker	4	—	(4) b Chappell	64
K W R Fletcher	c Marsh b Walker	4	—	(5) c Marsh b Lillee	1
*A W Greig	b Walker	18	—	(6) c Cosier b O'Keeffe	41
†A P E Knott	lbw b Lillee	15	—	(7) lbw b Lillee	42
C M Old	c Marsh b Lillee	3	—	(8) c Chappell b Lillee	2
J K Lever	c Marsh b Lillee	11	—	(9) lbw b O'Keeffe	4
R G D Willis	not out	1	—	not out	5
	b 2, lb 2, w 1, nb 2	7		b 8, lb 4, w 3, nb 7	22
		95			**417**

1–19, 2–30, 3–34, 4–40, 5–40, 6–61, 7–65, 8–78, 9–86, 10–95

1–28, 2–113, 3–279, 4–290, 5–346, 6–369, 7–380, 8–385, 9–410, 10–417

Lillee	13.3–2–26–6		Lillee	34.4–7–139–5
Walker	15–3–54–4		Walker	22–4–83–1
O'Keeffe	1–0–4–0		Gilmour	4–0–29–0
Gilmour	5–3–4–0		Chappell	16–7–29–1
			O'Keeffe	33–6–108–3
			Walters	3–2–7–0

Umpires: T F Brooks (A) and M G O'Connell (A)

The unquestionable highlight of the 1976–77 season was this one-off Test, to celebrate a hundred glorious years of sledging and sharp practice between the two nations. England, as usual, were a side in transition. Mike Brearley, Peter Willey and Geoff Miller had made debuts the previous summer; John Lever and Derek

Randall had been capped in India. For Australia, Max Walker replaced the injured Jeff Thomson, while David Hookes, aged twenty-one, made his debut after five centuries in six Sheffield Shield innings.

But who cares who was in the teams? No one did at the time. The Centenary Test was a celebration, a party. There were 214 former Test cricketers in attendance, including Percy Fender, born in 1892. (When reminded that in 1930 he had doubted Bradman's ability to succeed in England, he replied, 'An indiscretion of youth.') Greg Chappell tossed a specially minted commemorative gold coin; Tony Greig called correctly and put them in. 'I hope he doesn't live to regret it,' said Geoffrey Boycott in the commentary box. There was a little moisture under the surface, and Bob Willis, Chris Old, Lever and Derek Underwood all bowled superbly, but when Australia folded for 138, Chappell blamed the pressure of the occasion rather than the pitch. There must have been something going on, because England were then all out for 95. The authorities began to get nervous. Her Majesty The Queen was due to drop by at three o'clock on the fifth afternoon. At this rate the game would be long over and the ground deserted. Soon Australia were 53 for 3 in their second innings, with Rick McCosker unable to bat because a Willis bouncer had broken his jaw in the first innings. But the moisture in the pitch was gone; batting was becoming less fraught. Ian Davis, Doug Walters and Hookes all passed fifty, Hookes carving Greig's off-spin for five successive fours; Rodney Marsh scored a century; McCosker came in anyway at number ten, his face held together with steel girders; and when Chappell declared England's target was 463 runs in ten hours and fifty minutes.

There followed one of the great Test innings, which John Arlott would praise for 'its concentration, soundness, bravery and frequent handsome strokes'. After Bob Woolmer's dismissal, Derek Randall skittered to the wicket to join Mike Brearley. Always a nervous starter, he was helped on his way by some wayward bowling from Gary Gilmour (playing his last Test). When Lillee returned to the attack, Randall was the first batsman in the match to hook him. Later on he would doff his cap to the old monster, thus riling Lillee to even greater excesses of rage and violence. ('This is not a f***ing tea party, Randall.') On another occasion, he pointed at the stumps, as though to redirect Lillee's aim. England reached 189 for 2 at the end of the fourth day, with Randall on 87 not out. Just another 272 to win.

They didn't make it, of course, but they came magnificently close. Randall's 174 was the second-highest score by a batsman playing his first E vs A Test. When he had made 161 he was given out caught behind, but Marsh recalled him, as he hadn't caught the ball cleanly. When he was finally out, caught at short leg, he went out through the wrong gate and almost found himself in the royal enclosure. Australia's winning margin of forty-five runs was exactly the same as that of the first-ever Test match between the two sides, a hundred years earlier. (If that had happened today, people would have talked.) It must have been quite a day. The Queen turned up on time, and Lillee, explaining he was 'a bit of a royalist', asked for her autograph. Meanwhile, Tony Greig was busy recruiting a few more players for Kerry Packer's World Series Cricket. The Centenary Test was the eight-hundredth Test in one hundred years; in the forty years since, there have been over fifteen hundred more.

Julian's XIs

Meat & Joints

1	S. Rabbit	(Waikato Valley)
2	Deer	(E Troop 21st Hussars)
3	J. Ox	(Rayleigh)
4	A. Baron	(Glastonbury)
5	C. Beef	(Lawrenny)
6	Crown	(Swansea)
7	C. B. Roast	(Berkshire)
8	A. J. Lamb	(England, Marylebone Cricket Club, Northamptonshire, Orange Free State, Western Province)
9	H. W. Veal	(Monmouthshire)
10	H. J. C. Mutton	(South Australia)
11	Cutlet	(Noddle Island)

The Village Year

In the spring a young man's fancy lightly turns to thoughts of food. March is the month of our annual dinner, which has had several venues. One or two have since closed, and one or two others have asked that we not return. Our current base is an Iranian restaurant in west London, courtesy of Sammy, an Iranian Jew who always wears sunglasses and bats at number seven or eight, looking as though he's going to be out every ball but somehow always managing to stay there, a vital skill in village cricket. (He is also a valuable bowler: no talent whatsoever, but such overpowering self-belief he thinks he's Shane Warne. This is the sort of bowler a captain needs when the opposition are 200 for 1 and all your real bowlers have suddenly sustained acute hamstring injuries.)

We can't really talk about what happens at these dinners, because no one ever remembers. Last year's was held on a Monday, in the hope that this would stop people getting too drunk, but the dozen who turned up were the hardcore funsters, the sort of people who go on stag weekends where someone dies. The following morning you wake up and if you're in any kind of bed at all you emit a small cheer of relief. Cliff will surely have missed his last train back to Hastings and spent the night on a station bench that is his and his alone. I myself seem to have an unerring homing instinct and always end up back in my own bed, snoring like a dolphin and yelling obscenities in my sleep, apparently. Only a fool would have put anything in their diary for the following couple of days.

Is this any sort of fun? To be honest, no, but it does feel like a necessary rite. The season begins with the dinner and continues with the issuing of the fixture list, a pictorial affair that usually depicts someone playing a perfect forward defence, missing the ball completely and being bowled middle stump. Cricket, as we all know, is a game played in the mind, and all this pre-season faffing about demonstrates that. Far more sensible to play it in the mind, where every square cut goes for four, than on grass, every village cricketer's mortal enemy.

Alex
PEATTIE + TAYLOR

CHARITY CRICKET
IN AID OF
Wellbeing for Women

BEING UMPIRE IS A VERY DEMANDING AND RESPONSIBLE ROLE, ALEX, EVEN IN A CHARITY CRICKET MATCH

SUNIL GAVASKAR MAY BE ONE OF THE GREATEST BATSMEN IN THE HISTORY OF THE GAME, BUT WHEN HE WAS HIT ON THE PADS BY A STRAIGHT BALL I HAD NO HESITATION IN GIVING HIM OUT L.B.W...

I SHALL ALWAYS REMEMBER THE AUTHORITATIVE, ASSURED AND DECISIVE WAY I RAISED MY INDEX FINGER...

YOU CERTAINLY WILL

YOU'VE JUST PAID £8,000 FOR A HARRODS PICNIC HAMPER...

WHAT...? OH NO...

SOLD! TO THE GENTLEMAN IN THE GLASSES...

BANG

AUCTION

April

April Birthdays

1: Arnold Sidebottom (1954), David Gower (1957),
   Stephen Fleming (1973)
2: Dermot Reeve (1963), Lawrence Booth (1975),
   Michael Clarke (1981)
3: Neville Cardus (1888)
4: Bapu Nadkarni (1933), Paul Downton (1957), Jonathan Agnew
   (1960), Steven Finn (1989)
5: Les Jackson (1921), Colin Bland (1938)
6: Dilip Vengsarkar and Mudassar Nazar (1956),
   Liam Plunkett (1985)
7: Dennis Amiss (1943)
8: Alec Stewart (1963)
9: Alan Knott (1946)
11: Billy Bowden (1963), Ian Bell (1982)
12: Vinoo Mankad (1917)
14: Craig McDermott (1965), Umar Gul (1984)
15: John Bracewell (1958), James Foster (1980)
16: R. E. 'Tip' Foster (1878), Salim Malik (1963)
17: Norman Cowans (1961), Muttiah Muralitharan (1972)
18: Doug Insole (1926), Malcolm Marshall (1958)
19: Sydney Barnes (1873), Dickie Bird (1933), Jason Gillespie (1975)
20: Adolf Hitler (1889), Graeme Fowler (1957)
22: Jonathan Trott (1981)
24: Sachin Tendulkar (1973)
25: C. B. Fry (1872), Mike Selvey (1948), Monty Panesar (1982)
28: Jack Fingleton (1908), Mike Brearley (1942), Scyld Berry (1954),
   Andy Flower (1968)
29: Phil Tufnell (1966)

David Gower *(April 1)*

'David Gower makes batting look as easy as drinking tea,' said Sir Leonard Hutton. 'It's hard work making batting look effortless,' said Gower himself, raising a Roger Moore eyebrow.

Michael Clarke *(April 2)*

Australian batsman and captain who had all the talent, and not quite enough of the personality. In 2004, after Clarke had made a glorious century on his Test debut, his team-mate Darren Lehmann said he should play every Test for the next ten years, even if it meant forfeiting his own place. But Clarke wasn't to all Australian tastes: too many tattoos, too many endorsements, too many luscious blonde girlfriends. Only in 2012, when he made four Test double-centuries in a year, did his reputation miraculously improve.

Greg Baum in *Wisden* described his wonderful timing: 'Late in 2012 against Sri Lanka, while hampered by injury at Hobart and Melbourne, he would stab down on yorkers with no thought other than of survival, yet still the ball would squirt from his bat like a pip from an orange.' And yet within three years he was gone, strangely unmourned.

Bapu Nadkarni *(April 4)*

Anyone who says that cricket never really changes should study the career of R. G. 'Bapu' Nadkarni, who played forty-one Tests for India between 1955 and 1968. A useful all-rounder, Nadkarni appears in these pages because of the astonishing economy of his bowling. As H. Natarajan wrote on ESPNcricinfo, 'Batsmen faced with the problem of playing Bapu Nadkarni's left-arm spin had two scoring options to choose from: nil and negligible.' In 1960–61 against Pakistan, Bapu returned figures of 32–24–23–0 at Kanpur and 34–24–24–1 at Delhi. And against England in Chennai in 1964, he outdid himself: his figures of 32–27–5–0 included twenty-one consecutive maidens. According to Natarajan, 'His legendary parsimony and precision were the result of untiring research and development in the nets – he would bowl endlessly at a coin placed on a good length.' How would Jos Buttler fare against him? Slowly, I imagine.

Les Jackson *(April 5)*

Derbyshire paceman from 1947 to 1963, who was widely revered as one of the finest bowlers of his day. Fred Trueman called him 'the best six-days-a-week bowler I saw in county cricket'. Tom Graveney said he was 'the best bloody bowler in the country'. Ted Dexter said, 'County batsmen are inclined to talk more quietly or laugh a little louder at less funny jokes when they get near Derbyshire.' Jackson played in 418 matches and took 1730 wickets at an average of 17.38.

So why did he not play more than twice for England? His two Test matches were twelve years apart: one against New Zealand at Old Trafford in 1949, the other against Australia at Headingley in 1961. He took seven wickets at 22.14, but after both matches was summarily dropped without explanation.

Various excuses were given. Derbyshire prepared green wickets that suited their seam attack rather too well. Jackson was less than express pace. Freddie Brown, captain of England between 1949 and 1951, thought he lacked the stamina to come back for a second spell, even though he bowled an average of 886 overs a season. Blah blah blah.

But as his *Telegraph* obituary made plain, 'Ultimately, it is diffi-cult to avoid the conclusion that Jackson's omission was partly due to snobbery.' Jackson was a former coal miner. Sir Gubby Allen was the Old Etonian chairman of selectors when Jackson was at his peak. According to Trueman, 'My information is that [Allen] would not have Les at any price, and if that's true it's criminal.' Sir Gubby played twenty-five Tests but never took a hundred wickets in a season. Jackson did so ten times. But he was a coal miner from Derbyshire, and therefore beyond the pale.

Dear God, we think things are bad now, but we know nothing. No wonder the Australians hate us.

Alec Stewart *(April 8)*

Prolific opening batsman for England, compelled by circumstance to don the wicketkeeping gloves in more than half his Tests (which brought his average down below 40), Alec Stewart was a formidably well-scrubbed cricketer of a slightly military mien. He was born on 8.4.63, and in his 133 Tests, he scored exactly 8463 runs. Did he do this on purpose? His most regular opening partner, Michael Atherton, might have spotted the pattern, but The Gaffer? Surely not. Indeed, for some more religious followers of England cricket, this numerical confluence finally offers proof that God exists.

As it happens, I spotted Alec Stewart buying a round in the Fentiman Arms, round the corner from the Oval, in April 2018, and I seriously considered going up to him and saying, 'Did you know that . . . ? But I chickened out. Three pints more and I might have.

Alan Knott *(April 9)*

Wilfully eccentric England wicketkeeper who would never eat both meat and cheese in the same meal.

Ian Bell *(April 11)*

Synaesthesia is a perceptual phenomenon in which stimulation of one sensory or cognitive pathway leads to automatic, involuntary experiences in a second sensory or cognitive pathway. So, for example, colours have smells. Or letters and numbers have colours. Or in my case, certain inanimate objects forcibly remind me of famous international cricketers.

This is no joke, by the way. It's real.

For many years I had a sugar bowl that, for some reason, reminded me of Andrew Caddick. It may have been the large ear-like handles on each side.

And I had a teapot that reminded me of Mark Butcher. Unfortunately, it broke. As, eventually, did he.

My new teapot reminds me of Ian Bell. I can't explain why; it just does. I therefore think of Ian Bell every single day, probably before you are awake.

The technical term for this may be cricketaesia.

Muttiah Muralitharan *(April 17)*

Bishen Bedi thought he was a chucker. So did the umpire Darrell Hair, who no-balled him seven times in three overs at the MCG in 1995–96. But Rob Smyth, in his delightful short book *The Spirit of Cricket*, thought otherwise. 'Murali's sheer decency – his refusal to respond to often vicious abuse, his unbreakable smile, his omnipresent enthusiasm – is the very essence of the spirit of cricket.'

Doug Insole *(April 18)*

Essex batsman of the 1950s who played nine Tests for England and, after retirement, became a prominent administrator and éminence grise, with a finger in more pies than there were pies. As chairman of selectors, he was there when Geoffrey Boycott was dropped for slow scoring in 1967, and when Basil D'Oliveira wasn't picked for the South African tour of 1968–69. He was also the only male Test cricketer to have worked at Bletchley Park during the war. He went for an interview with a moustachioed officer called Major Bellringer. 'Bellringer asked me if I'd done any Morse,' Insole told Andrew Lycett in 2017. 'I replied that I'd done a bit at air-training camp. He then said they would quickly get me up to twenty-three words a minute. So I became an operator. I wasn't actually in the Army but in something called Special Communications Unit Number Three. I had no idea what I was doing, but I knew it was of some significance.' This was true: Insole was awarded the Bletchley Park war medal in 1969.

Dickie Bird *(April 19)*

As Matthew Engel wrote, 'He was the first umpire to combine the distinct roles of top-flight umpire and music-hall comedian.'

Adolf Hitler *(April 20)*

According to an article published in the *Daily Mirror* in 1930, Hitler was taught cricket by British PoWs during the First World War, but declared that it was 'insufficiently violent' for his purposes. In particular, he wished to abolish pads, which he considered 'unmanly and unGerman'.

Sachin Tendulkar *(April 24)*

What must it be like to be Sachin Tendulkar? No other cricketer has carried the burden of an entire nation's cricketing hopes for so long, other than possibly Bradman, but those were different times. Australia's population in the 1930s was between six and seven million. India's population in 1989, when Tendulkar first played Test cricket, was 852,736,160. For many of us, our first memory of the wee lad came in that same year, when at Lord's he ran around from the Mound Stand and took a wonderful low catch one-handed in front of the Compton Stand to dismiss Allan Lamb. He was seventeen at the time. 'Sachin Tendulkar is, in my time, the best player without a doubt,' said Shane Warne. 'Daylight second, Brian Lara third.' Tendulkar has spent more of his life playing international cricket than anyone else: 1359 days in all, which translates to 3.72 years. In Test matches, in 329 innings spanning twenty-four years, he never once batted at number three.

C. B. Fry *(April 25)*

Sussex and England batsman who is said to have moved from good to great by watching what K. S. Ranjitsinhji was doing at the other end and trying to emulate it. He also played in an FA Cup final, equalled the long jump world record, headed the England batting averages for six seasons and was a notable classical scholar. After he retired he had a box at Lord's, from where he would write his reports for the *Evening Standard* and entertain friends and acquaintances. At ten-thirty his chauffeur-driven Bentley would pick him up from Brown's Hotel, fully equipped with writing pads, binoculars, travelling rugs, a copy of Herodotus for passages of slow play, a box of Henry Clay cigars and, according to Denzil Batchelor, 'reserve hampers of hock and chicken sandwiches in case there was a strike of caterers in north-west London'. In the afternoon Mrs Fry would occasionally turn up: in youth she had been 'an honorary whip with the Duke of Beaufort's hounds, and the model for a G. F. Watts painting: an unusual double'. Years later, Batchelor went to 'Madam's' memorial service. 'Charles wrung me by the hand and said, to hide his emotion, "Look, I'll show you an infallible way to play a googly." He had picked up the cricket bat and was demonstrating imperiously, when the chapel bell rang.' At the Paris Peace Conference, Fry was said to have been offered the throne of Albania, and said no. (Later historians have suggested that this didn't actually happen, but I don't think we should let truth get in the way of a good story.)

C. B. Fry once met Hitler. In 1934, according to his autobiography, he went to Germany to try to strengthen links between the Boy Scouts and the Hitler Youth, and when he met the Führer they exchanged Nazi salutes. Fry also tried, but failed, to persuade Joachim von Ribbentrop that Germany should take up cricket and aspire to become a Test-playing country. Fry's autobiography went through a number of impressions and it was only between the third (1941) and the fourth (1947) that his words of admiration for Hitler were removed.

Jack Fingleton *(April 28)*

A stubborn opening batsman known for his dour defensive approach, Fingleton became a journalist and commentator in retirement, and one of cricket's most accomplished writers. Four months older than Donald Bradman, he didn't care for the great man one bit, and rarely missed an opportunity to have a pop at him in print. 'Douglas Jardine, who saw many great batsmen at close quarters, was once asked to name the greatest. He didn't hesitate. "Hobbs," said Jardine, "is number one every time. He was so good on bad pitches." The interviewer interposed another name. Jardine looked out of the window – and refused to answer.'

Phil Tufnell *(April 29)*

Why neutral umpires were introduced, no. 4592. Phil Tufnell was bowling for England against Australia at the MCG in 1990–91, and wasn't sure how many balls he had sent down. So he asked the umpire, Peter O'Connell, 'How many left, ump?' O'Connell looked Tufnell up and down and said, 'Count them yourself, you Pommy bastard.'

Quiz 1 Answers

1. Toby Roland-Jones.
2. Sir Jack Hobbs.
3. Sir Arthur Conan Doyle.
4. Graeme Smith.
5. It was the first to be measured at 100 mph.
6. Zaheer Abbas.
7. Darren Gough. (Mark Ramprakash won the year after.)
8. Sophia Gardens/SWALEC Stadium. (In Cardiff.)
9. Duncan Fletcher.
10. Shahid Afridi.

The Only Man

The only man ...
to become Prime Minister of the United Kingdom having once played first-class cricket is Sir Alec Douglas-Home. As Lord Dunglass he was, according to *Wisden*, 'a useful member of the Eton XI'. In the Eton–Harrow match of 1922, which was badly affected by rain, he scored 66, and then took 4 for 37 with his medium-paced outswingers. He played ten first-class matches for six different teams, Middlesex, Oxford University, H. D. G. Leveson-Gower's XI, Free Foresters, Harlequins and the MCC, with whom he toured South America under Pelham Warner. He played twice for Middlesex, once in 1924 and once the following year. Cricket, though, was gradually superseded by politics, and

he entered the House of Commons in 1931. Later succeeding to his father's title as the 14th Earl of Home (which sounds like something out of Mervyn Peake), he became Foreign Secretary and then, in 1963, after renouncing his peerage, Prime Minister, when he emerged as a surprise compromise candidate who wasn't as hated as much as all the other candidates. *Wisden* goes on, 'Despite all his honours, Alec Home never made an enemy and was much valued, in cricket as in politics, for his quiet charm and sagacity.' This didn't help him as Prime Minister, though, as he lasted in office for less than a year.

The only man ...
to win the Nobel Prize for Literature, having once played first-class cricket, is Samuel Beckett. He played twice for Dublin University against Northamptonshire in 1925 and 1926, scoring 35 runs in four innings and taking no wicket for 64. *Wisden* describes him as 'a left-hand opening batsman, possessing what he himself called a gritty defence, and a useful left-arm medium-pace bowler'. In later years he wrote increasingly in French, and no doubt sat in the bars of Paris with fellow expats discussing what the French for 'wicketkeeper' might be.* His gloom was legendary: once, sitting in glorious sunshine at Lord's, his companion said that such a prospect made one glad to be alive. Beckett responded, 'I wouldn't go that far.' When he won the Nobel in 1969 – coincidentally, on the fifty-fourth anniversary of W. G. Grace's death – his wife, Suzanne Dechevaux-Demesnil, said, 'This is a catastrophe.'

The only man ...
who has played Test cricket for England and has four of the same letter in his surname is Alan Mullally. Tall and languid, with a mop of blond hair and a look on his face of constant mild bemusement,

---

* *Gardien de guichet*

Mullally was a left-arm seamer who never quite fired in England colours, but nonetheless played nineteen Tests between 1996 and 2001. (Lawrence Booth has described him, not inaccurately, as 'tidy rather than terrifying'.) He is probably best remembered now as part of the Tail of Doom, when the England selectors unaccountably picked three number 11s to go in 9, 10 and 11. The trio, Mullally, Phil Tufnell and Ed Giddins, played against New Zealand at the Oval in 1999 and scored nine runs in six innings between them. Close observers thought they were lucky to get those. If Devon Malcolm had been playing, he'd probably have gone in at number 8.

The only man ...

ever to be knighted for services to cricket while still playing Tests was New Zealand's Sir Richard Hadlee, in 1990. (Sir Donald Bradman played two first-class games after being knighted, but no Tests.) Sir Richard was the first bowler to four hundred Test wickets and, by any standards, one of the greatest bowlers of all time. As Andrew Miller has written, 'Few players ... have carried the fortunes of their team to quite the same extent as Richard Hadlee.' He was still at the top of his game when he retired, aged thirty-nine, in 1990, having taken 5 for 53 against England at Trent Bridge, including a wicket with his very last ball. Glenn McGrath, as so often, went further, taking wickets off his last ball in Tests, his last ball in ODIs and his last ball in international T20s.

The only man ...

who played Test cricket and was later executed for murder was Leslie Hylton. A fast bowler who played in six Tests for the West Indies between 1935 and 1939, Hylton was hanged in Jamaica in 1955, a few weeks after his fiftieth birthday, for the murder of his wife Lurline. During his trial, he claimed to have been trying to shoot himself, but missed. As there were seven bullets in his wife's body, this excuse was disregarded. The date of the hanging coincided with the fourth Test between the West Indies and Australia in Barbados. The West Indian opener John Holt was going through a poor run with the bat, and dropped a couple of sitters in the slips. A banner in the crowd read 'Hang Holt, Save Hylton'.

The only man ...

since the Second World War to have taken a wicket for England with his first ball in Tests is the left-arm spinner Richard Illingworth, who bowled the West Indies' Phil Simmons at Trent Bridge in 1991. Illingworth, who is no relation at all to Ray Illingworth, subsequently became an international umpire, although the rules now requiring every umpire to be neutral mean that the only country in which he hasn't stood in a Test is his own.

Twenty men in all have taken a wicket with their first ball in Tests, and only one of them went on to take more than two hundred wickets in all: the Australian off-spinner Nathan Lyon. Who, by complete coincidence, is one of very few players to stop play by burning toast in the dressing room. It happened in 2017 when New South Wales were playing Queensland in the Sheffield Shield. The smoke alarm went off, the fire brigade was called and play was suspended for thirty minutes.

The only man ...

to play in a Football League match in the middle of scoring a first-class century was Chris Balderstone, for Leicestershire and Doncaster Rovers in September 1975. Balderstone, who played two Tests for England the following summer, was 51 not out when bad light stopped play early against Derbyshire at Chesterfield. As he had a bit of time, he got in his car and drove up to Doncaster, where he played a Division 3 match against Brentford, which ended 0–0. He then drove back to Chesterfield, slept like a lord and completed his century the following morning, finally being dismissed for 116.

The only man ...

to win the 440-yard hurdles at Crystal Palace in the middle of scoring a first-class century was W. G. Grace. He was eighteen years old, and in Jon Hotten's words, 'about to reshape the game in his image'. Playing for All-England against Surrey at the Oval in 1866, Grace had just completed his first-ever first-class century, and was not out overnight. So he hotfooted it to Crystal Palace and won the race, wearing his pink racing knickerbockers. The following morning, he carried on batting and eventually reached 224 not out. Four weeks later he returned to the Oval and made 173 for the Gentlemen of the South against the Players. Of Grace's 126 centuries, only two were scored in Tests, both of them at the Oval.

The only man ...

to tell Sir Donald Bradman how to bat and get away with it was Field Marshal Bernard Montgomery. According to Sir John Major (who seems a reliable source), Bradman had just scored his famous second-ball duck in his final Test match at the Oval in 1948. (If he had scored 4 he would have left the Test arena with a batting average of 100. As it was he had to live the rest of his life with a far-from-untidy 99.94.) As he returned to the pavilion, devastated by the turn of events, he was accosted by the bellicose Field Marshal. 'Bradman,' said Montgomery, 'can you spare me a moment? I would like to tell you where you went wrong.' No one knows what happened next, presumably because everyone else fled in abject terror.

It's not Montgomery's only connection with the great game, though. H. M. 'Monty' Garland-Wells was an English amateur who played for Oxford University and Surrey between 1927 and 1939, and captained Surrey in his last season. He was a middle-order batsman and a bowler of medium-pace cutters, who once bowled Donald Bradman for 32. During the Second World War, 'Garland-Wells' was used during the North Africa campaign as a secret code to refer to Field Marshal Montgomery. As *Wisden* put it, 'This was more impenetrable to the Germans than the most complicated cipher.'

The only man ...

to score a triple century in his final Test was Andrew Sandham of Surrey, whose 325 against the West Indies in Kingston in 1930 was the world's first Test triple-century. 'I would not have done [it] but for Joe Hardstaff, who was umpiring. I started with sore toes and after reaching 100 I said to Joe: "I'm off now." But he said: "No, you stay here and talk to me. I don't know anyone out here."' Every time he passed an important milestone he said he was going, but Hardstaff always found a reason for him to stay. 'By tea-time on the second day I had scored about 250 and somebody had been looking up the record by an Englishman in the West Indies. It was around 260 and Joe said: "Stay here and beat that."' Sandham's 325 stood as the highest innings in Test history for ninety-eight days, until Don Bradman scored 334 not out for Australia against England at Headingley – or did it? The fact is that the Kingston Test in which Sandham played had not been scheduled and wasn't initially deemed to be a real Test match. The MCC did not bestow Test status on the match until after Bradman's innings, so the record didn't exist until it had already been broken. The following summer, Jack Hobbs and Herbert Sutcliffe came back into the side (they had been given the West Indies tour off for good behaviour) and Sandham never played for England again.

The only man ...

to score three hundred runs in a single day in a Test match was, possibly inevitably, Donald Bradman. The date was July 11 1930, the place was Headingley, and Bradman, aged twenty-one, walked out to the crease after only eleven balls had been bowled. In his autobiography, Harold Larwood claimed he had got Bradman out caught behind when he was on 0. The umpires were unmoved. (And Larwood was wrong: the ball-by-ball details show that he didn't bowl to Bradman before he had scored.)

Bradman hadn't picked up a bat for a week. At lunch he was 105 not out, at tea he was 220 not out; he then slowed down a little (relatively speaking) to reach 309 not out by the close. 'To call him a run-getting machine as he has been called is a poor compliment,' wrote Plum Warner. 'That rather implies that the runs are ground out with a roar and a clash and a clatter, while as a fact he makes his runs easily and smoothly and naturally, with the mark of genius throughout.'

Eight Englishmen have scored two hundred runs in a day. Four of them were Walter Hammond. The others were R. E. 'Tip' Foster (a record-breaking 287 in 1905), Sir Leonard Hutton, Denis Compton . . . and only one man since 1954. That man is the nuggety Surrey left-hander Graham Thorpe, who hit 200 not out against New Zealand in Christchurch in 2001–02. Chris Cairns was unable to bowl or field because of a knee injury, but the runs don't make themselves. Thorpe's double-century was the third-fastest in Tests at the time – until Nathan Astle made 222 in 168 balls the following day. New Zealand needed 550 to win; they reached 451, thanks to Astle, and lost by a mere ninety-eight runs.

The only man . . .
(other than Samuel Beckett) to have both won the Nobel Prize for Literature and received an obituary in *Wisden* was the playwright and poet Sir Harold Pinter. Although not a first-class cricketer, Pinter was a cricket tragic of the first water, who once said, 'I tend to believe that cricket is the greatest thing that God ever created on earth . . . certainly greater than sex, although sex isn't too bad either.' For many years he ran a travelling team called The Gaieties – although, one has to say, his own personality was far from gay. Charles Collingwood, who has played Brian Aldridge

in *The Archers* since 1975, also used to run a cricket club, and like all of us, sometimes had to work quite hard to get eleven players to take the field. 'How well I remember the occasion when the last untried name on my list was H Pinter. Nervously I dialled the number at 8.30 on the morning of the game and, after what seemed like an eternity, the receiver was lifted.

'"Hello," a deep, husky voice said.

'"Is that Harold Pinter?"

'"Yes."

'With an audible tremor in my voice I enquired whether he would be free to play for the Stage against Richmond that afternoon.

'Rather surprisingly without a pause, he said, "Fuck off," and hung up.'

The only rabbit . . .
to have six Test pairs to his name – dismissed without scoring in both innings – was the New Zealand bowler Chris Martin, who was such a poor batsman he is better characterised as a ferret (goes in after the rabbits). Martin probably spent more time putting his kit on than actually batting, and his bats were renowned for the absence of red ball-shaped marks in and around their sweet spot, if indeed they had a sweet spot.

New Zealand has a long and honourable history of producing rabbits: Ewen Chatfield, Danny Morrison and Geoff Allott all come to mind. But Martin has a reasonable claim to the title of Worst Batsman Test Cricket Has Ever Seen. In 2009 Imran Coomaraswamy produced a valuable analysis of Martin's career figures on the ESPNcricinfo website, which we can now update slightly. In seventy-one Tests Martin scored 123 runs at an average of 2.36 per innings, just over half the number of wickets he took (233). Roughly a third of his innings resulted in ducks, another third found him stranded on 0 not out, and the other third produced single-digit scores. His only double-figure score, 12 not out, was achieved against the might of Bangladesh. His best against a major cricketing nation was 7. 'Getting Martin out,' said Brydon Coverdale on ESPNcricinfo, 'was as difficult as making a cup of tea.' Often left out of ODI teams, Martin once revealed that New Zealand coach John Bracewell had no misgivings about including him in the T20 team because the likelihood of him having to bat was minimal. He never, in any cricket, batted anywhere other than number 11. In March 2009, he survived five balls to allow his team-mate Jesse Ryder to complete a maiden Test century: the reaction was disbelief. But Martin was a good egg who clearly took all this in good heart: on the New Zealand TV comedy show *Pulp Sport*, he once made a cameo appearance, advertising his new video, *Learn to Bat Like Chris Martin*.

Geoff Allott, by the way, batted for 101 minutes before being dismissed against South Africa at Auckland in 1998–99. His final score was 0.

Favourite Tests

Port-of-Spain, April 21, 22, 23 1995

WEST INDIES vs AUSTRALIA: Third Test

Australia

*M A Taylor	c Adams b Ambrose	2	—	(2) c Murray b K C G Benjamin	30
M J Slater	c Murray b Walsh	0	—	(1) c Richardson b Walsh	15
D C Boon	c Richardson b Ambrose	18	—	c sub b Walsh	9
M E Waugh	c Murray b Ambrose	2	—	lbw b Ambrose	7
S R Waugh	not out	63	—	c Hooper b K C G Benjamin	21
G S Blewett	c Murray b W K M Benjamin	17	—	c Murray b K C G Benjamin	2
†I A Healy	c Richardson b Walsh	8	—	b Ambrose	0
B P Julian	c Adams b K C G Benjamin	0	—	b Ambrose	0
P R Reiffel	c Lara b Walsh	11	—	c Hooper b Ambrose	6
S K Warne	b Ambrose	0	—	c Hooper b Walsh	11
G D McGrath	c Murray b Ambrose	0	—	not out	0
	lb 6, w 1	7		lb 3, nb 1	4
		128			**105**

1–2 (2), 2–2 (1), 3–14 (4), 4–37 (3), 5–62 (6), 6–95 (7), 7–98 (8), 8–121 (9), 9–128 (10), 10–128 (11)

1–26 (1), 2–52 (2), 3–56 (3), 4–85 (5), 5–85 (4), 6–85 (7), 7–87 (6), 8–87 (8), 9–105 (10), 10–105 (9)

Ambrose	16–5–45–5		Ambrose	10.1–1–20–4
Walsh	17–4–50–3		Walsh	13–4–35–3
W K M Benjamin	6–3–13–1		W K M Benjamin	5–0–15–0
K C G Benjamin	8–2–14–1		K C G Benjamin	8–1–32–3

West Indies

S C Williams	c Taylor b Reiffel	0	—	c Warne b M E Waugh	42
*R B Richardson	c Healy b McGrath	2	—	not out	38
B C Lara	c Taylor b McGrath	24	—	not out	14
J C Adams	c M E Waugh b Reiffel	42	—		
C L Hooper	c Reiffel b S R Waugh	21	—		
K L T Arthurton	c M E Waugh b McGrath	5	—		
†J R Murray	c Healey b McGrath	13	—		
W K M Benjamin	c Slater b Warne	7	—		
C E L Ambrose	c Slater b McGrath	1	—		
C A Walsh	c Blewett b McGrath	14	—		
K C G Benjamin	not out	1	—		
	lb 4, nb 2	6		b 4	4
		136		(1 wkt)	98

1–1 (1), 2–6 (2), 3–42 (3), 4–87 (5), 5–95 (6), 6–106 (4), 7–113 (8), 8–114 (9), 9–129 (7), 10–136 (10)

1–81 (1)

McGrath	21.5–11–47–6		McGrath	6–1–22–0
Reiffel	16–7–26–2		Reiffel	6–2–21–0
Julian	7–1–24–0		Julian	3–0–16–0
S R Waugh	3–1–19–0		Warne	3.5–0–26–0
Warne	12–5–16–1		M E Waugh	2–0–9–1

Umpires: D R Shepherd (E) and C E Cumberbatch (WI)
Referee: Majid Khan (P)

In the 1980s and early 1990s the West Indies were unequivocally the best team in the world. In the '90s, Australia superseded them. But when, precisely? In *The Meaning of Cricket*, Jon Hotten points to the 1994–95 series in the West Indies, and specifically to the third Test, a match that Australia actually lost. Australia had won the first Test, in Barbados, by ten wickets, the first three-day defeat imposed on the home team in thirty years. Brendon Julian (4–36) and Glenn McGrath (3–46) bowled out the West Indies for 195 (Brian Lara 65, Carl Hooper 60), before Australia hit 346, with skipper Mark Taylor scoring 55, Steve Waugh 65 and Ian Healy 74 not out. Second time around the West Indies went for 189, with McGrath taking 5–68 and Shane Warne 3–64. The second Test match (of four) was a rain-ruined, low-scoring draw, so the West Indies badly needed a result. The pitch in Trinidad wasn't great. 'The Australians,' said *Wisden*, 'had a suspicion of trouble when they went looking for the pitch and could barely pick it out from the rest of the gumleaf-green square ... Fast bowlers looked at it and grinned like fat men about to tackle Christmas dinner.' Steve Waugh thought that anything approaching 150 would be competitive, but Curtly Ambrose and Courtney Walsh scythed through his team's upper order. Mark Waugh, the strokemaker's strokemaker, managed just two singles in twenty-five minutes before edging behind.

But his twin stood firm. He didn't like Ambrose and he didn't care who knew it. As the ball whistled around his ears, Waugh swore at the bowler and then faced him down, six feet away. Ambrose had to be forcibly restrained by his captain, Richie Richardson. 'It's Test cricket,' said Waugh afterwards. 'If you want an easy game, go play netball.' One could imagine Clint Eastwood saying something similar, possibly chewing on a cigarillo.

Where Ambrose had led, McGrath followed, and the outswing-ing yorker Lara edged to slip was reckoned by some to be the ball of the series. Australia had a deficit of just eight on first innings, but they could not make the most of it, collapsing from the relative comfort of 85 for 3 to a feeble 105 all out. The West Indies only needed 98 and chose to have a dash for it, which worked rather well. Lara hit the winning runs, a six off Warne. The match only took 164 overs and, but for rain, might have finished earlier than tea on the third day.

So 1–1 with one to play. But the continental plates of

international cricket had shifted. As Justin Langer said of Waugh, 'To stand up to the best fast bowler of our time and go toe to toe ... it gave us a huge boost.' On an altogether friendlier wicket at Kingston, the West Indies were dismissed for 265 and Australia put together a mountainous 531, formed around a fourth-wicket partnership of 231 between Mark Waugh, who made 126, and Steve Waugh, who hit exactly 200. He was last out after just under ten hours at the crease, facing 425 balls, of which more than 150 were short-pitched. According to Robert Craddock in *Wisden*, he 'had 17 fours, one six and six aching bruises at the end of his greatest innings'. Warne went to town in the second innings, with 4–70, and West Indies lost by an innings and 53 runs. We all know what happened after that. Within five years even England were beating the West Indies, while Australia were crushing all-comers with a Waugh-like grimace on their lips and all the charm of a rainy fortnight in Margate. Happy days, for them at least.

Julian's XIs

Body Parts

1	C. H. Tongue	(Cambridge University)
2	D. Shoulder	(Barton)
3	B. M. Brain	(Gloucestershire, Minor Counties, Worcestershire)
4	E. M. Balls	(Lords and Commons)
5	H. Heart	(Frankford)
6	J. M. Kidney	(Barbados)
7	P. S. Ear	(Colston's School)
8	M. Liver	(Garstang, Garstang Second XI, Garstang Third XI)
9	H. Kneebone	(Wangaratta)
10	A. Arm	(Sulhamstead and Ufton Second XI)
11	J. Leg	(Kirkby Portland Second XI)
12th man	T. M. Head	(Adelaide Strikers, Australia, Royal Challengers Bangalore, South Australia, Worcestershire, Yorkshire)

The Village Year

Many teams train hard and practise assiduously in order to hit the ground running when the first game comes along. We tend to hit the ground and go splat. For some reason I have an image in my mind of Ben, a big burly batsman and one of our best players, dropping an absolute sitter at square leg in the first over of the first game of the season, against our old rivals the Railway Taverners. The batsman went on to score a century. Of course he did. Even the players who have privately netted and rehearsed their swishing off drives with a ruler in the mirror all winter can't get going. You can almost hear the knees creak. There's also a more fundamental problem, in that players who have found form in the warmth and on the fast wickets of indoor nets now come out and bat in the cold and the wet on the stodgiest wickets known to mankind. As I once said, nets precede a nought.

In April 2017, as always, our footballing players were unavailable, as they were all in pubs watching football, so I had to scout about a bit to fill the team. One of our old players, Andrew, who hadn't played for us in fifteen years, said he'd like to make a comeback, and he had a seventeen-year-old son who played a bit as well. Phew! I thought. Two birds with one stone. The Railway Taverners looked young and disturbingly hungry (it turned out that the pub kitchen was closed and they hadn't had any lunch). Andrew said his son Joe was an opening batsman, so when we won the toss, we batted. Joe took the first ball. He looked very good. In line, middle of the bat, played to his feet. Second ball went for four. So did the third. As we watched, with wonder and increasing delight, Joe did something I've only ever seen the very best batsmen do in first-class cricket. Wherever the ball was bowled, he somehow got into exactly the right position to hit it for four, or occasionally six. He saw it so early it was as though he knew where it was going before the bowler did. Joe scored 184, his father scored 48 not out in about seven minutes and we won the game. What are you up to next Sunday? I said to Joe afterwards. Unfortunately he was busy, as he has been almost every Sunday since.

May

May Birthdays

1: Sonny Ramadhin (1929), Gordon Greenidge (1951)
2: Brian Lara (1969)
3: Sadiq Mohammad (1945), David Hookes (1955)
4: Martyn Moxon (1960), Ravi Bopara (1985)
6: Neil Foster (1962)
8: Robin Hobbs (1942), Pat Cummins (1993)
11: Ian Redpath (1941)
12: Rob Key (1979)
14: Bob Woolmer (1948)
15: Ted Dexter (1935)
17: Alfred 'Tich' Freeman (1888), Bhagwat Chandrasekhar (1945)
18: Hedley Verity (1905), Graham Dilley (1959)
19: Gilbert Jessop (1874)
20: Deryck Murray (1943), Keith Fletcher (1944)
21: Isa Guha (1985)
22: Erapalli Prasanna (1940)
23: Denis Compton (1918), Graeme Hick (1966)
24: Martin McCague (1969)
25: Robert Croft (1970)
26: Glenn Turner (1947), Paul Collingwood (1976)
27: Frank Woolley (1887), Ravi Shastri (1962), Michael Hussey (1975), Mahela Jayawardene (1977)
28: Jeff Dujon (1956), Misbah-ul-Haq (1974), Ashwell Prince (1977)
29: T. C. 'Dickie' Dodds (1919)
30: Maurice Tate (1895), George Headley (1909), Jagmohan Dalmiya (1940), Bob Willis (1949)
31: Steve Bucknor (1946)

Brian Lara *(May 2)*

As Rob Smyth notes, at the end of his Test career no other player had made more than 3059 runs in defeats. Lara made 5316. 'In the 2000s alone, he played eight innings in excess of 150 in defeat. Often his team were not just beaten, but thrashed.' Apparently Lara wasn't that popular with his team-mates. Maybe they would have liked him more if he had kept getting out for 0, like all of them.

Martyn Moxon *(May 4)*

Yorkshire opener of the 1980s and 1990s who suffered two extraordinary pieces of bad luck. In one of the ten Tests he played, he made 99 for England against New Zealand at Auckland in 1987–88. Early in this innings, he swept the ball for three runs off the middle of his bat, only to see the umpire give it as three leg byes. In the following Test he was set to right this terrible wrong, and at the end of the third day was 81 not out. The last two days were washed out by rain and not another ball was bowled. Moxon never did make a Test century.

Robin Hobbs *(May 8)*

Essex leg-spinner of the late 1960s and early 1970s who played seven Tests for England. Hobbs was not best buddies with his Test captain, Ray Illingworth, who didn't like him or rate him and didn't care who knew it. In his last Test against Pakistan in 1971, played on a seamers' wicket at Headingley, Hobbs did not take a wicket and never looked like taking one. He was unimpressed. 'I went up to the changing room to get my bag and said goodbye to the lads. I didn't change, I went down in my whites, jumped in my red Mini and drove home to Ingatestone. I'd been decorating my house and I was so angry that I got a tin of red paint and I wrote "F*** Illingworth" all round the walls of my lounge. Later on David Acfield helped me paint over it. It took ten coats to get rid of it.'

Ted Dexter *(May 15)*

In 1976 Dexter published, with Clifford Makins, a novel called *Testkill*, a murder mystery set against the drama of an Ashes Test at Lord's. I read somewhere that it's one of the worst novels ever written, so of course I had to read it. It's actually quite efficiently done. The sex is appalling, the women are unlike any women who have ever walked the earth, the sexual politics are not so much dated as carbon-dated, everybody drinks constantly (champagne for breakfast, pink gins for lunch), the murders make no sense at all, and the murderer is someone you'd barely noticed, who turns out to be as mad as a March Pietersen. The hero, Jack Stenton, is a former public schoolboy with a short temper (and an even shorter attention span), who used to bat with some style for England but now, aged forty-five, is plying his trade as a journalist. Hmm, wonder where that character came from? But the story does rattle along, and the dramatis personae include characters not unlike Gubby Allen and E. W. Swanton. As it happens, both of them are horribly murdered. Wishful thinking, maybe?

Gilbert Jessop *(May 19)*

'As a hitter, Jessop stands absolutely alone; others, such as C. I. Thornton and Bonnor, may have driven the ball farther and higher, but no cricketer that has ever lived hit it so often, so fast, and with such a bewildering variety of strokes. His very stance, like a panther's crouch, bespoke aggression ... Length had no meaning for him; it was the length ball he hit best, and he hit it where the whim or the placing of the field suggested.' (H. S. Altham)

'A shortish man, dreaded by the Civil Service Commissioners and Merchant Banks as the most effective office-emptier in history. He *assaulted* bowling, redirecting balls like stones from a catapult ... His cricket career ended in 1916 when he was forgotten in a heat-treatment box.' (J. L. Carr)

Denis Compton *(May 23)*

'One afternoon Compton came in from batting at the tea interval, and was enduring with his usual indulgence the shafts of genially abusive humour which are a long tradition of the Middlesex dressing-room. Someone, probably Walter Robins, said: "It's a funny thing a strong chap like you can't drive the ball straight. We never see you hit it over the bowler's head." Compton said: "Yes, it is funny; look out for the third ball after tea.' A few minutes afterwards the third ball bowled came whistling straight and true into the Members' seats in front of the pavilion, and, as the umpire was signalling "six" Compton waved his bat cheerfully to his companions.' (E. W. Swanton)

John Arlott once bumped into Compton and his Middlesex teammate Bill Knightley-Smith in St John's Wood High Street. 'Ah,' said Arlott. 'It's Knightley-Smith. And Twice-Nightly Compton.'

T. C. 'Dickie' Dodds *(May 29)*

Dashing Essex opening batsman of the 1940s and 1950s who, according to his obituary in the *Daily Telegraph*, 'hit sixes in accordance with his religious convictions'. Most other God-fearing cricketers eventually abandon the game for full-time worship, but Dodds took the view that the best way to glorify God was to play cricket in the right spirit – which, in his case, meant smashing the ball out of the ground.

Like many of his contemporaries, Dodds lost many of his best years to the Second World War. In those days he was mainly a leg-spinner, and served with the Signals in India and Burma. In Bombay he played for a Service XI, captained by our old friend Douglas Jardine. Dodds's leg-breaks were being carted to all parts, so he asked Jardine if he could move a fielder to the boundary. Jardine was enraged. 'You and I are amateurs,' he barked. 'It is only professionals who ask to have their field shifted when they are hit for four.'

Dodds regularly hit the first two deliveries of decent bowlers for four and six. After retirement, he was delighted to hear Ian Botham on the radio describing his great feats against Australia in 1981. 'You've got to enjoy it, let it speak for itself, let it take you over,' said Botham. 'You know, Dickie,' a priest told Dodds later, 'that is the perfect expression of the Holy Ghost.'

Maurice Tate *(May 30)*

Took a wicket with his first ball in Test cricket, when he and Arthur Gilligan bowled South Africa out for 30 in 12.3 overs in 1924. In 1924–25, touring Australia, Tate took thirty-eight wickets at 23.18. No Englishman has since taken more. For the definitive word on Tate, though, here's J. L. Carr:

'Maurice Tate took 2783 wickets (average 18) and was the greatest medium-fast bowler of his era. He never bowled a no-ball, and his single wide was a floater carried off by the wind. Arms semaphoring, his final footfall struck the turf so hard that cover-points reported slight earth-shocks. His *best* ball was an outswinger which moved in line of middle and off but, at the last instant, swerved outwards. His *unplayable* ball was this bowled in a Brighton sea-fret.'

George Headley *(May 30)*

West Indian titan who, with Learie Constantine, held his team together in the 1930s. When Headley was out cheaply, the West Indies would usually be all out for less than a hundred. In just twenty-two Tests he scored 2190 runs at an average of 60.93. 'So accomplished was his batsmanship that Anglo-Australian writers liked to call him the "Black Bradman",' wrote Ramachandra Guha. 'His own compatriots thought this inexact as well as patronising: they would rather refer to the Don as "the White Headley".' C. L. R. James thought him second only to Bradman, although 'Bradman's curious deficiency on wet wickets has been the subject of much searching comment. George's superior record has been noticed before, and one critic, I think it was Neville Cardus, has stated that Headley has good claims to be considered *on all wickets* the finest of the inter-war batsmen.'

And it all might not have been. When England were touring the West Indies in 1929–30, the entire Headley family were about to emigrate to the United States. But George's passport was delayed. So he played for Jamaica against the tourists, scored a century, was picked for the West Indies, and never looked back. On such tiny threads of mischance are great careers forged.

Bob Willis *(May 30)*

Took 8 for 43 against Australia at Headingley in 1981, when Australia needed 130 to win and could only muster 111. England cricket fans of a certain age know all these statistics by heart, and when they shut their eyes they can still see Willis running in from the Kirkstall Lane End like a crazed wildebeest. His run-up was long and not a thing of beauty. 'I don't go as far as that on my holidays,' said another (unidentified) fast bowler. Frank Keating compared his run-up to 'a 1914 biplane tied up with elastic bands trying vainly to take off'.

In 2011, at a Lord's Taverners dinner celebrating the thirtieth anniversary of the match, Willis was asked what had got into him to enable him to take 8 for 43. 'Heroin,' he replied. (Note from lawyer: this was a joke.)

After retirement, Willis was recruited to the Sky Sports commentary team, where he swiftly became renowned for his Eeyore-like gloom and relentless pessimism. As tastes changed, and cricket commentary became more upbeat, Willis was removed from the frontline and found a more comfortable niche in the mid-evening highlights slot, where he tells it like it is: that everyone played appallingly, that the world is going to hell in a handcart, and we would all be better off if we ended it all now.

Friends and Enemies

Playing as I do an entirely social form of the game – in which it's important that team-mates actually like one another – I have long been fascinated by the extent to which real cricketers actually get on, either with their team-mates or their opponents. Some are clearly very sociable, to the point of falling down drunk in one or two cases; some are less so. One of the very few Test cricketers I have ever met is Michael Atherton, with whom I worked on some project many years ago in Cornwall. I asked him if he had made any good friends while playing. He looked at me as though I was mad. 'Well, Gus Fraser, I suppose,' he said before falling silent. He had not been out there to make friends. I wouldn't have been there for any other reason. But then he played a hundred Tests and my average with the bat is five and a half. Different strokes for different folks, as they say.

There are, of course, some legendary antipathies. I read somewhere that Dilip Vengsarkar of India and Malcolm Marshall absolutely hated each other. Apparently, in his first Test, Marshall had been batting and Vengsarkar, fielding at slip, had claimed a catch off his pad. Marshall was given out for nought and left the field in tears. Thereafter, whenever Vengsarkar came in to bat, Marshall upped his pace by 10 mph, peppered the Indian batsman with bouncers and usually got him out cheaply. If you're going to get on the wrong side of someone, it's probably wise not to make it one of the best fast bowlers who ever lived.

Here are a few prominent cricketers discussing team-mates, opponents, friends, enemies.

Steve Waugh on Devon Malcolm

'I always found facing Devon Malcolm a difficult assignment, largely due to his unpredictability and genuine pace. He was a match-winner, but throughout his career he didn't fit the mould required by the English selectors. He was poorly managed, plagued by inconsistent selection and hampered by team strategies. Australia, as a team, breathed a sigh of relief whenever a steady medium-pacer was picked in front of him ... On his day, he was as quick as anyone I'd ever faced.'

The Nightwatchman

Mark Nicholas on Robin Smith

'I have long thought that the flaw in Robin is that he listens willingly but does not always hear. By the time his Test career ended prematurely in 1996, he was a marginally less good version of exactly the same batsman [Allan] Lamb met in the middle at Headingley in 1988. Most cricketers change. The nature of the hurdles they face, the opponents who study them and the march of time demand that technique, method and approach become subject to rethinks. Robin had stayed pretty much the same, if understandably scarred by the years of battle. At his best, he was exceptional, but he had fewer gears than others less gifted. This was the reason the England selectors, who could not possibly have understood his complex character and the upbringing that came with it, were to mess him about in the latter half of the career.'

A Beautiful Game, 2016

Michael Atherton on Angus Fraser

'His personal example was outstanding. I cannot remember a time that he did not give his absolute all on the field. Of course, playing for your country, that should be a natural state of affairs, but all players go through phases – and I'm not talking about "form" here – where off-the-field problems impact upon their state of mind and ability to focus and concentrate. It always seemed to me that Gus gave his all to every ball that he bowled ...

'In and around the dressing room, he was a valuable source of honest reaction. One of the earliest changes I noticed as captain was that other players became more guarded when they spoke in my company, less willing to be as direct or critical as they had previously been for fear of upsetting someone who might have some influence to bear on selection ... Gus, though, remained loyal. Not loyal to me, but loyal to his instincts, his need for honesty and directness. He was quite happy to tell me when I behaved foolishly. In the Sydney Test [of 1995], for example, he was quite clear that he thought I had messed up in declaring on Graeme Hick. He was not afraid to criticise selections I had made or field placings, or the content of teamtalks. Leaders must never fight shy of surrounding themselves with people who will hold them to account and tell them things they may not wish to hear. It is so valuable.'

Team Mates, 2016

Angus Fraser on Mike Atherton

'A natural mistimer of the ball.'

Quoted by Atherton himself in the *Sunday Telegraph*, 1998

Mike Selvey on Angus Fraser

'Eeyore without the *joie de vivre*.'

Wisden, 1996

Vic Marks on Viv Richards

'We knew Richards was phenomenal right from the start. I remember the first middle practice at Taunton in April 1974. A cheerful, earnest pace bowler by the name of Bob Clapp, who would become an even better teacher, charged in; Richards rocked forward and then back and square cut with awesome certainty. As the ball smashed into the boundary boards Peter Roebuck and I looked at one another in tacit agreement. We were not going to get into the team ahead of this man.'

Team Mates, 2016

Vic Marks on Chris Tavaré

'At county level Tavaré frequently belied his reputation. He could tear attacks apart. This was more likely to happen in one-day cricket when he would gently advance down the pitch, head still, bat raised, the ominous precursor to him smashing the ball as hard as anyone in the game. He could deliver the most devastating of innings, though anyone newly arrived in his dressing room would not have a clue from Tavaré's demeanour about the outcome of his latest visit to the crease. Whether he had been dismissed for nought or 150 the bat would be gently returned into a meticulously well-ordered coffin before he sat down to mull over what had just happened.'

Team Mates, 2016

Mark Nicholas on batsmen sharing secrets

'[David Gower] said that after a rough time against Dennis Lillee, he approached Greg Chappell for some advice. Chappell told him he was playing the wrong half of the ball. "Dennis is running it across you, so you have to play the outside half of the ball. You're committed to the inside half." Good grief. Gower said he understood it and responded with some better returns.

'Justin Langer told Ian Chappell he was sick of getting hit by the short ball. Chappell told him to focus on the hand that had the ball in it and nothing else – in other words, not a general area but specifically the ball in the hand. "You pretty much can't get hit if you do that: your eye and brain will work faster than the ball." Langer was staggered at the improvement. I wish I'd asked Chappell the same question forty years ago.'

A Beautiful Game, 2016

Steve Waugh on Shane Warne and Daryll Cullinan

'Warne owned the head-space of Cullinan, one of South Africa's better batsmen of the 1990s, and they both knew it. Every time Cullinan made his way to the crease when the ball was within Shane's sizeable grasp, we could see him shrinking both mentally and physically with each painstaking step, as if the inevitable guillotine was hovering above. It was always just a matter of time.'

The Meaning of Luck, 2013

Mike Brearley on Ian Chappell and Andy Roberts

'[Chappell] found Roberts's short ball harder to deal with than anyone else's. It was always straight, and, arriving around chest height, was never wasted. Chappell would fend the ball off, duck and take blows, waiting for a short ball just outside off stump that would give him room to swing his arms and pull or hook. Just once, during a World Series match, he got such a ball and pulled it away for four. Never again, Chappell said. Recently he had commented on this to Roberts. Roberts remembered it well. He wasn't going to give him such a ball again. And he never did.'

On Form, 2017

Geoff Marsh (Australian coach) on Sir Donald Bradman

'We had him down for a seminar in 1997 ... to come and meet the players. One of the questions I asked was, "What sort of things did you do when you were out of form?" And he looked at me and said, "I can't answer that." I asked him why. He said, "Well, when I played, I was never out of form."'

Quoted in *On Form*, 2017

Mike Selvey on Wayne Daniel

'Histrionics were not for him. If he beat the bat he was sanguine, a stare perhaps, but then a wipe of a glistening brow and the march back to his mark, moaning about how tough life was having to walk back into the breeze. Just once we saw him angry. He was batting at Hove in the semi-final of what was to be the last Gillette Cup. It was a tricky pitch and Middlesex had been struggling. In those days, the viewing area for teams was on top of the pavilion, square to the pitch, and from here it was obvious that Arnold Long, the Sussex keeper, was standing a long way back for Imran Khan, who was galloping down the hill and bowling with great rapidity. For reasons best known to himself, Imran decided to bounce Wayne. It was not a wise move, something instantly recognised by Long, who even before the ball smacked into his gloves was heard to shout, "You c***!" The recipient of the bouncer was incandescent when he returned to the dressing room, eyes blazing, the whites turned red. He threatened reprisal and, to the tune of 6 for 15 from ten overs, duly delivered. He was utterly brutal.'

Team Mates, 2016

David Lloyd on Jack Simmons

'Jack Simmons joined Lancashire very late in life for a professional cricketer. He came into county cricket at the age of twenty-nine after playing for a host of clubs around the Lancashire leagues. During his time at Lancashire he developed into a genuine character and never lost his amateur ways ...

'Jack was never too thrilled with pre-season training. The diet was always starting tomorrow; the leg always played up a bit which prevented any running. Oh, and he was thinking about packing up smoking.

'We used to finish our morning sessions with a three-to-five-mile run around Chorlton and Old Trafford. Simmo knew every short cut there was. He was spotted in various places which bore no resemblance to the route we were supposed to take. He was seen alighting from an articulated wagon at the gates of Old Trafford, having flagged the driver down and told him he was lost. He was also seen slumped in the doorway of the Throstle's Nest pub suffering from an acute stitch ...

'Jack's appetite is legendary and not without good reason. After all, he has had one delicacy in a local chip shop named after him on the menu. It is the imaginatively named "Jack Simmons Special", consisting of pudding, chips and peas with a fish on top ...

'Returning home from an away fixture one night Jack asked me to drop him off at his favourite chippy. He ordered one of his famed specials and then sat on the wall outside and proceeded to demolish the lot.

'"Why don't you take them home and eat them there?" I enquired.

'"No," he said. "If I did that, Jacqueline wouldn't make me any supper."'

Team Mates, 2016

Tony Lewis on Ray Illingworth

'On the field with him you sense that he knows every blade of grass by name. At Lord's, the Father Time weather vane turns by one degree behind his back and he will announce "wind's on the move".'

Daily Telegraph, 1994

Ian Botham on Ray Illingworth

'If I had my way, I would take him to the Traitor's Gate and personally hang, draw and quarter him.'

Independent, 1996

Paul Nixon on Hansie Cronje

'I loved the challenge of testing myself against Hansie. We competed against each other every day and pushed ourselves to the absolute limit ... He was a physical machine who brought a new intensity to our training and nets and never flagged. Around the club [Leicestershire], he commanded natural authority with his 1300 Championship runs, his mastery of run-chases, and his helpful attitude towards the younger batsmen.

'He was the perfect man to have around, really, and it seemed innocuous when the jokes started flying around about his legendary love of money. As quickly as he earned admiration for his approach to cricket, Hansie attracted a reputation as the tightest man at the club. Early into his stay he latched onto Gordon Parsons, his brother-in-law (Gordon was married to Hansie's sister, Hester) and began heading to his house every night for dinner. This, we concluded, was mainly because he was too stingy to buy his own food.'

Keeping Quiet: The Autobiography, 2012

Mike Brearley on Ted Dexter

'His main failing was that he easily became bored. In all three matches that I played under him in South Africa in 1964–65 there were periods in which he lost interest and was more concerned with getting his golf-swing right at square leg than with who should be bowling or with what field. He was an excellent theorist on the game; but when his theories failed to work, or he had no particular bright ideas, he would drift; and the whole team drifted with him. I would guess that Dexter was, in those day, more interested in ideas than in people.'

The Art of Captaincy, 1985

Matthew Hayden on Justin 'Alfie' Langer

'Connections are hard to contrive. They either happen or they don't. But from our very first partnership, Alfie and I just clicked, and I felt amazingly lucky to have found such a connection with someone who also happened to be my opening partner for Australia. And as with any best mate, it's not always about talking. When we were having that cigar under the stars we didn't need to talk much.

'We were more compatible technically than most people realise. Before we arrived, people used to talk about the benefits of a left- and right-handed combination, because bowlers had to constantly adjust their lines when the strike was rotated. The assumption that it was easier bowling to two lefties, because you could use the same plan. Not true – at least not with us.

'You couldn't bowl outside off stump to Alfie because he'd just nick you down to third man for fun. In fact, I always felt that's when he was in supreme form, when he was playing those cheeky little nudges through slips that looked half-accidental, but were actually the result of beautifully late, soft hands.

'In contrast, that wide ball was not my favourite delivery. For much of my career I didn't enjoy the cut shot, and my footwork was programmed to let dangerous balls go, not defuse or deflect them as Alfie so deftly did. My wrists were trained to turn to steel, his to rubber.

'We were products of our cricketing education. Because I learnt on seaming decks at the Gabba, balls that were pitched around off stump and moving away set off warning bells for me. But Alfie, like Damien Martyn, had learnt on the high, true-bouncing decks of Perth, where you can use the pace of the ball with soft hands to glide it to the third man boundary. Our partnership was a great argument for having different wickets in Australia, because you develop batsmen with different strengths. And it's another reason why I will always argue against "drop-in" pitches, which are more docile and lack character.'

Standing My Ground, 2010

Phil Tufnell on Ian Botham

'And then into the dressing room, for the first time in two years, exploded Ian Botham. This was what I had signed up for.

'It is hard to describe the wave of relief that washed over me when I heard the noise with which Botham announced his entrance. The sound itself is hard to describe, emanating as it appeared to do from a deep underground cavern, then booming from his mouth like the horn of an ocean-going liner announcing its imminent departure. Incorrectly aimed, the vibrations from one of Botham's belches might be capable of laying waste to a small market town. To me, though, it sounded like the music of the gods. As I sat in the corner of the changing room at the Oval, watching this living cricketing icon completely grip the attention of every single person just by being there, I offered up a silent prayer.

'"Thank God," I thought. "Thank God there is someone here who will stop everyone looking at *me*. Thank God there is someone here who is not blindly going to obey the regime if he doesn't think it is right. Thank God Beefy has come to save me.

'"Come on, lads," said one of the hierarchy. "Let's do a couple of laps."

'"Yeah, right. In a minute," said Beef.

'And I thanked God again.'

The Autobiography: What Now?, 1999

Ted Dexter on Peter May

'I found myself batting with him in my first Test innings on a dank day at Old Trafford against New Zealand. Tony MacGibbon, Johnny Hayes and Bob Blair were big raw-boned pace bowlers, the pitch was damp, the light not good and the ball was moving about. Peter May played and missed a few times, and I certainly did. The situation was quite awkward.

'I got the impression that he considered me to be something of a young scallywag, and he was probably right, but he offered me plenty of encouragement. He had been very kind and welcoming, as he always was, but I did not yet feel that I knew him very well. Suddenly he walked down the pitch and said, "There's nothing for it, I think they've got to go." The next thing I knew, the ball was whistling over extra cover and to all parts as he simply took the attack apart.

'It was part of the oddity about Peter that here was this quiet and reserved man, yet the moment he got a bat in his hand he was all aggression. During one of his early Tests in the West Indies, he went in and hit his first ball, or certainly one of his first, for six. Len Hutton, his captain, was batting at the other end, and enquired of him what was going on. Peter replied that he had not quite got to it, so thought he ought to carry on through with the shot. A power and a tension were present in his batting which were not obvious in his normal demeanour.'

Ted Dexter's Little Cricket Book, 1996

Derek Pringle on Graham Dilley

'A personable man, with a fondness for a pint and a fag, he was, in truth, probably too gentle to be the consummate fast bowler. From the side, though, he had all the attributes to be one, save that which tends to separate the hugely talented from the very best: a rigorous self-belief.'

The Promise of Endless Summer, 2013

Geoffrey Boycott on Derek Underwood

'The face of a choirboy, the demeanour of a civil servant and the ruthlessness of a rat catcher.'

Opening Up, 1980

Vic Marks on Chris Lewis

'The enigma with no variation'

Observer, 1994

David 'Bumble' Lloyd on Dermot Reeve

'I don't like you Reeve. I never have liked you. You get right up my nose and if you come anywhere near me, I'll rearrange yours.'

Quoted in *Dermot Reeve's Winning Ways*, 1997

Tony Greig on Geoffrey Boycott

'His ability to be where the fast bowlers aren't has long been a talking point among cricketers.'

After Boycott had turned down an offer
to join the Kerry Packer circus, 1978

Mike Brearley on Geoffrey Boycott

'As I stood at the non-striker's end, I felt a wave of admiration for my partner; wiry, slight, dedicated, a lonely man doing a lonely job all these years.'

The Ashes Retained, 1979

Pat Pocock on David Gower

'Real officer class. Languid self-possession. Confront him with a firing squad and he'd decline the blindfold.'

After Gower was appointed England captain, 1989

Shane Warne on Sachin Tendulkar

'He was unstoppable. I'll be going to bed having nightmares of Sachin just running down the wicket and belting me for six. I don't think anyone, besides Don Bradman, is in the same class.'

Interview, 1998. Tendulkar averaged 113
against the Australian tourists in India in that series

JULIAN'S XIs

Vegetable

1	V. Squash	(Riversdale)
2	Y. Yam	(HMS *Iron Duke*)
3	C. E. Neep	(Bury and West Suffolk)
4	A. Swede	(Buckinghamshire Under-15s)
5	W. Radish	(SS *Britannic*)
6	S. Gourd	(India Blind)
7	A. L. Pease	(Worcestershire Club and Ground)
8	G. Onions	(Dolphins, Durham, Durham Cricket Board, England, Marylebone Cricket Club)
9	J. Marrow	(Guildford Clergy)
10	A. Leek	(Leek)
11	S. E. Kale	(Manawatu, New Zealand Schools, Southern Hawke's Bay)
12th man	G. Caper	(Chelsea Club)

The Village Year

In May, the season is beginning to bed in properly. Some players return from their winter activities rather slowly, almost with reluctance, while others start the summer with an almost manic enthusiasm, but by the end of the month you should have a reasonable idea of how the season is going to pan out. Most cricket teams operate on roughly a five- to seven-year cycle. For two or three years in the middle of the cycle, the team will be very settled. The regulars play almost every week, and it's very hard for newcomers, or even returning oldcomers, to get a look in. But then one person gets injured, another gets sent away for work, one or two retire because their knees or eyes have gone, and openings in the team emerge. This is a crucial point in a team's history. I have known teams that were essentially groups of friends who simply enjoyed each other's company, and when a few drift off it's too hard for new players to come into the team, which seems like a closed shop of old in-jokes and even older wicketkeeping gloves. Teams like this often just fade away, but not without a couple of seasons of absolute incomprehension, as it becomes harder and harder to raise a team and more and more games have to be cancelled.

Personally, I favour a policy of permanent recruitment. I learned this from Harry Thompson, with whom I ran the Captain Scott Invitation XI for many years. If Harry went to a party he would always be on the lookout for potential cricketers. Maybe someone who hadn't played for a few years, or someone who had never played but had always fancied it, or someone currently playing for another team but not happy there. At the time I thought he was a fanatic, but years later I do exactly the same thing. We had a game recently at Smarden in Kent, and we only had six players. I threw myself on the mercy of social media, and somehow we came up with five players in the last couple of days. Of these five, three never played for us again, but two became absolute regulars, and were cornerstones of the team by the end of the season. This was a clear result. People come along and they like it or they don't. It's entirely out of your control, although I find that a decent pair of new wicketkeeping gloves helps no end.

June

June Birthdays

1: John Masefield (1878)
2: Mark and Steve Waugh (1965), Angelo Mathews (1987),
   Steve Smith (1989)
3: Wasim Akram (1966)
4: Ben Stokes (1991)
6: Frank Tyson (1930), Asif Iqbal (1943), Mike Gatting (1957),
   Aleem Dar (1968)
8: Ray Illingworth (1932), Derek Underwood (1945)
10: Ian Blackwell (1978)
11: Rachael Heyhoe Flint (1939), Matthew Engel (1951)
12: Terry Alderman (1956), Javed Miandad (1957)
13: K. S. Duleepsinhji (1905), Chris Cairns (1970)
16: 'Billy' Griffith (1914), Tom Graveney (1927)
17: Brian Statham (1930), Shane Watson (1981)
18: Moeen Ali (1987)
19: Walter Hammond (1903)
20: Allan Lamb (1954)
21: John Edrich (1937), Jeremy Coney (1952)
23: Sir Leonard Hutton (1916), Ramnaresh Sarwan (1980)
24: Brian Johnston (1912), Vernon Philander (1985),
    Stuart Broad (1986)
25: Vic Marks (1955)
27: Kevin Pietersen (1980), Dale Steyn (1983)
28: Mushtaq Ahmed (1970), Wahab Riaz (1985)
30: The Maharaja of Porbandar (1901), M. J. K. Smith (1933),
    Sanath Jayasuriya (1969)

John Masefield *(June 1)*

Poet Laureate from 1930 to 1967, who wrote a poem called 'The Oval (1882)', which contains the following couplets:

> Boyle took the ball; he turned; he ran; he bowled,
> All England's watching heart was stricken cold.

> Peate's whirling bat met nothing in its sweep.
> The ball put all his wickets in a heap.

In his introduction to *The Faber Book of Cricket*, Michael Davie nominates these as the worst couplets ever written about cricket, by anyone.

Steve Waugh *(June 2)*

Asked by an interviewer what his favourite animal was, Steve Waugh said, 'Merv Hughes'.

In his 168 Tests, Waugh was involved in twenty-seven run outs – not an enormous number, by any means, but what's interesting is that on twenty-three of those occasions, it was his partner who was run out. Shane Warne called him 'the most selfish cricketer I've played with'.

Wonderful sledger, though. In a Sheffield Shield match, he was getting ready to face his first ball and taking his time about it: taking guard, scratching out his mark, looking around at the field, generally faffing about. Finally, in the field Jamie Siddons lost his rag. 'For fuck's sake, mate, it's not a fucking Test match!' he yelled.

'Of course not,' said Waugh. 'You're here.'

Ben Stokes *(June 4)*

'A number six who comes out as all number sixes should, in a genuine fury, reeking of cigars and body odour, with a sense of bristling disdain for his opponents, for the five batsmen ahead of him and for the five still to come.' (Barney Ronay in the *Guardian*)

In the fracas outside a Bristol nightclub in 2017, which necessitated his absence from England's catastrophic tour of Australia that winter, Stokes punched his man thirteen times in around sixty seconds – thought to be an all-comers' record for the Bristol area.

Mike Gatting *(June 6)*

In his first Test, as a twenty-one-year-old tyro in Pakistan in 1977–78, Mike Gatting was given out lbw in both innings, for 5 in the first to the bowling of Abdul Qadir and for 6 in the second to the bowling of Iqbal Qasim. The umpire in both cases? Standing in his fourth Test, Shakoor Rana.

In 1984–85 India were playing England at Calcutta. Chris Cowdrey was bowling, and David Gower was the fielding captain.

'Do you want Gatt a foot wider?' said Cowdrey.

'No,' said Gower. 'He'd burst.'

Ray Illingworth *(June 8)*

The Yorkshire Brearley, whose captaincy added an extra dimension both to his own cricket and to England's. Won in Australia in 1970–71, and my greatest regret in life is that I wasn't quite old enough to be aware of it at the time. Left Yorkshire under a cloud, as everyone does, and led Leicestershire to countless trophies. One of his team-mates there was future BBC cricket correspondent Jonathan Agnew. 'While Leicester were in the field, he used to think out loud, running his ideas past senior players like Brian

Davison and Chris Balderstone, and was always entirely focused on the game, as if he was waiting for the moment to pounce.' After a spell behind the microphone saying everything twice – behind the microphone, he had a tendency to say everything twice – he became a grumpy and increasingly less effective coach and manager of England, but in his day Illingworth was a great man. As he once said, 'I've heard it said that this game at Test level is fifty per cent in the mind, fifty per cent in the heart, and bugger technique, and that's not far off the mark.' Or, as Sir Richard Hadlee once said, 'Ninety per cent of cricket is played in the mind.'

Ian Blackwell *(June 10)*

A left-arm spinner and powerful middle-order batsman, Blackwell played for Derbyshire (1997–99), Somerset (2000–08), Durham (2009–12) and one Test for England, scoring four runs and taking no wickets. But he was a much loved player, if only for his palpable girth in an era of slender and muscular players who ate only boiled chicken and salad and said no to cake at tea. Asked by the England selectors to lose several stone, he commented, 'If they want me to get down to that weight I will have to cut a leg off.'

Terry Alderman *(June 12)*

In the 1989 Ashes series – the unspeakable horror of which is seared on the mind of every true Englishman – the wicket-to-wicket bowling of Terry Alderman traumatised poor Graham Gooch, who kept missing and eventually asked to be left out of the team. When someone scrawled 'THATCHER OUT' on a wall, someone else added 'lbw b Alderman 0'.

Before the 2005 Ashes series, Alderman was asked what he thought of England's premier spinner Ashley Giles. 'I definitely believe if any of our batsmen get out to Ashley Giles in the Tests they should go and hang themselves,' he replied. 'But I am confident that won't happen.' Giles dismissed each of the Australian top eight at least once in the series.

Tom Graveney *(June 16)*

As Francis Wheen has said, 'Apart from Gower, the only England player I've seen who deserved an Arts Council grant for his batting. His 165 at the Oval in 1966, when aged nearly forty and facing the likes of Hall and Griffith, was one of the loveliest innings ever.'

Walter Hammond *(June 19)*

Impossibly stylish right-hander in the 1920s and 1930s for Gloucestershire and England, who but for Bradman would surely have been recognised as the best batsman in the world. Touring Australia in 1928–29, he scored 905 runs at an average of 113.12. Only one man has scored more in a series: Bradman. As Ramachandra Guha wrote, 'Theirs was one of the great rivalries of cricket, and it was usually the Australian who came out on top.' As a professional, Hammond could never captain England, so in 1938 he announced that he had taken a job outside cricket and would henceforth play as an amateur. The world opened its doors to him. Not only was Hammond named captain of England for the 1938 Ashes series, he was elected to life membership of Gloucestershire and elected a member of the MCC, which still actively barred professionals. That summer he captained the Gentlemen against the Players, becoming the only man ever to have led both teams. Not even Bradman managed that.

John Edrich *(June 21)*

Played fifty-seven innings against Australia without ever being out for 0.

Sir Leonard Hutton *(June 23)*

Here's Neville Cardus: 'He has emerged from a hard school. It has never been for Hutton a case of roses all the way; he had to dig the cricket out of his bones; a bat and the Yorkshire and England colours didn't fall into his mouth like silver cutlery ... There is no softness in Hutton's psychological or, therefore, in his technical make-up.' Or as Alan Ross put it, 'Like probably all men who can do one thing better than anyone else in the world, he seemed at moments unutterably wearied by it. The context of Hutton's cricket, the bleak decade when he almost alone in England – Compton and Bedser were allies – preserved its dignity, has been such that grace and levity seemed almost excluded as indecencies.' Ross said something of the sort to Hutton himself, who replied, 'I am Yorkshire bred and born you know, I have bought a drink but not too often.'

The BBC radio announcer John Snagge, once relaying the County Championship scores, said, 'Yorkshire 232 all out, Len Hutton ill ... No, I'm sorry, that should read, "Len Hutton 111".'

Brian Johnston *(June 24)*

Sir Alec Douglas-Home's daughter Meriel had two godfathers. One was the Conservative Prime Minister Neville Chamberlain. The other was the cricket commentator Brian Johnston.

When, in 1991, his fellow commentator Jonathan Agnew explained Ian Botham's thigh accidentally coming into contact with the stumps as 'he just didn't quite get his leg over', Johnners went off into fits of giggles. Both in 2005 and in 2012, astoundingly, this was voted the greatest piece of sporting commentary of all time.

Stuart Broad *(June 24)*

As a small child, Stuart Broad once bounced on Courtney Walsh's lap. He wasn't much bigger as a teenager. On his sixteenth birthday he was still only 5 feet 6 inches tall.

Vic Marks *(June 25)*

Before his third England tour to India in 1984–85, the Somerset off-spinner noted that the loss of his right arm was insured for £40,000 (an increase of £10,000 on the previous year), his spinning finger was worth £8000 and his little toe had been valued at £1200. At such prices, who needs a little toe? (*See* November 24.)

Kevin Pietersen *(June 27)*

On Pietersen's retirement in 2018, Andy Bull wrote in the *Guardian*, 'What [can] metrics tell you about Pietersen's achievements? How do you quantify the extravagance of his talent, chart the radical shock of watching him hit those shots? You weigh Pietersen's game by the memories you are left with, the moments you can still see in your mind when you close your eyes. Pietersen made more of those than any other postwar English player but for Ian Botham and Denis Compton.'

Pietersen played for England for nearly ten years, which, given his personality, was probably his greatest achievement. On his first tour there, the Australians christened him 'Figjam', which stood for 'Fuck I'm good, just ask me.' The teacher and writer Jonathan Smith quotes the psychotherapist Anthony Storr thus:

'Genius is most significantly found in unresolved people.' Smith goes on: 'Many of the most interesting pupils I have taught are angular; they're not easy or chummy. They may not get on all that well with their peers, and may well not be particularly keen to get on with you.' Pietersen's supporters, oddly, seem to share these characteristics. My friend Maxie, who skirts on the edge of sanity anyway, was so furious at his hero's dropping after the disastrous Ashes tour of 2013–14 that he unilaterally withdrew his support for the England team and now cheers on Australia. He blamed Alastair Cook, whom he regarded as a placeman and a mediocrity. Pietersen's former team-mates, it turns out, all blamed Pietersen. Pietersen, in an unusually scabrous autobiography, blamed his former teammates. Everyone blames someone. It's the English way.

Mushtaq Ahmed *(June 28)*

Sussex had never won the County Championship before, in 164 years of trying. But after several seasons with Somerset and one unimpressive year with Surrey (eight wickets at 38.12), a small and increasingly rotund former Pakistani leg-spinner joined the south coast county and spent six seasons with them. In those six, Sussex won the Championship three times, in 2003, 2006 and 2007. In those years, Mushtaq took 103, 102 and ninety wickets respectively. No one else has taken a hundred wickets in a season since Courtney Walsh in 1996. Has any overseas signing ever been so effective?

Mushtaq's captain Chris Adams was once heard to say that when the pitch was seriously spinning he sometimes delayed introducing Mushtaq 'to make more of a game of it'. My friend Roger was at Hove for the decisive game of 2003, their first championship. Sussex needed only three batting points to win, and when they gained them, he looked around and realised that many of his fellow spectators were in tears. Some of them had waited more than seventy years for this.

The Maharaja of Porbandar *(June 30)*

Ruler of the small state of Kathiawar, appointed captain of India on their first tour of England in 1932. Owing to an unfortunate shortage of talent, he played only four of the twenty-six first-class matches and stood down from the captaincy in favour of C. K. Nayudu for the one Test. A leg glance for two was his only scoring shot all tour, and he didn't bowl. But as *All Out Cricket* noted, he is almost certainly the only first-class cricketer in history to own more Rolls-Royces (seven) than his batting average (six).

Quiz 2

1. Which Test cricketer, who played the first of her Tests in the same team as Rachael Heyhoe Flint, and the last of her Tests in the same team as Charlotte Edwards, died in September 2017 at the age of fifty-eight?
2. Only two bowlers have taken hat-tricks twice in Test matches since the Second World War. One of them is Pakistani. Name him.
3. The other is English. Name him.
4. Who wrote this in a national newspaper in 2017: 'Mason Crane has an unforgettable name and this winter became the first English spinner to play in the Sheffield Shield since ... well, me, actually.'
5. W. G. Grace is one of the few England cricketers to have also represented his country at another sport. What sport was it? (He was captain of his country's team in the first decade of the twentieth century.)
6. In the early 1930s, three friends, who had known each other at Eton and Oxford, shared a flat in London. One was William Douglas-Home, playwright and younger

brother of Sir Alec. Another was Jo Grimond, future
leader of the Liberal Party. Which future cricket
commentator was the third?

7. Who, in 2009, was the first woman ever to be selected by
Wisden Cricketers' Almanack as a Cricketer of the Year?

8. Which captain of the England cricket team, who was
born in 1900 and died in 1958, had as his family motto
'Cave, adsum', meaning 'Beware, I am here'?

9. In 1900 a cricket team called Devon County Wanderers
embarked on a tour of Paris and surrounding areas,
during the course of which they recorded which
achievement, utterly uniquely?

10. In September 2008, the final of the Cockspur Cup took
place at Lord's between Kibworth, from Leicestershire,
and Malden Wanderers from Surrey. One Malden
batsman was called James Bond. He should have been
out caught at long-off, but you only live twice, and
shortly after that, he was run out for 27. Where was he in
the batting order?

Answers next month.

Miles Kington

I was a big fan of Miles. He wrote for *Punch* in the 1960s and 1970s, *The Times* in the 1980s, and the *Independent* in the 1990s and 2000s. He was one of the most prolific humorous journalists of his day, or indeed any other day: only Craig Brown, of current writers, approaches his workrate and his consistency. He died of cancer in 2008 and had typically sent in his last column only a couple of days earlier. At the time I had a good friend on the *Independent*, and he told me that the editorial staff had been surprised, even shocked, by how upset their readers were after he died. They were even more surprised when the newspaper's sales figures dipped substantially in subsequent weeks. People had been buying the paper purely to read the Kington column. There can be no greater praise.

This is a piece he wrote for *Punch* in June 1974, when India were touring. I loved it then, I loved it when I reread it in *The Punch Book of Cricket*, and I love it now.

Indian Cricket – The Way to Truth?

Miles Kington's armchair guide to this now fashionable ancient cult

Cricket is nothing new in this country. For many years there have been small clubs all over Britain devoted to this ancient belief, where the few devotees could meditate and do their exercises in the privacy of deserted stands and pavilions. And over the last half dozen years it has actually won a certain mass popularity, thanks to Sunday afternoon TV performances and knock-out competitions. But according to the experts, this kind of cricket is a crude and sensationalised version of the true mystical art.

'It's just a lot of clever tricks,' says Guru Ristspinna, one of

India's top practitioners. 'Always, the Western world takes something like Kung Fu or Karate and sees only the flashy, sensational side of it, chopping wood in half with the hand or lying on beds of nails. Many folk in Britain now think that cricket is a matter of clouting a ball immense distances, and bowling as fast as possible. But true cricket is all about the control of the body. Cricket lies in the mind.'

A team of Indian cricketers is in Britain at this very moment, demonstrating the true art to a public who have probably never seen the real thing before. Much of it is based on the Venkataraghavan, the scared book of Indian hand movements, which describes the 105 different positions for the fingers. A master of the art can use his fingers to control the cricket ball and make it do anything he wants – a true master can perform such difficult feats as Moving It Both Ways, Finding The Edge, Beating The Bat and Lifting It Off A Length.

'A truly great bowler,' says Ristspinna, 'enters into an almost mystical relationship with the ball, and they become one. He delights in using as many variations as possible, unlike most English bowlers, who think that sheer speed and aggression is the secret. It is only when he rids his soul of aggressiveness and learns the subtlety of the slow spin that he becomes an entire man. The deity of Indian bowling is the god Bedi, who is reputed to have been able to bowl the ball slowly, yet still evade the batsman, the wicket and the wicketkeeper. This is known technically as Bedi byes.'

But the main difference between our crude form of cricket and the true creed is that the British still see cricket as a martial art, as something to be won. The basic ritual of cricket is the 'match', a stylised game. The English try to beat the other side; the Indians go beyond that.

'An enlightened cricketer is not interested in winning or losing – he has already rid himself of such primitive emotions. The true cricketer thinks the important thing is not to win or lose or even to take part but to be a better person afterwards. He may easily go into a trance while at the wicket; some top-flight batsmen seem almost motionless, lost in contemplation of some distant object such as a spectator, or two spectators, if there are two.

'Time, remember, has no meaning for the real cricketer, which is why we disapprove so strongly of your Sunday afternoon traves-ties. One of the most important parts of the ritual is the creation of symbolic patterns by positioning the eleven devotees on the open ground, or Placing The Field, and this alone could take all day. It is said that the ancient Indian hero Gavaskar stood motionless for three years on one leg, his chin sunk in his hands and his brow furrowed. On the first day of the fourth year, he opened his mouth suddenly and said, "And a man on the square leg boundary."'

Not a martial art, then, though a skilled cricketer could no doubt do tremendous damage with the lethal three-foot-long 'bat'; not a religion, as Sikhs and Hindus can join without abandoning their own creed; not a philosophy, even. What is it, briefly? A way of life? 'More than that,' says the Guru. 'It is a man's only way of expressing eternity.'

Some ancient Indian books on the art of cricket:

The Venkataraghavan. The sacred book of hand movements, written in marvellous medieval Hindu prose. 'And the second finger shall be laid along the seam like a lion stretched out at the watering place when the blood-red sun of the Ghats goes down behind the ... '

The Perfumed Wicket. A loving disquisition on the little-noticed erotic side of cricket. The unknown author finds sensual delight in everything from the tying on of the pads to patting and stroking the pitch, for which he describes thirty-one different techniques.

The Tale of Chandrasekhar. Long, involved epic describing a mythical cricket game lasting six years in which each delivery is narrated in some detail, with ten side-chapters on the Mogul Invasion that held up the match for two years. The hero is the engaging slow-right-arm off-spinner elephant god Chandrasekhar.

The Poems of Prasanna. More lyrical than practical, these 585 poems dwell on the glory of the morning dew and how to make the ball rise sharply off it.

Some mystical terms used commonly in cricket:

Googly: the state of mind in which one expects one thing and receives another.

Wisden: the state of grace towards which all cricketers strive.

Draw: the outcome of a meeting between an irresistible bowler and an irremovable batsman, the conflict between good and evil.

New ball: symbol of rebirth and regeneration.

Rain stopped play: in the parched heartlands of India, the whole year is geared to the moment when, after months of suffocating dry heat, the heavens open, the monsoon arrives and the losing side gratefully secures the draw.

Boundary: the imaginary circular line which encloses all civilisation and beyond which lie only hecklers, transistors and men with no shirts.

Forward defensive stroke: the basic position in cricket, a simple exercise which a batsman repeats for an hour or two until he feels in the exalted state of mind where he may attempt some more exotic movement such as the sweep, hook or cut.

Umpire: an all-present, all-seeing deity who is basically benign but always aloof.

Favourite Tests

Leeds, June 6, 7, 8, 9, 10 1991

ENGLAND vs WEST INDIES: First Test

England

*G A Gooch	c Dujon b Marshall	34	—	not out	154
M A Atherton	b Patterson	2	—	c Dujon b Ambrose	6
G A Hick	c Dujon b Walsh	6	—	b Ambrose	6
A J Lamb	c Hooper b Marshall	11	—	c Hooper b Ambrose	0
M R Ramprakash	c Hooper b Marshall	27	—	c Dujon b Ambrose	27
R A Smith	run out	54	—	lbw b Ambrose	0
†R C Russell	lbw b Patterson	5	—	c Dujon b Ambrose	4
D R Pringle	c Logie b Patterson	16	—	c Dujon b Marshall	27
P A J DeFreitas	c Simmons b Ambrose	15	—	lbw b Walsh	3
S L Watkin	b Ambrose	2	—	c Hooper b Marshall	0
D E Malcolm	not out	5	—	b Marshall	4
	lb 5, w 2, nb 14	21		b 4, lb 9, w 1, nb 7	21
		198			252

1–13 (2), 2–45 (1), 3–45 (3), 4–64 (4), 5–129 (5), 6–149 (6), 7–154 (7), 8–177 (9), 9–181 (10), 10–198 (8)

1–22 (2), 2–38 (3), 3–38 (4), 4–116 (5), 5–116 (6), 6–124 (7), 7–222 (8), 8–236 (9), 9–238 (10), 10–252 (11)

Ambrose	26–8–49–2
Patterson	26.2–8–67–3
Walsh	14–7–31–1
Marshall	13–4–46–3

Ambrose	28–6–52–6
Patterson	15–1–52–0
Marshall	25–4–58–3
Walsh	30–5–61–1
Hooper	4–1–11–0
Richards	4–1–5–0

West Indies

P V Simmons	c Ramprakash b DeFreitas	38	—	b DeFreitas	0
D L Haynes	c Russell b Watkin	7	—	c Smith b Pringle	19
R B Richardson	run out	29	—	c Lamb b DeFreitas	68
C L Hooper	run out	0	—	c Lamb b Watkin	5
*I V A Richards	c Lamb b Pringle	73	—	c Gooch b Watkin	3
A L Logie	c Lamb b DeFreitas	6	—	c Gooch b Watkin	3
†P J L Dujon	c Ramprakash b Watkin	6	—	lbw b DeFreitas	33
M D Marshall	c Hick b Pringle	0	—	lbw b Pringle	1
C E L Ambrose	c Hick b DeFreitas	0	—	c Pringle b DeFreitas	14
C A Walsh	c Gooch b DeFreitas	3	—	c Atherton b Malcolm	9
B P Patterson	not out	5	—	not out	0
	lb 1, nb 5	6		lb 1, nb 6	7
		173			**162**

1–36 (2), 2–54 (1), 3–58 (4), 4–102 (3),
5–139 (6), 6–156 (7), 7–160 (8), 8–165 (9),
9–167 (5), 10–173 (10)

1–0 (1), 2–61 (2), 3–77 (4),
4–85 (5), 5–88 (6), 6–136
(3), 7–137 (8), 8–139 (7),
9–162 (9), 10–162 (10)

Malcolm	14–0–69–0
DeFreitas	17.1–5–34–4
Watkin	14–2–55–2
Pringle	9–3–14–2

Malcolm	6.4–0–26–1
DeFreitas	21–4–59–4
Watkin	7–0–38–3
Pringle	22–6–38–2

Umpires: H D Bird (E) and D R Shepherd (E)

These were the days of the West Indies hegemony, when their fast bowlers and even faster batsmen swept aside most Test teams with practised ease. These were also the days when home teams did not, as a matter of routine, prepare pitches that suited only them. England arrived at Headingley, where it was nominally June but actually February, to find a capricious pitch that swung and seamed, under dismal grey Yorkshire skies, with thousands of dismal grey Yorkshiremen in the stands. The West Indies had a bowling attack that, even now, makes batsmen gulp: Curtly Ambrose, tall, rhythmical, unrelentingly accurate; Patrick Patterson – in Mike Selvey's words 'a shuffling run and muscular, inelegant action but uncompromisingly rapid'; Courtney Walsh, bowling wide of the crease and angling the ball into the body; and Malcolm Marshall, very possibly the best of them all, 'with the tricks of Paul Daniels and the variations of Elgar', said Selvey, not exaggerating one bit.

England, meanwhile, had two debutants, Graeme Hick, who had served his seven years' qualification, and twenty-one-year-old Mark Ramprakash. Lucky old them. Their bowling attack was very slightly less terrifying: Phillip DeFreitas, Devon Malcolm, chugging Steve Watkin from Glamorgan making his debut, and good old Derek Pringle. The most optimistic spin you could put on our prospects was utter humiliation.

Viv Richards won the toss and inserted England, who struggled to 198, their seventh failure to reach 200 in nine innings at Headingley. Robin Smith counter-attacked effectively before being run out by Ambrose from third man, and Ramprakash looked solid, if terrifyingly young. DeFreitas then produced one of his more disciplined spells in England colours to bowl out West Indies for 173 and procure a wholly unexpected first-innings lead. At 156 for 5, the visitors had seemed set fair, but these were no conditions for tail-enders.

In their second innings, however, England were soon in familiar trouble at 38 for 3. Twice Ambrose was on a hat-trick, with both Allan Lamb and Robin Smith departing first ball. Ramprakash stuck around for another 27 – extraordinarily, his final batting average in Tests – but this was the Graham Gooch show. As he said, 'All I could do was to fight every ball and hope that runs would come from somewhere. Even on a pitch like that, if you can stay there for a session, things don't seem quite so bad. The ball gets older and often bowlers get frustrated because they think they should be bowling a side out.'

Selvey continues: 'What makes this innings so extra special, though, was the balance between defence and attack.' Gooch wasn't trying to save the game. He wanted to win it. 'For seven and a half hours, in tricky conditions, he kept at bay one of the most formidable pace attacks that has taken the field.'

I watched every minute. It was a monumental innings, a triumph of talent, determination, concentration and pure unyielding will. You didn't dare go to the loo. In 331 minutes, Gooch hit eighteen fours and scored two-thirds of his side's runs, and became the first England opener to carry his bat since Geoffrey Boycott in 1979–80. Selvey thought 'it deserves to be ranked not just as the finest innings ever played by an England captain, or even the finest by an England batsman, but perhaps one of the truly great innings of all time'.

To put it in context, the West Indies scored only eight more than Gooch in their own second innings. Although Devon Malcolm had one of his off days, DeFreitas and Pringle bowled a typically nagging length to batsmen who, in the main, self-destructed. England's victory, by 115 runs, was their first at home to the West Indies since 1969. Amazingly, they won another Test later in the series, to draw it 2–2.

Favourite Tests

Lord's, June 29, 30, July 1 2000

ENGLAND vs WEST INDIES: Second Test

West Indies

S L Campbell	c Hoggard b Cork	82	—	c Gough b Caddick	4
A F G Griffith	run out	27	—	c Stewart b Gough	1
W W Hinds	c Stewart b Cork	59	—	c Ramprakash b Caddick	0
B C Lara	c Stewart b Gough	6	—	c Cork b Caddick	5
S Chanderpaul	b Gough	22	—	c Ramprakash b Gough	9
*J C Adams	lbw b Gough	1	—	lbw b Cork	3
†R D Jacobs	c Stewart b Cork	10	—	c Atherton b Caddick	12
C E L Ambrose	c Ramprakash b Cork	5	—	c Ramprakash b Caddick	0
F A Rose	lbw b Gough	29	—	c & b Cork	1
R D King	not out	12	—	lbw b Cork	7
C A Walsh	lbw b Caddick	1	—	not out	3
	b 1, lb 8, w 2, nb 2	13		lb 8, nb 1	9
		267			**54**

1–80 (2), 2–162 (1), 3–175 (4), 4–185 (3), 5–186 (6), 6–207 (7), 7–216 (8), 8–253 (9), 9–258 (5), 10–267 (11)

1–6 (1), 2–6 (3), 3–10 (2), 4–24 (4), 5–24 (5), 6–39 (6), 7–39 (6), 8–39 (8), 9–41 (9), 10–54 (10)

Gough	21–5–72–4
Caddick	20.3–3–58–1
Hoggard	13–3–49–0
Cork	24–8–39–4
White	8–1–30–0
Vaughan	3–1–10–0

Gough	8–3–17–2
Caddick	13–8–16–5
Cork	5.4–2–13–3

England

Batsman	Dismissal 1	Runs 1		Dismissal 2	Runs 2
M A Atherton	c Lara b Walsh	1	—	lbw b Walsh	45
M R Ramprakash	c Lara b Ambrose	0	—	b Walsh	2
M P Vaughan	b Ambrose	4	—	c Jacobs b Walsh	41
G A Hick	b Ambrose	25	—	c Lara b Walsh	15
*†A J Stewart	c Jacobs b Walsh	28	—	lbw b Walsh	18
N V Knight	c Campbell b King	6	—	c Jacobs b Rose	2
C White	run out	27	—	c Jacobs b Walsh	0
D G Cork	c Jacobs b Walsh	4	—	not out	33
A R Caddick	c Campbell b Walsh	6	—	lbw b Ambrose	7
D Gough	c Lara b Ambrose	13	—	not out	4
M J Hoggard	not out	12	—		
	lb 5, nb 3	8		b 3, lb 8, w 1, nb 12	24
		134		(8 wkts)	191

1–1 (2), 2–1 (1), 3–9 (3), 4–37 (4), 5–50 (6), 6–85 (5), 7–100 (7), 8–100 (8), 9–118 (9), 10–134 (10)

1–3 (2), 2–95 (3), 3–119 (4), 4–120 (1), 5–140 (5), 6–140 (7), 7–149 (6), 8–160 (9)

Bowler	Figures	Bowler	Figures
Ambrose	14.2–6–30–4	Ambrose	22–11–22–1
Walsh	17–6–43–4	Walsh	23.5–5–74–6
Rose	7–2–32–0	Rose	16–3–67–1
King	10–3–24–1	King	8–2–17–0

Umpires: S Venkataraghavan (I) and J H Hampshire (E)
Referee: G T Dowling (NZ)

In the long, slow, grim tale of the West Indies' decline, from world-crushing behemoths to the sorry rabble they have since become, this Test comes around halfway down. Having previously failed to win a Test outside the Caribbean for three years, they had obliterated England in three days at Edgbaston, primarily thanks to their immaculate fast bowlers Curtly Ambrose and Courtney Walsh, whose standards had never wavered. As Martin Johnson wrote in *Wisden*, 'While Walsh and Ambrose regularly honed in on a spot the size of a dinner-plate, England's spread was more of tablecloth dimensions, and the disparity in pressure on the respective batting line-ups was vast.'

At Lord's a ruddy young fast-medium bowler called Matthew Hoggard made his debut, replacing poor Ed Giddins, and their captain Nasser Hussain had had to withdraw after cracking his thumb in an Essex game. Step forward The Gaffer, for Alec Stewart reassumed the skippership barely a year after being sacked for all the usual failures. Under grey skies Stewart won the toss and put the West Indies in, but Andrew Caddick, so effective at Lord's against Zimbabwe back in May, had one of his more anonymous days. Was there ever a more frustrating bowler for England? It's amazing, when you consider what happened later, that at one point West Indies were 162 for 1. Sherwin Campbell found his two favourite shots, the cut and the square drive, happily fed by the England bowlers, and Wavell Hinds played as though he were facing Ilford's Second XI, which maybe he was. But Hinds was given out when he wasn't, Brian Lara went cheaply and by the end of the day's play West Indies were 267 for 9.

The following day, I would be working in west London during the afternoon with a fellow writer who didn't like cricket – that partnership didn't last long – but I could watch the morning play at home. With Mark Ramprakash unaccountably opening, England were soon 9 for 3, and never really recovered. Again, Walsh and Ambrose simply bowled better, on a pitch that appeared to have more juice than before, although that may just have been because Caddick wasn't bowling on it. The West Indies led by 133 on first innings.

I left the house after the final England wicket and spent just under an hour on the London Underground. When I emerged I went to a nearby sweet shop and bought (as I remember) a Twix. And as I did so, I saw on the telly above the counter that the West Indies were 50 for 9 in their second innings. What? Sorry, what?

And who was the destroyer? Darren Gough, barrel-chested heart and soul of the England team? Dominic Cork, the pop-eyed adrenalin junkie? No, it was Somerset's own grizzled enigma, Andrew Caddick, who had ripped the heart out of the West Indies innings with 5 for 16. As I watched on the highlights later that evening, and a few times again, as I had ingeniously remembered to tape them, it was a compelling performance, as brutal as his first innings bowling had been insipid.*

So England had a chance. They needed just 188 to win, but this pitch was now bouncing and seaming all over the place, they were playing Walsh and Ambrose, and they basically weren't very good. But after Ramprakash's inevitable early dismissal, Michael Atherton and Michael Vaughan (a late replacement for Hussain) bedded in. Every one of the ninety-two runs they added was cheered to the rafters by a Lord's crowd who don't usually cheer anything, other than possibly the arrival of lunch. Ambrose went past the outside edge again and again, but the pair played with sublime self-control and rock-hard temperaments. They both fell in the forties and the middle order came and went, in the way it sometimes has. At 140 for 6 the West Indies were again favourites. Now Dominic Cork came to the crease, looking positively demented with competitiveness. Cometh the hour, cometh the loon. Gough defended stoically at the other end; the crowds cheered; the bowlers tired; and the runs, one by one by one, were somehow scored, although we knew not how. How could Walsh and Ambrose bowl so well and still end up on the losing side? By their faces afterwards, you could tell that they didn't know either.

---

* The West Indies still had one wicket left in their first innings as Friday's play started. Then both England and the West Indies were all out, and then England began their reply. It's the only time in Test history when parts of all four innings were played in a single day.

Julian's XIs

Vegetable 2nd XI

1	A. Bok	(Burma Lads)
2	C. Choi	(Cosmos)
3	W. Fennel	(Knutsford)
4	Cress	(Shelburne)
5	I. H. Romaine	(Bermuda)
6	D. C. Collard	(Cambridgeshire)
7	S. Green	(Easton and Martyr Worthy Second XI)
8	H. W. Chard	(Gloucestershire)
9	S. Carrot	(Basford Mill Second XI)
10	S. C. J. Broad	(England, Hobart Hurricanes, Kings XI Punjab, Leicestershire, Nottinghamshire)
11	G. Bean	(Brazil Cricket Association)
12th man	G. Beet	(Derbyshire, Marylebone Cricket Club)

The Village Year

Every June we play a team called St Radegund, who all went to Cambridge a long time ago and haven't got round to moving away. They play on a spectacularly lovely ground in a Cambridgeshire village, the sort where there's a tree at square leg. (Or at least, there was until it was struck by lightning.) Their leader, Steven, sits with a bottle of Ventoux by him as he scores and by the end of the innings it's an empty bottle of Ventoux. They're our sort of team.

In truth, St Radegund are far better than us and almost always thrash us. But they have a weakness, and it's our best bowler Andy. They genuinely fear him. In his youth Andy was a bit of a tearaway. Now he's sixty-odd and bowls tasty off-spin. He has a tendency, before each ball, to stand there and think for a bit, as though deciding what he wants to do. He then does what he wanted to do. (Very few bowlers can do this.) And he utterly has the hex on St Rad. Every year before we play them, Steven sends me an email asking me if Andy is playing. If he is, I tell him he's not; if he isn't, I tell him he is. We still never beat them, but if Andy is rolling in from the Pavilion End he will almost certainly take 6 for 33 and we will secure a last-minute squeaky-bum draw. In 2018, Andy dropped out on the Friday with childcare issues and we were all out for 34.

In most games we play, of course, it's the players on the other side who have a hex on us. The batsman who always scores a century, the bowler who always takes five wickets, the fielder who always takes the brilliant juggling slip catch having dropped everything else all season. In one fixture, it's the umpire. He's very, very old, this umpire, and he has taken and passed all the exams. He will square up to anyone who questions his technical competence. And yet he will never give any batsman on the home team out lbw, and he gives out to our batsmen at the drop of a hat. He's the difference between the teams, and he doesn't even know it. Last year he was indisposed, and we smashed them. Same players as ever on both sides; totally different result. We play them again this year hoping beyond hope that he has died of old age. Cricket: the game with a moral centre.

July

July Birthdays

3: Ewen Chatfield (1950), Richard Hadlee (1951), Henry Olonga (1976), Harbhajan Singh (1980)

4: Alec and Eric Bedser (1918), Jan Brittin (1959)

5: Tony Lock (1929)

6: Tony Lewis (1938), Makhaya Ntini (1977)

7: MS Dhoni (1981)

8: Alec Waugh (1898), Sourav Ganguly (1972)

9: Sir George Edwards (1908)

10: Sunil Gavaskar (1949), Scott Styris (1975), Salman Butt (1984)

12: Graham Roope (1946), Alan Mullally (1969)

13: Ashley Mallett (1945), Larry Gomes (1953)

14: Arthur Coningham (1863), Geraint Jones (1976)

16: Shaun Pollock (1973)

17: Bob Taylor (1941), Kim Barnett (1960)

18: W. G. Grace (1848), Dennis Lillee (1949)

20: Maurice Leyland (1900)

21: Barry Richards (1945)

22: Tom Cartwright (1935), Trent Boult (1989)

23: Clive Rice (1949), Graham Gooch (1953)

24: Zaheer Abbas (1947)

25: Bill Bowes (1908)

27: Bryan 'Bomber' Wells (1930), Allan Border (1955), Jonty Rhodes (1969)

28: Sir Garfield Sobers (1936)

30: Jimmy Anderson (1982)

31: Sir Gubby Allen (1902)

Alec and Eric Bedser *(July 4)*

How to tell between these extremely identical twins? According to Surrey wicketkeeper Arthur McIntyre, Eric had a slight scar under his chin.

As teenagers, both Alec and Eric bowled medium-fast. They decided that some variation was required, so they tossed a coin, and Alec won. From then on Eric concentrated on bowling off-breaks, and as a better batsman than Alec played for Surrey as an all-rounder.

Alec, meanwhile, went on to play for England, and his 236 wickets in fifty-one Tests between 1946 and 1955 stood as a world record for several years. As the 1950s wore on and Alec's bowling lost a bit of nip, so Eric came into his own, and in 1961, after Alec had retired, Eric took seventy-two wickets, more than in any other season.

Alec served as an England selector for twenty-three years and spent twelve of them as chairman. When he dropped Geoff Miller from the team, he wrote him a letter. 'It's a prized possession,' said Miller many years later, when he in turn had become chairman of selectors. 'Apart from outlining the reasons why I'd been dropped it also encouraged me to keep performing in county cricket and to not lose heart. It was so considerate I use it as a template now whenever I need to let players know they've been left out.'*

---

* Astoundingly, there was another set of twins called Alec and Eric Bedser, born in May 1948 in East London in South Africa and named after the elder Alec and Eric, who were already well established as cricketers. The younger Alec and Eric also became decent players; Alec played for Border in the Currie Cup, before dying in a car crash in 1981 at the age of thirty-three.

Tony Lock *(July 5)*

Left-arm spinner, in the same near-medium-pace mould as Derek Underwood, and later an inspirational captain for Western Australia. Fred Trueman thought him the best close catcher he had ever seen. After Jim Laker took nineteen wickets on a brutally spinning wicket at Old Trafford in 1956, and Lock took only one, the pair of them didn't speak for a whole month. As Peter Richardson, who scored a hundred on the opening day of that Test, later wrote, 'Lockie would attack; Jim would chip away. It was no secret they didn't get on. They were always competing.'

Alec Waugh *(July 8)*

Older, shorter, balder novelist brother of Evelyn, known as 'Uncle Sex' to his family for his libidinous ways, who moved to Morocco late in life on the proceeds of his bestseller, *Island in the Sun*. He said that he missed only one thing about his old life in London: his collection of *Wisdens*. (*See also* October 28.)

Sir George Edwards *(July 9)*

Guildford leg-spinner, friend of the Bedsers and, in 1979, President of Surrey CCC who, for all his eminence, wouldn't be listed here but for one fact. It was Sir George who, as a young aircraft engineer, told Barnes Wallis about backspin when he was developing the Dambusters bomb. 'In the early days, I was doing the experimental trials and Wallis and others were of the opinion that the bomb needed topspin on it. I was quite sure that it didn't – that it needed backspin because as a bit of a bowler I knew enough about the difference between topspin and backspin, especially as far as water went. I had some difficulty in convincing the powers that be that that was how it was, and I finally convinced them by getting a catapult built with an arrangement so that I could fire one with a bit of backspin and another with no spin at all, and then fire another with topspin. And to everybody else's surprise, the one with top-spin screwed itself in, the one with no spin hardly bounced at all, but the one with backspin skittered along the lake ten or a dozen times.' Spin-bowling expertise won the Second World War: you read it here first.

Sunil Gavaskar *(July 10)*

'His lack of privacy surpasses anything that a British sportsman has to endure,' wrote Vic Marks in 1985. 'Sunil and Pammie, his wife, have not been out shopping together for years, and even when they held a small drinks party in their Kanpur garden, the balconies and tree of the neighbouring households were lined with spectators.'

Arthur Coningham *(July 14)*

Australian all-rounder who played one Test at Melbourne against England in 1894–95 and also toured England in 1893. But Arthur Coningham was also a bit of a character, once described as having 'the audacity and cunning of an ape, and the modesty of a phallic symbol'. In his only Test he took a wicket with his first ball. Later on he was no-balled, and in his wild rage he deliberately hurled the next ball at England captain A. E. Stoddart's head. On his tour of England, during which he was awarded a medal after diving into the Thames to save a boy from drowning, he is said to have started a fire in the outfield during a match in Blackpool 'to keep warm'. Trained as a chemist, he was made bankrupt, and once discharged became a bookmaker, carrying a satchel embossed with the words CONINGHAM THE CRICKETER. In 1912 his wife divorced him after he committed adultery in a beach shed. He died in a mental institution in 1939, aged seventy-five. His son, Sir Arthur Coningham, was a First World War flying ace and went on to become an Air Marshal of the RAF.*

W. G. Grace *(July 18)*

'No monument, no portrait, no book can adequately represent either the vitality of W. G. or his superb skill in the game he loved,' said Lord Hawke, in an uncharacteristically mellow moment. K. S. Ranjitsinhji said, 'He turned the old one-stringed instrument into a many-chorded lyre.' 'W. G.'s batting had grandeur and not elegance,' wrote A. A. Thomson. 'It was massive and ingenious.'

'There is something monumental in his stance at the wicket, wholly free from a false refinement, without extraneous elegances,' said Andrew Lang. 'His is a nervous, sinewy, English style, like that of Fielding.' 'Leaving the ball alone never won matches,' said W. G. himself. When he scored his hundredth first-class hundred, Old Parson Wickham was behind the stumps, and swore that Grace only let four balls go by.

Or, as Matthew Engel put it, 'He exists in our imagination halfway between a child's conception of God, and Edward VII as played by Timothy West.'

Henry Allingham, who died in July 2009 at the age of 113, was famously the last survivor of the Battle of Jutland. Among many obituaries was one in *Wisden*, which recorded that 'beyond reasonable doubt', he had been the last person alive to have seen W. G. Grace bat. (For London County against Surrey in 1903.)

---

* Thanks to Martin Williamson and Ben Pobjie for their invaluable research.

Dennis Lillee *(July 18)*

David Frith wrote, 'He is one of the great fast bowlers of the twentieth century, possessing a full set of gear changes, a knowledge of aerodynamics equal to Lindwall's, an abundance of stamina and determination, and more courage than is given to most.' In 1972 Lillee was terrifying. I watched him on television, mainly from behind the sofa. Already, since his great career-threatening injury, very slightly less than express pace, he had such wonderful control and such unanswerable aggression. His eyes gleamed, his moustache bristled audibly. The hair is all gone these days – he even went bald as though he had meant to – but I note that the moustache remains: greyer, slightly abbreviated, but still a statement of intent. He remains the template for the incredibly angry fast bowler the world over. (*See also* November 4.)

Bryan 'Bomber' Wells *(July 27)*

Tubby off-spinner for Gloucestershire and Nottinghamshire in the 1950s and 1960s, with an extraordinarily brief run-up. He said he took two steps when he was cold and one step when he was hot. Inevitably, some batsmen were unprepared for Bomber's delivery. As a young man, playing for the Gloucestershire Nondescripts against Witney, he bowled out a batsman called Len Hemming. But Hemming didn't seem to be ready, so the captain called him back. Next ball, Bomber bowled him again. 'If you think I'm staying here for him to get his bloody hat-trick, you've got another think coming,' said Hemming. Bomber wasn't much of a batsman, and his running between the wickets left much to be desired. One team-mate was once left stranded in mid-pitch by Bomber's failure to call.

'Can't you say anything?' he shouted.

'Goodbye,' said Bomber.

Garfield Sobers *(July 28)*

As well as scoring 8032 runs (at 57.78), taking 235 wickets and bagging 109 catches in ninety-three Tests between 1953 and 1973, Gary Sobers was born with an extra finger on each hand. They were both removed during childhood. Would his figures have been better or worse if they hadn't been?

In 1997 Sir Garfield won a prize believed to be about two hundred thousand pounds in the Lotto, the Barbados lottery. He also liked the horses, and occasionally the horses liked him. Josh Gifford, the highly successful racehorse trainer, had a dog called Sobers.

Jimmy Anderson *(July 30)*

As well as taking a few wickets over the years, Jimmy Anderson holds the England record (eighteen) for the most consecutive innings without scoring more than 5.

Gubby Allen *(July 31)*

Refused point blank to bowl bodyline on the 1932–33 tour of Australia. Which was very impressive, but eighty-five years on, it's hard not to see this through the old amateur–professional prism that blighted English cricket for so long. Both Douglas Jardine and Allen were amateurs, so if Allen wanted to take the field wearing a red nose and clown trousers, there was very little Jardine could do about it. Whereas Harold Larwood and Bill Voce were professionals, and they did what they were told. Larwood was the one compelled to apologise to Australia in writing; Larwood was the one who never played for England again. Meanwhile Sir Gubby Allen, knighted for ruling English cricket with a rod of iron, moved into a small house next to Lord's and had his own private entrance to the ground. He died in 1989, aged eighty-seven, having apparently turned into a tortoise.

Quiz 2 Answers

1. Jan Brittin.
2. Wasim Akram.
3. Stuart Broad.
4. Vic Marks.
5. Bowls.
6. Brian Johnston.
7. Claire Taylor.
8. Douglas Jardine.
9. They won the cricket gold medal at the Paris Olympics. (It's the only one ever awarded. They didn't even know they were competing in the Olympics until after the game was over.)
10. 007.

The Only Man

The only man ...

to have played first-class cricket and died on the *Titanic* was John B. Thayer II, an American businessman with the Philadelphia Railroad Company. In his youth he had attended the University of Philadelphia, where he had captained the lacrosse team in 1879 and also played baseball. In 1884 he was part of the Philadelphian team that visited England, and took twenty-two wickets at 21 each. In all he played seven games now recognised as first-class, three for the Philadelphians, four for an 'American Born' side, and all seven at the Germantown Cricket Club in Pennsylvania. He scored

138 runs at 11.50 and took six wickets at 26.83. Thayer and his family were first-class passengers on the *Titanic*, and as the ship sank he made sure his wife and maid boarded lifeboats. His son Jack dived in the water and, unlike Leonardo DiCaprio, found an overturned collapsible boat and survived. When all of the lifeboats were gone, one eyewitness reportedly saw Thayer looking 'pale and determined by the midship rail aft of lifeboat 7'. No doubt he was waiting for the ultimate umpire to raise a single digit. His body was never recovered.

The only man ...

to captain England at both cricket and football was R. E. 'Tip' Foster. He also holds the record for the highest score on Test debut – 287 for England against Australia in 1903–04. It was the highest score in Tests for twenty-seven years (until surpassed by Andrew Sandham's 325) and remains the third-highest score by any batsman against Australia. He was one of seven brothers who all played cricket for Worcestershire. The others were B. S. (1902–11), G. N. (1903–14), H. K. (1899–1925), M. K. (1908–34), N. J. A. (1914–23) and W. L. (1899–1911). Not for nothing was the county commonly known as 'Fostershire'. In 1899, against Hampshire, Wilfred and Tip both scored their maiden first-class centuries in the first innings, and followed up with two more centuries in the second innings. This is a unique occurrence in the County Championship, although Ian and Greg Chappell both scored two centuries in a Test match in 1974.

Tip also played as a forward for the Corinthians in the early 1900s, and was capped five times by England. C. B. Fry played as a full back in one of those games. In 1913 Tip's diabetes was worsening and he was sent to South Africa to recuperate. He died there the following year, aged just thirty-six.

The only man ...

to play in both cricket and football World Cups is Sir Vivian Richards, who played for Antigua in the qualifying rounds of the 1974 football World Cup, and for West Indies in the 1975, 1979 and 1983 cricket World Cups.

The first woman to play in both cricket and football World Cups was England's Clare Taylor, who won the cricket cup in 1993 and played in the football team in 1995. She was an amateur throughout her sporting career and worked for the Royal Mail. 'The amount of time I spend away on unpaid leave has got beyond a joke,' she said.

The only woman to play in both cricket and football World Cup finals is Ellyse Perry of Australia. She took part in the 2009 cricket World Cup and the 2011 football World Cup, when the Matildas reached the quarter finals.

The only father and son ...

who both scored centuries on their Test debuts are Lala Amarnath (in 1933) and Surinder Amarnath (in 1976). Strangely enough, neither of them ever scored another. Another son, Mohinder, also played for India and scored eleven centuries in sixty-nine Tests, but none on debut. His Test career actually spanned eighteen years (December 1969 to January 1988) and, according to Wikipedia, 'behind his seemingly lethargic demeanour were nerves of steel'. Imran Khan believed that in 1982–83, Mohinder was the best batsman in the world. He was also (a wonderful quiz question, this) Man of the Match in both the semi-final and final of the 1983 World Cup, which India of course won.

The only man ...

to be born in one country and then play Test cricket for two other countries was the off-spinner John Traicos. Athanasios John Traicos, to give him his full name, was born of Greek parentage in Zagazig, Egypt, in 1947 and brought up in Southern Rhodesia, which in cricketing terms was then treated as a province of South Africa. Traicos made his Test debut for South Africa against Australia in 1970 and played three Tests, but South Africa were then excluded from international cricket for twenty years because of apartheid. Traicos continued to play for Southern Rhodesia – later Zimbabwe – and represented them at the 1983 World Cup, where they famously beat Australia. Zimbabwe received Test status in 1992, and in the team for their inaugural Test was none other than Traicos, now aged forty-five. This appearance came a record twenty-two years and 222 days after his last Test appearance, and in that match he recorded his Test-best figures of 5 for 86. He played three more Tests before retiring because of business commitments. (He was a lawyer and, unusually for a Test player, had to pop into the office every day for a couple of hours before he went to play cricket.) At forty-five years and 304 days on the last day of his last match, Traicos was the oldest Test player since Pakistan's Miran Bux thirty-eight years before, and the twelfth-oldest of all time.*

The only bestselling author ...
to catch fire while playing at Lord's was Sir Arthur Conan Doyle, for the MCC against Kent in 1903. '[Bill Bradley's] first delivery I hardly saw, and it landed with a terrific thud upon my thigh,' he wrote in *Memories and Adventures*. 'A little occasional pain is one of the chances of cricket, and one takes it as cheerfully as one can, but on this occasion it suddenly became sharp to an unbearable degree. I clapped my hand to the spot, and found to my amazement that I was on fire. The ball had landed straight on a small tin

---

* Miran Bux was forty-seven years and 302 days old on the last day of the match between Pakistan and India in 1954–55, and probably felt it. The oldest of all, of course, was Wilfred Rhodes, who was fifty-two years and 165 days old when he played for England against the West Indies in 1929–30. He may not have executed a huge number of diving stops on the cover point boundary that day.

vesta box in my trousers pocket, had splintered the box, and set the matches ablaze.'

Conan Doyle wasn't the only medical doctor playing for the MCC that day. The other was W. G. Grace. The Kent captain, meanwhile, was the unimprovably named Cuthbert Burnup.

The first twins ...

to play Test cricket in the same team were not Mark and Steve Waugh, as everyone thinks, but Rosemary and Elizabeth Signal of New Zealand, against England in 1984. It was Rosemary's only Test, but Elizabeth played six in all. The sisters were also the first twins to play a one-day international in the same team.

As for the Waugh brothers, Steve made his Test debut in 1985–86 (Mark didn't play for another five years). Steve had made his first-class debut for New South Wales in 1984–85, batting at number nine and bowling medium pace. In his first twenty-six Tests, he averaged only 30.62 and hadn't yet scored a century. But for once the selectors stuck with him, and he came good – very, very good indeed, to be precise – on the 1989 tour of England, when he wasn't dismissed until the third Test, and ended up with 506 runs at 126.5.

The only two families ...

to play Test cricket in three consecutive generations are the Headleys and the Khans. George Headley, who scored 2190 runs at 60.83 in twenty-two Tests for the West Indies, was one of the greatest batsmen of all time, at his best before the Second World War. His son Ron Headley played twice for the West Indies in 1973, but more prolifically for Worcestershire, for whom he scored more than twenty-one thousand runs between 1958 and 1974. And Ron's son Dean Headley, a fast-medium bowler of great spirit with a distinctively shaped head, played fifteen Tests for England between 1997 and 1999, taking sixty wickets at 27.85. He would have played many more but for injury.

Meanwhile, on the subcontinent, Jahangir Khan played four Tests for India in the 1930s, and after independence served as an administrator in Pakistan. He famously killed a bird in flight while bowling for the MCC against Cambridge University in 1936. (The bird is now stuffed and displayed prominently in the MCC Museum.) His son Majid Khan was possibly the most elegant batsman of his time and a member of the ferociously good Pakistan team of the 1970s, playing sixty-three Tests and scoring 3931 runs. Against New Zealand in 1976, he became only the fourth Test batsman to score a century before lunch on the first day. And Majid's son Bazid Khan played a single Test against the West Indies in 2005, scoring 23 and 9. His father and two uncles, Imran Khan and Javed Burki, all captained Pakistan, although obviously not at the same time.

The only man ...
to score double centuries in both innings of a first-class match was Arthur Fagg, who did so in 1938 for Kent against Essex. He scored 244 in the first innings and an undefeated 202 (in 170 minutes) in the second of a drawn match. He played five Tests for England but didn't do a lot. But he played for Kent until 1957, scoring more than twenty-seven thousand runs and fifty-eight centuries, before becoming a first-class umpire, and stood in eighteen Tests between 1967 and 1975. When I was eleven (in 1971) I thought Arthur Fagg was the funniest name in the history of the world.

Two players have scored a triple century and a century in the same match, and both in Tests: Graham Gooch, with 333 and 123 for England against India at Lord's in 1990, and Kumar Sangakkara with 319 and 105 for Sri Lanka vs Bangladesh at Chittagong in 2013–14.

The only three men ...

to score 99 on Test debut are Arthur Chipperfield (in 1934), Robert Christiani (in 1947–48) and Asim Kamal (in 2003–04). And the fact that we've never heard of any of them suggests it's something you want to avoid doing if at all possible. (They played fourteen, twenty-two and twelve Tests respectively.)

The only man ...

who played Test cricket but neither batted, bowled nor took a catch in the field was poor Jack MacBryan, an amateur and the leading Somerset batsman in the years after the First World War. In 1924 he was selected for England against South Africa at Old Trafford. But only 66.5 overs were played, owing to incessant rain, and for some reason he was never picked again. He had fifty-nine years to rue his ill fortune, finally dying in 1983, aged ninety.

The only Test cricketer ...

to be mentioned by name in an Oscar acceptance speech was thanked by Sir Tim Rice, when accepting the award for Best Original Song for 'Can You Feel the Love Tonight' from the Disney film *The Lion King*. 'I'd also like to thank Denis Compton, a childhood hero of mine.' A spokesman for the Academy of Motion Picture Arts and Sciences said, 'We don't know who Denis Compton is. He doesn't appear to be at Disney Studios or have anything to do with *The Lion King*.'

The only Kent opening batsman ...

ever hired to write an agony uncle column for an Australian women's magazine under the pseudonym 'Dr Love' was David Fulton, who scored over twelve thousand runs for the county between 1992 and 2006. The magazine was *For You*, and probably for him as well.

The only man ...

to have the number 356 tattooed on his ankle to indicate that he was Australia's 356th Test player is Michael Slater. He also has a car registration plate with the number 356 on it. But he wasn't actually the 356th. Brendon Julian, who made his debut in the same match, was deemed to have been the 356th because Julian comes before Slater alphabetically. But because Australia batted first, and Slater opened the batting, Julian did not take the field until the second day and therefore becomes 357, while Slater moves up to 356. The Australian Cricket Board were in a generous mood, though. They recognised that the mistake was theirs and that the original demarcation should stand, thus saving Slater a return visit to the tattoo parlour.

The only man ...

to have captained England and appeared in a film with Elizabeth Taylor was C. Aubrey Smith. He only played one Test, against South Africa in 1888–89 at Port Elizabeth, taking 5 for 19 in the first innings. Smith was a fast bowler whose unusual curving run-up, which started near long-off, earned him the nickname 'Round the Corner Smith'. He began acting on the London stage in 1895, appeared in early films for the embryonic British film industry, and later went to Hollywood, where he was typecast in officer and gentleman roles. In 1932 he founded the Hollywood Cricket Club, and imported grass from England to create a pitch. Errol Flynn, David Niven, Leslie Howard and Boris Karloff were among many illustrious team-mates. When a young Laurence Olivier booked into the Chateau Marmont Hotel to begin his first day as a film star in America, there was a note from Smith waiting for him: 'There will be nets tomorrow at 9 a.m. I trust I shall see you there.' Decades after his cricketing career had ended, when he had long been a famous face in films, Smith was spotted in the Lord's pavilion.

'That man over there seems familiar,' said one member to another.

'Yes,' said the second. 'Chap called Smith. Used to play for Sussex.'

The only woman …

to have played Tests for England and worked for MI6 was Eileen Ash, who was still driving her yellow Mini around the streets of Norwich in 2017 at the age of 106. Under her maiden name of Whelan, she played three Tests in 1937 as a medium-pace bowler, and took ten wickets at 20.90. In *The Nightwatchman*, the spy writer Andrew Lycett asked her about her years as a spook, but she didn't want to talk about it. But we do know that her spying career lasted from 1938, when she first appeared for the Civil Service cricket team, to 1948, when she left MI6 to go on a tour of Australia.

The only man …

to take sixteen wickets in a Test match at Lord's (on his debut, as it happens) was Bob Massie of Australia. It was 1972 and conditions were perfect for swing, but even so, the movement that Massie achieved was prodigious. The England batsmen could hardly lay a bat on the ball, while all the bowler had to do was to make sure the ball was on line and wickets would necessarily follow. And yet Massie only played five more Tests. Why?

One possible solution to this ancient mystery was supplied in *Ted Dexter's Little Cricket Book*. Back in '72 Dexter was writing for the *Sunday Mirror* and watched the Test in its entirety. His suspicions were aroused.

I telephoned Tony Greig to ask him exactly what was happening out in the middle. He said it was a routine occurrence – they were using lip ice, and had done so also at Old Trafford in the first Test. I had never even heard of lip ice, let alone how it could be used to the bowler's advantage. He explained that it was the clear stuff applied to the lips to stop them burning in hot climates. Now it was being used to polish the ball. I asked if I could quote him. He refused that, but assured me it was happening ...

I went down to the chemist and asked for a sample of every brand of lip ice they had in stock. I received some quizzical looks, but got them, went home, got out an old ball and a rag impregnated with lip ice, and started to polish. I got the shock of my life. The ball came up like a mirror ...

In those days I still felt a little sensitive to the fact that I was a fairly recently retired ex-cricketer and felt that it might be letting the side down to expose a matter like this. I went to see the Australian manager, Bob Steele, to warn him that we had rumbled his bowlers and would be running the story in a big way. It was a fairly terse interview in which he was totally non-committal. There was no doubt, however, that from then on the ball stopped swinging in the way it had at Lord's. I am sure that action was taken by the manager, who might not have even known himself what had been going on before I told him. Bob Massie took four more wickets in the first innings of the next Test at Trent Bridge, but then bowled another 109 overs in the series, taking a mere three more wickets.

Interesting, eh? As the writer and philosopher George Santayana has said, 'Those who cannot remember the past are condemned to repeat it.'

The greatest threat to Britain's national security ...
occurred at the height of the Cold War, according to the historian and constitutional expert Professor Peter Hennessy. It was during the Lord's Test in 1963, which had a thrilling finish. 'Every television screen in the Ballistic Early Warning System room was tuned to Lord's. The Russians could have taken us out at any time.'

Favourite Tests

Leeds, July 16, 17, 18, 20, 21 1981

ENGLAND vs AUSTRALIA: Third Test

Australia

J Dyson	b Dilley	102	—	(2) c Taylor b Willis	34
G M Wood	lbw b Botham	34	—	(1) Taylor b Botham	10
T M Chappell	c Taylor b Willey	27	—	c Taylor b Willis	8
*K J Hughes	c & b Botham	89	—	c Botham b Willis	0
R J Bright	b Dilley	7	—	(8) b Willis	19
G N Yallop	c Taylor b Botham	58	—	(5) c Gatting b Willis	0
A R Border	lbw b Botham	8	—	(6) b Old	0
†R W Marsh	b Botham	28	—	(7) c Dilley b Willis	4
G F Lawson	c Taylor b Botham	13	—	c Taylor b Willis	1
D K Lillee	not out	3	—	c Gatting b Willis	17
T M Alderman	not out	0	—	not out	0
	b 4, lb 13, w 3, nb 12	32		lb 3, w 1, nb 14	18
		401 for 9 dec			**111**

1–55, 2–149, 3–196, 4–220, 5–332,
6–354, 7–357, 8–396, 9–401

1–13, 2–56, 3–58, 4–58,
5–65, 6–68, 7–74, 8–75,
9–110, 10–111

Willis	30–8–72–0
Old	43–14–91–0
Dilley	27–4–78–2
Botham	39.2–11–95–6
Willey	13–2–31–1
Boycott	3–2–2–0

Botham	7–3–14–1
Dilley	2–0–11–0
Willis	15.1–3–43–8
Old	9–1–21–1
Willey	3–1–4–0

England

G A Gooch	lbw b Alderman	2	—	c Alderman b Lillee	0
G Boycott	b Lawson	12	—	lbw b Alderman	46
*J M Brearley	c Marsh b Alderman	10	—	c Alderman b Lillee	14
D I Gower	c Marsh b Lawson	24	—	c Border b Alderman	9
M W Gatting	lbw b Lillee	15	—	lbw b Alderman	1
P Willey	b Lawson	8	—	c Dyson b Lillee	33
I T Botham	c Marsh b Lillee	50	—	not out	149
†R W Taylor	c Marsh b Lillee	5	—	c Bright b Alderman	1
G R Dilley	c & b Lillee	13	—	b Alderman	56
C M Old	c Border b Alderman	0	—	b Lawson	29
R G D Willis	not out	1	—	c Border b Alderman	2
	b 6, lb 11, w 6, nb 11	34		b 5, lb 3, w 3, nb 5	16
		174			356

1–12, 2–40, 3–42, 4–84, 5–87, 6–112, 7–148, 8–166, 9–167, 10–174

1–0, 2–18, 3–37, 4–41, 5–105, 6–133, 7–135, 8–252, 9–319, 10–356

Lillee	18.5–7–49–4		Lillee	25–6–94–3
Alderman	19–4–59–3		Alderman	35.3–6–135–6
Lawson	13–3–32–3		Lawson	23–4–96–1
			Bright	4–0–15–0

Umpires: B J Meyer (E) and D G L Evans (E)

Two days before the Headingley Test, I turned twenty-one. After university I had scurried back to the parental home in north London and was now preparing for my birthday party on the Saturday of the Test. Most friends were coming down from one university or other; a few would stay several days in sleeping bags on the floor. The most adhesive turned out to be my good friend Richard, who arrived in time for the first day's play, found the seat nearest to the TV, lit a cigarette, poured a glass of whisky and sat down to watch. For the next five days he remained a beacon of stillness and concentration. I'm not sure he missed a single ball.

After a string of disappointing performances Ian Botham had been sacked as England captain and replaced by Mike Brearley. England decided to play four seamers and brought in Chris Old for John Emburey. If they had played three seamers, the one to be left out would have been Bob Willis, who had bowled thirty-two no-balls at Lord's. But the Headingley pitch promised awkward bounce and, if the cloud remained, swing and seam. 'It was mid-July, but it felt like mid-April,' wrote Brearley. He told umpire David Evans that you could bowl out a side for 90 if all went well. Australia therefore made 401 for 9. Botham took 6 for 95, but when Dennis Lillee and Terry Alderman came in to bowl, they made the ball talk. It usually said, 'You're out.' England made 174, about par for the pitch, thought Brearley. As we were laying out food and drink for my party, England followed on, Graham Gooch was out for 0 and the batsmen were offered the light.

Sunday was a rest day, both for the Test players and for us. In my house, much bacon was consumed.

On Monday morning England were swiftly 41 for 4. Peter Willey and Geoffrey Boycott resisted grittily for three and a half hours, before Boycott was lbw to Alderman. England were 135 for 7, still 92 behind. Botham was one of several players who had booked out of the team hotel. When he came in to bat, he initially batted with some care, scoring 39 in eighty-seven minutes. It was Graham Dilley who started the onslaught. Botham then joined him, driving Alderman to all parts, and memorably leaping down the pitch and thumping him for a straight six. The poet Gavin Ewart wrote, 'One particular six, a tremendous one, parabola-tall, / Made one pretty sorry for the ball.' Dilley and Botham put on 117 runs in eighty minutes. When Dilley was out England were twenty-five runs ahead with only two wickets left. Botham and Old then clubbed another sixty-seven runs, and after Old was out

Botham protected Willis so effectively they added another thirty-one. At the close we were 351 for 9, and leading by 124. How did any of us sleep that night?

Willis was soon out on Tuesday, and Australia needed 130. They were quickly 56 for 1. Brearley had opened with Botham and Dilley, and then brought on Willis, bowling uphill and into the wind. Nothing was happening. Willis changed ends. Brearley told him to bowl faster and straighter and hold nothing back. He bowled the perfect bouncer, fast and straight, at Trevor Chappell's head. Chappell lobbed it up to Bob Taylor. Last over before lunch, Kim Hughes, on 0, edged a short ball to Botham at third slip. Brearley started to think that it could be done. England hadn't won a Test match in over a year. Three balls later Graham Yallop fended another short, fast, lifting ball to Mike Gatting at short leg. Australia were 58 for 4 at lunch.

Thirteen minutes after lunch Old bowled Allan Border: 65 for 5. He had been bowling uphill with tireless accuracy, and conceded only eleven runs off his first eight overs. Next over Dyson tried to hook Willis and gloved the ball behind: 68 for 6. Then Rodney Marsh, also trying to hook, got a top edge and Dilley took the catch at long leg: 74 for 7. Next over Willis had Lawson caught behind: 75 for 8. And yet Australia only needed fifty-five to win. In the next four overs Lillee and Ray Bright scored thirty-five of them. Oh God oh God oh God. You always felt that Willis would get them out sooner or later, but we were rapidly running out of later. Finally Lillee spooned up a ball to mid-on, where Gatting ran in, dived and caught it inches above the ground. Then Willis to Bright, the perfect ball for a tail-ender, a fast yorker on middle stump. England had won by eighteen runs.

After the match, Willis looked like a zombie. In my house, Richard switched off the TV, took a sip of whisky and idly wondered if he might have a bath.

JULIAN'S XIs

Saltwater Fish

1	W. H. A. D. Moray	(Household Brigade)
2	Whiting	(West Indian Wanderers)
3	G. Turbot	(South Wilts)
4	Herring	(Marylebone Cricket Club)
5	G. Sprat	(Finchley)
6	R. T. B. Snook	(Stragglers of Asia)
7	D. J. Skate	(Ringwood)
8	S. M. Pollock	(South Africa, Africa XI, Dolphins, Durham, ICC World XI, KwaZulu-Natal, Mumbai Indians, Natal, Warwickshire)
9	Ray	(West Bromwich Albion Football Club)
10	J. Sardine	(Windward Islands)
11	C. W. Smelt	(Ottery St Mary)
12th man	T. Crabb	(Kew)

The Village Year

Each July we play a team from West Mersea, on a tidal island just off the coast of Essex. It's the furthest we ever drive – at least two hours for most of us – and it's one of the most popular fixtures on the list. Partly this is because they are lovely. But it's also because of their wondrous hospitality. The teas are magnificent, and most years they put on a big meal afterwards, which everyone stays for. It's the trencherman's fixture, which means pretty much everyone on the team. By the end of the evening several of my team look five months pregnant.

Tea is the *ne plus ultra* of cricketing repasts. *Wisden* 2000 reported that a village team from Stoke Canon in Devon had actually disbanded because of the quality of their teas. The club had not managed to replace their regular cake-baker and tea-brewer after she retired in 1993, and the men were compelled by necessity to make the teas themselves. 'Some of the players made really terrible sandwiches,' said the captain. 'Our teas became notorious.'

Skating quickly over the question of how difficult it is to make a passable sandwich, I can sympathise. We play only away fixtures and so very rarely have to provide a tea for anyone. But we're excellent at consuming them, and we're even better at appreciating a really good tea. Players who drop every ball that reaches them and rarely score a run before September can nonetheless make sounds like 'MMMMMM!' when chomping through their half-time cheese-and-pickle sandwiches, because they know that everyone will benefit: the home team, who depend on the tea-makers utterly; the tea-makers themselves, who can never be complimented too much; and their own team, who will be invited back next year. A few good performances at tea pretty much nails your place in the side.

My own preference is for salad cream sandwiches, which only cricketers have eaten since 1969, and peanut butter and banana sandwiches, which make it hard to open your mouth afterwards. Some kind of chocolate cake, bourbon biscuits, and several cups of hot, sweet builders' tea completes the repast. YUM.

August

August Birthdays

1: Sir Frank Worrell (1924), Graham Thorpe (1969)
4: Colin Dredge (1954)
7: John Woodcock (1926), Greg Chappell (1948),
   Dominic Cork (1971)
8: Bill Voce (1909), Angus Fraser (1965), Kane Williamson (1990)
10: Chris Read (1978)
12: Peter West (1920), Eddie Barlow (1940)
13: Robin Jackman (1945), Shoaib Akhtar (1975)
14: Ramiz Raja (1962)
15: Jack Russell (1963)
16: Lord Hawke (1860), Jeff Thomson (1950),
    Shivnarine Chanderpaul (1974)
18: Godfrey Evans (1920)
20: John Emburey (1952)
21: Simon Katich (1975)
22: Percy Fender (1892)
23: Jack Bannister (1930), Mark Butcher (1972)
27: Sir Donald Bradman (1908), Mark Ealham (1969),
    Mohammad Yousuf (1974)
28: Lasith Malinga (1983)
31: Clive Lloyd (1944), Chris Rogers (1977)

Frank Worrell *(August 1)*

'His greatest contribution,' said Learie Constantine, 'was to destroy for ever the myth that a coloured cricketer was not fit to lead a team.'

Greg Chappell *(August 7)*

The *Guardian*'s Frank Keating once shared a car with him. 'We sat together in the back of the chauffeured limousine. I started with time-of-day small talk. I received not a single word in reply. When we arrived at his London hotel, the Waldorf, he was asleep. I gently woke him. He got out, and slammed the door without a word to me or the driver. Ever since, I have been in awe, or certainly wary, of his cold-fish disdain.'

It should be the first rule of public life: never be unnecessarily rude to a journalist. Later on in the same piece, Keating remembers the famous ODI between Australia and New Zealand, in which, with one ball left, New Zealand needed six to win. Greg Chappell famously ordered his younger brother Trevor to bowl the last ball underarm and along the ground, which made it impossible to hit. Wrote Keating: 'The captain's long suspected meanness of spirit was at last fully revealed.'

Dominic Cork *(August 7)*

Hilariously competitive England swing bowler of the 1990s who took 131 Test wickets at 29.81 but, even more importantly, appeared as a contestant on the sixth series of ITV's *Dancing On Ice*. 'I love the sequins, the music, the costumes, the lot!' he said, not at all camply. The judges were less convinced. 'The thing I like about your performance is when it's over,' said one of them. Corky was the sixth contestant to be eliminated: he was lucky to get that far.

In June 1995, the journalist Patrick Kidd was doing his A levels, when he suddenly perceived the presence of Mr Crickmore, the exam's invigilator, maths teacher and a regular school umpire. Mr Crickmore gave a small cough, then dropped a piece of paper on Patrick's desk. As he walked on, Patrick slowly unfolded it and read the message. 'Dominic Cork has taken 7 for 43,' it read. 'England win the Lord's Test.'

Angus Fraser *(August 8)*

Perpetually exhausted large-bottomed fast-medium England bowler of the 1990s, who carried all his nation's hopes for far too long. 'Angus Fraser deals in parsimony and red-faced effort,' wrote Mike Selvey in *Wisden*. 'He is perennially grumpy, kicks savage lumps from the turf at a conceded leg-bye, and could murder a mis-fielder . . . Runs are a commodity to be hoarded, not frittered away on the undeserving. This is Scrooge in flannels.' Ray Illingworth didn't rate him and kept leaving him out of the England team, which said more about Illingworth than it did about Fraser. Peter Lever, a bowler in a similar mould, gave him the ultimate tribute: 'I know from watching him bowl that that man could never tell me a lie.'

Jeff Thomson *(August 16)*

His bowling was once timed at 99.97 mph, 'but that's rubbish,' says Jeff. 'I was much faster than that.'

Simon Katich *(August 21)*

Splendidly gritty Australian opener who, in coming after the great pairing of Hayden and Langer, was probably not as appreciated as he should have been. Also following in Hayden's footsteps, Katich won his heat of *Celebrity MasterChef Australia* in October 2009, offering crusted salmon with lemon wilted spinach and creamy potato mash, despite not having a sense of smell. 'The only problem I have is I don't know when something is burning,' he said afterwards.

Percy Fender *(August 22)*

Talented all-rounder of the 1920s and '30s whom many contemporaries believed to have been the best captain never to have led England. As Ronald Mason wrote, 'Tall, angular, beaky, balding, surprisingly reminiscent in appearance of Groucho Marx, [he] looked about as unpromising material for an all-round cricketer as could be conceived. He looked decades older than he really was, and his large horn-rimmed spectacles over the assertive turfed moustache gave him the air of a fierce cashier peering angrily among the ledgers for a lost sixpence.'

In 1977, aged eighty-five, Fender wrote to the *Daily Telegraph*:

'Exactly fifty years ago (Saturday 27 August) an odd thing happened at Lord's ... Middlesex, winning the toss, had lost five wickets in seven consecutive deliveries – all clean bowled and with a chance of a hat-trick twice in one over ... In all the bowler had taken six wickets in 11 deliveries – a record which stood for 45 years until Pocock, another Surrey slow spin bowler, took six wickets in nine consecutive deliveries against Sussex at Eastbourne in 1972.'

What Fender was too modest to mention was that it was he who had taken all these wickets.

'Many of those who played in the Lord's game have now passed on,' he continued, 'and having gone out to grass in the country, I shall be alone with the "glass of wine" which I always associate with Happy Memories.'

Sir Donald Bradman *(August 27)*

With a Test average of 99.94, Bradman was statistically by far the best batsman ever to walk the earth, although some commentators note a weakness on sticky wickets. According to Neville Cardus, 'perhaps his most remarkable innings in a Test match occurred at Lord's during 1930, which was his "wonderful year" ... Ponsford and Woodfull scored 162 for the first wicket, then Bradman in two hours and forty minutes before half-past six scourged the England attack for 155 not out. The power and the ease, the fluent, rapid, vehement, cold-blooded slaughter were beyond sober discussion.' The Australian Broadcasting Corporation's mailing address in every capital city of Australia is PO Box 9994. The code phrase that told Allied troops of the assault on the monastery at Monte Cassino in March 1944 was 'Bradman will be batting tomorrow'. Among Nelson Mandela's first words when he was released from Robben Island after twenty-seven years were 'Is Don Bradman still alive?' Bradman was never out in the nineties in a Test match. He was out for 89 once, and later said he had in fact made 90 because one of his runs had been counted as a leg-bye.* Once he reached 100 in Tests, as he did twenty-nine times, he scored an average of another eighty-five runs. In the thirty Tests he played that Australia won, he averaged 130.1, and he converted twenty-three of twenty-seven fifties he scored into hundreds. He could be a slow starter: in more than 10 per cent of his innings he scored less than 2. A variety of dahlia is named after him. There are twenty-two roads named after him in Australian state capitals (Victor Trumper has eight). The English journalist Jack Ingham once wrote, 'It is strange, but I think true, that all the time, day and night, somewhere in the world somebody is talking about Bradman.'

---

* If this run had been counted, it would have brought his career average up to 99.957.

All in a Name

This research (and many of the words) are courtesy of Steven Lynch and his readers on ESPNcricinfo:

c Beet b Root

Derbyshire's teams either side of the Great War often featured wicketkeeper George Beet and Fred Root, a medium-pacer who later played for England after moving to Worcestershire. Although Beet was a keeper, there was only one instance of 'c Beet b Root' for epicures to savour, the unfortunate batsman being Sussex's Herbert Chaplin at Derby in 1913.

Lillee c Willey b Dilley

This famous scorebook entry was recorded – not long after a commentator had pointed out the possibility of it happening – during the second innings of the first Test between Australia and England at Brisbane in 1979–80. It was also the first time it could have happened, as this was Graham Dilley's Test debut.

Cook c Mustard b Onions

In a county game between Kent and Durham in 2007, Simon Cook was caught behind by keeper Phil Mustard off the bowling of the England fast bowler Graham Onions. Gourmets across the world waited for the Durham pair to play against the Namibian all-rounder Kola Burger, but sadly it was not to be.

Lamb c Kourie b Rice

Playing for Western Province against Transvaal at Johannesburg in February 1980, Allan Lamb was caught by Alan Kourie off the bowling of Clive Rice. This was in the final of South Africa's domestic competition – sadly the one-day one rather than the Currie Cup (in which Lamb was once c Cook b Rice for 130).

Marks v Spencer

Playing for Oxford University against Sussex in the Parks in 1975, the future England off-spinner Vic Marks was dismissed in each innings (caught by John Snow both times) by the burly medium-pacer John Spencer. In the same fixture the following year, Victor returned the favour: Spencer b Marks 6.

Lee c Lee b Lee

At Lord's in June 1933, the Middlesex batsman Harry Lee was caught by his brother Frank, playing for Somerset, off the bowling of another brother, Jack: the unique scorecard entry was 'HW Lee c FS Lee b JW Lee 82'. Harry later wrote: 'I do not believe that brothers had ever before behaved so unbrotherly in a first-class game.'

As well as being unique in all cricketing history, 'Lee c Lee b Lee 82' is thought to be the shortest scorecard entry, in terms of characters, involving three names, ever recorded in first-class cricket. (If we discount the caughts, the bowleds and the numbers, it adds up to nine.) And there are more.

In Tests, eleven characters (if you delete the initials):
    G A Hick c D C Boon b T B A May
    (England vs Australia, The Oval, 1993)

In ODIs, ten characters:
    A Rath c T P Ura b M D Dai
    (Hong Kong vs Papua New Guinea, Hong Kong, 2016–17)
    M M Ali c T M Head b A J Tye
    (England vs Australia, Adelaide, 2017–18)

In T20 internationals, twelve characters:

D R Smith c M S Wade b B Lee
(West Indies vs Australia, Gros Islet, 2011–12)
C S Baugh c M S Wade b B Lee
(West Indies vs Australia, Bridgetown, 2011–12)
S Kami c A Vale b J B Reva
(Nepal vs Papua New Guinea, Dublin, 2015)

What of the longest scorecard entry in Test cricket? No one is entirely sure, but 'A I Kallicharran c sub (Yajurvindra Singh) b Venkataraghavan' must be a contender. (Yajurvindra Singh's main distinction is that he took seven catches on his Test debut, playing for India against England at Bangalore in 1976.)

The question of the longest scorecard entry in county cricket was brought up in the letters pages of *The Times* in May 2009, when Christopher Collins of Alton in Hampshire suggested one from the recent Hampshire vs Sussex match:

'C C Benham c Hamilton-Brown b Martin-Jenkins 1'

Swift to reply was the serial writer of letters to newspapers, Malcolm Watson (from one of whose books this exchange has been taken). 'Sir,' he wrote, 'A quick glance amongst the obvious candidates reveals that "J Birkenshaw c Ingleby-Mackenzie b Shackleton 0" exceeds Christopher Collins's suggestion by two characters and the very next dismissal in the same match (Hampshire vs Leicestershire, May 1962), "J van Geloven c Ingleby-Mackenzie b Sainsbury 3" by one character, each without the involvement of a second double-barrelled name.' For some bizarre reason *The Times* did not print this letter.

But they did print the one they received the following day from Michael Openshaw in London NW3:

'Sir, Christopher Collins looks for the longest dismissal in terms of characters. I cannot answer for county cricket but the match between Andhra Pradesh and Kerala – reported in *The*

Times of November 17, 1990 – has this line: Chamundeswaranagh c Balasabramaniam b Anantapadmanabhan 2'

A line that probably takes longer to say than the innings took to watch.

For long names, of course, one needs look no further than Sri Lankan cricket. W. P. U. J. C. Vaas, despite having only four letters in his surname, has forty-eight letters across his five forenames. And he's still not the cricketer with the longest name who has represented Sri Lanka internationally. Here are the top ten, as compiled by criclife.com:

1= (59 characters): Gihan Rupasinghe (full name Rupasinghe Jayawardene Mudiyanselage Gihan Madushanka Rupasinghe)

1= Akila Dananjaya (full name Mahamarakkala Kurukulasooriya Patabendige Akila Dananjaya Perera)

3　(55 characters): Hemantha Wickramaratne (full name Ranasinghe Pattikirikoralalage Aruna Hemantha Wickramaratne)

4　(53 characters): Sachithra Senanayake (full name Senanayake Mudiyanselage Sachithra Madhushanka Senanayake)

5　(52 characters): Chaminda Vaas (full name Warnakulasuriya Patabendige Ushantha Joseph Chaminda Vaas)

6　(51 characters): Ranjith Madurasinghe (full name Madurasinghe Arachchige Wijayasiri Ranjith Madurasinghe)

7= (49 characters): Chanaka Welegedara (full name Uda Walawwe Mahim Bandaralage Chanaka Asanka Welegedara)

7= Prasanna Jayawardene (full name Hewasandatchige Asiri Prasanna Wishvanath Jayawardene)

7= Tissara Perera (full name Narangoda
   Liyanaarachchilage Tissara Chirnatha Perera)
10 (48 characters): Hemantha Boteju (full name
   Jayawardene Welanthanthrige Hemantha
   Devapriya Boteju)

In case you were wondering, Rangana Herath (full name Herath
Mudiyanselage Rangana Keerthi Bandra Herath) is eleventh.

Celebrities

Huge numbers of famous people love, esteem and sometimes even play cricket. And who can blame them? On the field of play, no one is ever going to be so uncool as to ask for an autograph. Mick Jagger can hang around Lord's for years without being bothered, as all the men in egg-and-bacon ties will pretend they don't know who he is. Although, in certain circumstances, outrageous fame can get in the way of normal life (*see* Hugh Grant).

Lily Allen

Showed the excellent taste we had all guessed at when interviewed by Jonathan Agnew for *Test Match Special* during the 2009 Ashes series. 'I like the beauty of the game,' she said, 'the whites against the green, the pace of it, and the fact that you're allowed to drink in the stand, which you can't do at football.'

Clement Attlee

In 2005 the *Guardian* quoted historian Paul Addison, who had been asked what aspect of modern Britain would have most upset Clement Attlee, the country's first post-war Prime Minister. Rupert Murdoch winning the TV rights to Test cricket, Addison said.

Johnny Borrell

The Razorlight frontman is a famous cricket nut, and in May 2007 took his American film-star girlfriend Kirsten Dunst to a Test match at Lord's. Is that not the definition of true love? Or possibly a monumental tactical error, for Dunst watched Collingwood scratch out a century against the West Indies and dumped Borrell before the summer was out.

Guy Burgess and Donald Maclean

The two spies, who defected to the Soviet Union in 1951, are said to have participated in what Burgess's biographer Andrew Lownie called 'one of the strangest sporting events to have been held in Moscow'. It was, of course, a cricket match, in which Maclean captained a Gentlemen's team against a Players' side skippered by *Daily Worker* correspondent Dennis Ogden. Burgess was the umpire, and 'the wives prepared a splendid tea of cucumber and caviar sandwiches', according to the spy writer Andrew Lycett. The game was played on a relatively smooth patch of grass at the dacha of Robert Dagleish, an expatriate translator and former diplomat. The Players won by fifty-four runs after an explosive innings by someone identified only as 'a former American spy who adopted a baseball stance'. We don't have a precise date, but we know this match took place in the summer of 1963. The last real Gentlemen vs Players match took place at Lord's in 1962. It's rather comforting to think of this ancient tradition continuing, for one match at least, in class-bound Soviet Russia.

Kenneth Clarke, CH, QC, MP

In 2010 the Lord Chancellor, Kenneth Clarke, admitted losing the key to the red box containing his official papers while watching a Test match against Pakistan at Trent Bridge. Interviewed on *Test Match Special*, he denied that he had lost it deliberately so he could watch the game without having to work. 'Honestly, if they send the key, I will do the papers tonight,' he said.

Coldplay

The band's bassist Guy Berryman was asked to sponsor Gloucestershire village club Slaughters United in 2010, and promptly sent them a cheque for £750. Lead singer Chris Martin used to play for Countess Wear CC in Devon – possibly because his father was their president – and also turned out for Great

Rissington, just down the road from Slaughters. 'A local umpire recalls having a chat with Chris after one game and asking him what he did for a living,' Slaughters secretary Paul Heming told the *Independent*. 'He told him, "I'm in this band called Coldplay. We've just made our first album and we think it might do quite well." And everyone at the bar went, "Yeah, yeah".'

Hugh Cornwell

The erstwhile lead singer of The Stranglers experienced an epiphany while watching Devon Malcolm hit a six against India at Old Trafford in 1990. In his autobiography he wrote, 'Unexpectedly I suddenly identify with this character and recognise that the effort being made to fight his way of the straitjacket situation in which the Indian bowlers have placed him, perfectly mirrors my own current, repressed state within the group. As I watch the ball soar high over the turf, it comes to me in a flash that I should leave The Stranglers, tonight, after the gig.'

Russell Crowe

The Oscar-winning Hollywood actor and professional Australian actually has Kiwi roots: Martin and Jeff Crowe, New Zealand captains both, are his cousins. In 2002 he announced that he was building his own cricket ground on his six-hundred-acre estate at Coffs Harbour, New South Wales. 'I might have more than five thousand Test runs,' said Martin, 'but he makes forty million bucks a movie.'

John Fowles

The author of *The French Lieutenant's Woman* was the mainstay of Bedford School's bowling attack between 1942 and 1944, bowling swing and seam, and had a trial for Essex. He believed that a 'secret gate-key to all [Pinter's] work' was 'his very intense and evident love of cricket'. (*See* Harold Pinter.)

Hugh Grant

Louche, libidinous leading man and, for two or three years in the early 1990s, an unlikely stalwart of my own team at the time, the Captain Scott Invitation XI. In 1993 we were playing on Palewell Common in East Sheen, and my old friend Terence asked Hugh what he was working on. 'Oh God,' said Hugh, with a sigh. 'It's appalling. I'm starring in a film and it's so bad that it'll end my career. I'll be lucky ever to work again.'

The film came out the following summer. It was *Four Weddings and a Funeral*.

Not long after the film's release, we were playing at Ardley with Fewcott in Oxfordshire. It was one of the less reliable pitches on which we played. If a team made 50 it was doing well, and 31 was once a winning score. Word clearly got round that Hugh, by now a major star, was taking part, and when he came out to bat he was accompanied by a crowd of about fifty teenage girls, variously screaming, swooning and, in one or two outrageous cases, rubbing themselves up against him. He never played for us again.

Miles Jupp

The comedian and host of BBC Radio 4's *News Quiz* went on *Celebrity Mastermind* and chose 'The life and career of Michael Atherton' as his specialist subject. He won.

John le Carré

Went to prep school in Berkshire, where he was taught by R. C. Robertson-Glasgow. Le Carré kept wicket at Sherborne, and his brother Tony appeared for Dorset in the Minor Counties Championship. His conman father financed Learie Constantine's court case against the Imperial Hotel in London, which had refused him accommodation on racist grounds in 1943; and once lent Ray Lindwall and Keith Miller £100 and £150 respectively when they were short of readies. In *The Tailor of Panama*, Geoffrey

Cavendish has the voice of an 'upper-class cricket commentator on a sunny summer's afternoon'.

McFly
In 2006, the boyband set off the fire alarm playing cricket backstage before a concert at the Sheffield Arena. The ball hit the alarm, thus causing a two-hour delay in preparations.

Martin McGuinness
IRA hard man, Sinn Féin politician and, finally, an almost cuddly deputy first minister of Northern Ireland turned out to have been a rabid cricket fan for more than forty years. When Kevin O'Brien scored all those runs against England in the 2011 World Cup, McGuinness said he was a national hero. And he was as thrilled as anyone when England beat Australia in the 2005 Ashes. Politics has never seemed more complicated than this.

Sir John Major
In 2005 the former Prime Minister (and onetime President of Surrey CCC) revealed the text of a poem he had once written when trapped on the front bench during a Test match:

> Oh Lord, if I must die today,
> Please make it after close of play.
> For this I know, if nothing more,
> I will not go, without the score.

Peter O'Toole
The Irish actor and part-time hellraiser became a friend of Don Wilson, the former Yorkshire off-spinner then coaching at Lord's, and used to drop in at the Indoor School for the odd net. On one occasion Imran Khan turned up, wanting some bowling practice. O'Toole was the only batsman available. 'Peter was bruised from

head to foot,' said Wilson, 'but he loved it. It was like he was Lawrence of Arabia all over again.'

Harold Pinter

The legendarily bad-tempered playwright once wrote a poem about Len Hutton, his all-time hero, who he said he was too shy ever to contemplate meeting. This is it, in full:

> I saw Len Hutton in his prime,
> Another time, another time.

He sent it to his friend, fellow playwright and drinking partner Simon Gray. The following day he rang him to find out what he thought.

'I haven't finished it yet,' said Gray.

Daniel Radcliffe

The *Harry Potter* star queued at the 2007 Lord's Test for the autographs of Sachin Tendulkar and Andrew Strauss. 'I am a geek,' he told the *Independent* in 2012. 'I'm obsessed with cricket.' He also said that he had been having nightmares in which Strauss was chasing him with a cricket bat. (Well, we all have *those*.)

Keanu Reeves

Interviewed in 2003 on *The Tonight Show*, the actor and good-looking slacker Keanu Reeves, who had just been filming in Australia, mounted a stirring defence of the great game. 'But doesn't it go on for days and days?' asked the mystified host Jay Leno. 'Cricket's cool,' said Reeves. 'In five days you have time to, like, get real into it.'

Christian Vieri

As he is a footballer I had to look him up to see who he was. But the much-travelled Italian striker turns out to have been brought up in Australia, and only returned to Italy as a teenager. An interviewer once asked him which player he had idolised as a boy. 'Allan Border.' Allan who? Who did he play for? 'Australia,' said Vieri, obviously enjoying this. He has a bat signed by him too.

Charlie Watts

Rolling Stones drummer of impeccable sartorial taste, and pretty good sporting taste too. He nominated John Arlott's commentary of Jim Laker taking nineteen wickets against Australia at Old Trafford in 1956 as one of his desert-island discs.

Bill Wyman

Former Rolling Stones bassist and regular participant in celebrity matches. In 1994 he took a one-handed catch in the gully to dismiss Brian Close. In his other hand was a cigarette. In 1995 he took what he claimed was the first televised hat-trick at the Oval. His victims were the ITN newsreader Trevor McDonald, the Sky Sports presenter Charles Colvile and BBC football man Gary Lineker.

Favourite Tests

The Oval, August 18, 19, 20, 21 1994

ENGLAND vs SOUTH AFRICA: Third Test

South Africa

G Kirsten	c Rhodes b DeFreitas	2	—	(2) c & b Malcolm	0
P N Kirsten	b Malcolm	16	—	(1) c DeFreitas b Malcolm	1
W J Cronje	lbw b Benjamin	38	—	b Malcolm	0
*K C Wessels	lbw b Benjamin	45	—	c Rhodes b Malcolm	28
D J Cullinan	c Rhodes b DeFreitas	7	—	c Thorpe b Gough	94
J N Rhodes	retired hurt	8	—	(9) c Rhodes b Malcolm	10
B M McMillan	c Hick b DeFreitas	93	—	(6) c Thorpe b Malcolm	25
†D J Richardson	c Rhodes b Benjamin	58	—	(7) lbw b Malcolm	3
C R Matthews	c Hick b Benjamin	0	—	(8) c Rhodes b Malcolm	0
P S de Villiers	c Stewart b DeFreitas	14	—	not out	0
A A Donald	not out	14	—	b Malcolm	0
	b 8, lb 10, w 1, nb 18	37	—	lb 5, nb 9	14
		332			**175**

1–2 (1), 2–43 (2), 3–73 (3), 4–85 (5), 5–136 (4), 6–260 (8), 7–266 (9), 8–301 (10), 9–332 (7) (J N Rhodes retired hurt at 106)

1–0 (2), 2–1 (1), 3–1 (3), 4–73 (4), 5–137 (6), 6–143 (7), 7–143 (8), 8–175 (5), 9–175 (9), 10–175 (11)

DeFreitas	26.2–5–93–4
Malcolm	25–5–81–1
Gough	19–1–85–0
Benjamin	17–2–42–4
Hick	5–1–13–0

DeFreitas	12–3–25–0
Malcolm	16.3–2–57–9
Gough	9–1–39–1
Benjamin	11–1–38–0
Hick	2–0–11–0

England

G A Gooch	c Richardson b Donald	8	—	b Matthews	33
*M A Atherton	lbw b de Villiers	0	—	c Richardson b Donald	63
G A Hick	b Donald	39	—	not out	81
G P Thorpe	b Matthews	79	—	not out	15
A J Stewart	b de Villiers	62	—		
J P Crawley	c Richardson b Donald	5	—		
†S J Rhodes	lbw b de Villiers	11	—		
P A J DeFreitas	run out	37	—		
D Gough	not out	42	—		
J E Benjamin	lbw b de Villiers	0	—		
D E Malcolm	c sub b Matthews	4	—		
	b 1, w 1, nb 15	17		lb 6, nb 7	13
		304			205

1–1 (2), 2–33 (1), 3–93 (3), 4–145 (4),
5–165 (6), 6–219 (7), 7–222 (5), 8–292 (8),
9–293 (10), 10–304 (11)

1–56 (1), 2–180 (2)

Donald	17–2–76–3		Donald	12–1–96–1
de Villiers	19–3–62–4		de Villiers	12–0–66–0
Matthews	21–4–82–2		Matthews	11.3–4–37–1
McMillan	12–1–67–0			
Cronje	8–3–16–0			

Umpires: R S Dunne (NZ) and K E Palmer (E)
Referee: P J P Burge (A)

South Africa had won the first Test by a hideous 356 runs; the second Test was a batsman-friendly draw, in which Peter Kirsten and Graeme Hick both scored centuries. England needed to win this one to tie the series, so they dropped Angus Fraser (as you do) and Phil Tufnell (after just one Test back in the side) and brought in Devon Malcolm, and Joey Benjamin for his only Test. Selectors were jittery men in those days.

The visitors' grim, unsmiling captain Kepler Wessels won the toss and chose to bat on a fast and true pitch, and would have been surprised to be effectively 136 for 6 just after lunch, with Jonty Rhodes in hospital with suspected concussion. He had ducked so low into Malcolm's bouncer that the bowler nearly appealed for lbw. But burly all-rounder Brian McMillan (who, in appearance, I always thought had something of Gérard Depardieu about him) and wicketkeeper David Richardson battled through the crisis, and the visitors' final score of 332 seemed about par. England's skipper Michael Atherton was then given out lbw to the first ball he had faced. Athers looked at his bat and shook his head meaningfully as he left the crease, for which dissent he was fined half his match fee (£1250) and reprimanded by the perennially furious match referee Peter Burge. Despite fifties from Graham Thorpe and Alec Stewart, England were struggling against the pace of Allan Donald and Fanie de Villiers. But the support bowling was less ferocious, and after Phillip DeFreitas, who amazingly hadn't been dropped all summer, and Darren Gough had had a swish, first innings parity appeared to be in sight.

At which point, England's genuine number eleven, Devon Malcolm, came to the crease. Malcolm was one of the nicest guys who ever played for England. Strikingly swift on his day, he didn't really look like a fast bowler: he wore glasses, he couldn't field and his radar was worse than Steve Harmison's. First ball from de Villiers was short and nasty and hit Malcolm on the grille of his helmet, right between the eyes. As de Villiers said later, 'I must admit we were laughing a bit, because he really looked like he couldn't play. I think us giggling was what probably upset him.' Malcolm wasn't hurt, but he was very cross. 'You guys are going to pay for this,' he said. 'You guys are history.'

Really, if there's a single lesson cricket has to teach us, it's Never

Make a Fast Bowler Angry. Malcolm took the new ball, with steam visibly issuing from his ears, and in ninety-nine balls he took 9 for 57. *Wisden* called it 'the most devastating spell by an England bowler since Jim Laker wiped out the Australians in 1956'. He started with a caught and bowled, and you wouldn't have put much money on that. A bouncer was then hooked down long leg's throat, wicketkeeper and slips took four catches, all from devilish lifting balls, and two batsmen were bowled by brisk, pinpoint yorkers. As Alec Stewart later put it, 'No one can honestly say they enjoy the challenge of rapid quick bowling, but some enjoy the challenge more than others, and a few South Africans were not prepared to really fight for their team-mates or their country.' Or, in the slightly pithier words of DeFreitas, 'The South Africans, they crapped it a bit. He got it right and bowled quick.'

England needed 204 to win. The one-day international squad had been announced that morning and Graham Gooch wasn't in it. He came in and, in Daryll Cullinan's words, 'absolutely murdered Allan [Donald] . . . On top of Devon's spell, that was about it for us. I'd played with AD since school days and it was the first time I'd seen a batsman, on that sort of pitch, do that to him. It was brilliant to watch.' It certainly was. We all thought it was the beginning of a new, aggressive, successful England team. It wasn't, of course, but that's another story.

Favourite Tests

Birmingham, August 4, 5, 6, 7 2005

ENGLAND vs AUSTRALIA: Second Test

England

M E Trescothick	c Gilchrist b Kasprowicz	90	—	c Gilchrist b Lee	21
A J Strauss	b Warne	48	—	b Warne	6
*M P Vaughan	c Lee b Gillespie	24	—	(4) b Lee	1
I R Bell	c Gilchrist b Kasprowicz	6	—	(5) c Gilchrist b Warne	21
K P Pietersen	c Katich b Lee	71	—	(6) c Gilchrist b Warne	20
A Flintoff	c Gilchrist b Gillespie	68	—	(7) b Warne	73
†G O Jones	c Gilchrist b Kasprowicz	1	—	(8) c Ponting b Lee	9
A F Giles	lbw b Warne	23	—	(9) c Hayden b Warne	8
M J Hoggard	lbw b Warne	16	—	(3) c Hayden b Lee	1
S J Harmison	b Warne	17	—	c Ponting b Warne	0
S P Jones	not out	19	—	not out	12
	lb 9, w 1, nb 14	24	—	lb 1, nb 9	10
		407			182

1–112 (2), 2–164 (1), 3–170 (4), 4–187 (3), 5–290 (6), 6–293 (7), 7–342 (8), 8–348 (5), 9–375 (10), 10–407 (9)

1–25 (2), 2–27 (1), 3–29 (4), 4–31 (3), 5–72 (6), 6–75 (5), 7–101 (8), 8–131 (9), 9–131 (10), 10–182 (7)

Lee	17–1–111–1		Lee	18–1–82–4
Gillespie	22–3–91–2		Gillespie	8–0–24–0
Kasprowicz	15–3–80–3		Kasprowicz	3–0–29–0
Warne	25.2–4–116–4		Warne	23.1–7–46–6

Australia

J L Langer	lbw b S P Jones	82	—	b Flintoff	28
M L Hayden	c Strauss b Hoggard	0	—	c Trescothick b S P Jones	31
*R T Ponting	c Vaughan b Giles	61	—	c G O Jones b Flintoff	0
D R Martyn	run out	20	—	c Bell b Hoggard	28
M J Clarke	c G O Jones b Giles	40	—	b Harmison	30
S M Katich	c G O Jones b Flintoff	4	—	c Trescothick b Giles	16
†A C Gilchrist	not out	49	—	c Flintoff b Giles	1
S K Warne	b Giles	8	—	(9) hit wkt b Flintoff	42
B Lee	c Flintoff b S P Jones	6	—	(10) not out	43
J N Gillespie	lbw b Flintoff	7	—	(8) lbw b Flintoff	0
M S Kasprowicz	lbw b Flintoff	0	—	c G O Jones b Harmison	20
	b 13, lb 7, w 1, nb 10	31		b 13, lb 8, w 1, nb 18	40
		308			279

1–0 (2), 2–88 (3), 3–118 (4), 4–194 (5), 5–208 (6), 6–262 (1), 7–273 (8), 8–282 (9), 9–308 (10), 10–308 (11)

1–47 (1), 2–48 (3), 3–82 (2), 4–107 (4), 5–134 (6), 6–136 (7), 7–137 (8), 8–175 (5), 9–220 (9), 10–279 (11)

Harmison	11–1–48–0	Harmison	17.3–3–62–2
Hoggard	8–0–41–1	Hoggard	5–0–26–1
S P Jones	16–2–69–2	Giles	15–3–68–2
Flintoff	15–1–52–3	Flintoff	22–3–79–4
Giles	26–2–78–3	S P Jones	5–1–23–1

Umpires: B F Bowden (NZ) and R E Koertzen (SA)
Third Umpire: J W Lloyds (E)
Referee: R S Madugalle (SL)

Led by Michael Vaughan with a glint in his eye and an almost antipodean self-belief, England had lost the first Test at Lord's by a terrible margin: 239 runs. But at Edgbaston, just before the coin was tossed, a stroke of luck. Australia's opening bowler

Glenn McGrath trod on a ball during practice and tore his ankle ligaments. Michael Kasprowicz, rather less terrifying, replaced him. Ricky Ponting won the toss and elected to field. Why not? Conditions demanded it and England needed to be crushed underfoot like ants.

But this was a new England. Marcus Trescothick stood there and simply banged it through extra cover for four, time and time again. Later on, Andrew Flintoff played himself back into form with a innings of magnificent violence. He was out just before tea; then Kevin Pietersen, in his second Test, took over. After eighty overs, England had made 407, the most runs conceded in a day by Australia since 1938. Five different men hit sixes: the scoring rate was 5.13 an over.

Early next morning, Matthew Hayden hit his first ball straight to cover, to record his first duck in forty months and sixty-eight innings. Joy! But Justin Langer, hit on the head in Steve Harmison's first over, bedded in for the long haul. The middle order seemed strangely diffident: from the relative security of 194 for 3, Australia subsided to 308 all out, leaving Adam Gilchrist high and dry on 49 not out. England's lead was a useful 99, which looked even better when Shane Warne bowled Andrew Strauss on the second evening with a vicious turner. On the third morning Brett Lee reduced them further to 31 for 4, before Warne took over and had them tottering at 131 for 9. A lead of 230: would it be enough? But Flintoff was still there, and with Simon Jones, one of the better number elevens in the world, he started clumping the ball around in his usual way. One over from Michael Kasprowicz went for 20, another from Lee for 18. The last pair added 51. Australia needed 282 to win.

If we had been playing anyone else, you would assume that was too many. But Australia had an aura, an unshakeable self-belief. They won the easy games, they won the hard games. Even when things started badly, they invariably ended up well. So when they ended the third evening on 175 for 8, we did not feel entirely safe.

The eighth wicket had come off the last ball, when Michael Clarke, the last recognised batsman, missed Harmison's slower one and was bowled. On day four they would need 107, with only two wickets left. They couldn't do it. Could they?

In *Wisden*, Steven Lynch said that if the remaining two Australian wickets had fallen quickly the following morning, the match would still have been remembered as a classic. But remembered as viscerally as we now remember it? Shane Warne and Brett Lee added 45 before Warne trod on his wicket. Lee and Kasprowicz then whittled away the English lead with luck, skill and great aplomb. 50 ... 40 ... 30 ... 20 ... 10 ... I was in a car driving to a cricket match and refused to turn on the radio. My friend Robin was in the back seat, listening to it on headphones. Then, with three runs required and all hope lost, Harmison dug in a short one, Kasprowicz gloved behind, and an extraordinary, wondrous victory was ours.

When the Old Trafford Test began four days later, a DVD entitled *The Greatest Test* was already on sale. As Lynch said, no one was arguing with the description.

JULIAN'S XIs

Herbs & Spices

1	C. Dill	(Bermuda Select XI)
2	Bay	(Royal Army Service Corps)
3	Thyme	(Gentlemen of Worcestershire)
4	J. Parsley	(Dragoons)
5	R. D. Minty	(Jersey)
6	A. F. A. Mace	(Norfolk, Norfolk Club and Ground)
7	Sage	(Catterick Garrison)
8	A. Ginger	(Oxfordshire)
9	A. Garlick	(Duke of Norfolk's XI)
10	Salt	(Combined Services XI)
11	C. W. A. Pepper	(Highgate School)

The Village Year

Some fixtures expire very quickly: the teams find out they're incompatible and they each quietly move on. Others take years to die. We had been playing Sir Tim Rice's team, the Heartaches, for the best part of twenty years, but in that time we got older and worse and they got younger and better. The last four or five games we played were little short of embarrassing. But we got on terribly well with them, and we had been playing them for so long that our children who had played with their children when they were small met those children once again, when grown up, at parties, and got on as well as their parents did.

The last few years of this fixture took place at Arundel Castle, which is exactly the sort of place we've wanted to play: posh, scenic and grand, with actual paying spectators, who may have felt a little cheated by the standard of cricket they witnessed. The pitch there is astonishingly flat, and the grass is Lord's perfect. This isn't a ground that is just mown with a machine. Trained grass nibblers are employed each morning to chew down each blade to a uniform length. You could play snooker on it.

And to say they crushed us would be no exaggeration. One year someone scored 196. He would have reached 200 if he hadn't had a brainstorm in the nervous 190s and holed out. Another year Torquil, their astoundingly posh opening batsman, hit the ball with such force that in stopping it at extra cover, I hurt my hand so badly that I didn't play for a month. I was supposed to be captaining and I just felt relief that I could hand over to someone else. Sitting with the opposition, my hand covered by frozen peas, I saw for the first time how old, grey, fat and arthritic our team had become. We needed more than new blood. We needed oxygen tanks. I looked at Sir Tim and he looked at me, and the fixture quietly died there and then.

'I've had enough, Bernard ... I want you out.'

September

September Birthdays

1: David Bairstow (1951), Clare Connor (1976)

2: Chris Tremlett (1981)

3: J. W. H. T. Douglas (1882), Basil Butcher (1933), Geoff Arnold (1944)

4: Lance Klusener (1971)

5: Mark Ramprakash (1969)

6: Saeed Anwar (1968)

7: Norman 'Mandy' Mitchell-Innes (1914)

8: Siegfried Sassoon (1886), Geoff Miller (1952), Jos Buttler (1990)

9: Fred Spofforth (1853), S. S. Abid Ali (1941), Neil Fairbrother (1963), Graham Onions (1982)

10: K. S. Ranjitsinhji (1872), Belinda Clark (1970), Eoin Morgan (1986)

12: Wes Hall (1937)

13: Robin Smith (1963), Shane Warne (1969)

14: Paul Allott (1956), Kepler Wessels (1957)

15: Colin Ingleby-Mackenzie (1933), Mike Proctor (1946), Abdul Qadir (1955), Patrick Patterson (1961), Nathan Astle (1971)

16: Mickey Stewart (1932)

17: Peter Lever (1940)

18: Derek Pringle (1958), Darren Gough (1970)

21: Learie Constantine (1901), Curtly Ambrose (1963), Chris Gayle (1979)

22: Martin Crowe (1962)

23: Henry Blofeld (1939), Moin Khan (1971)

24: Pat Pocock (1946)

25: Bishen Bedi (1946), Hansie Cronje (1969), Claire Taylor (1975), Adam Lyth (1987)

26: Ian Chappell (1945), Jonny Bairstow (1989)

27: Bill Athey (1957), Brendon McCullum (1981)

28: Majid Khan (1946)

29: Trevor Howard (1913), David Steele (1941), Chris Broad (1957), Mark Nicholas (1957)

30: Darrell Hair (1952)

David Bairstow *(September 1)*

Red-haired, combative Yorkshire wicketkeeper who won four Test caps, appeared in twenty-one one-day internationals and, to the shock and dismay of all, took his own life in 1998, aged forty-six. His son Jonny, who would follow him into the England team, was eight at the time. In his *Wisden* obituary, Matthew Engel described Bairstow as 'perhaps the only unequivocally popular man in Yorkshire'. 'He wasn't a great wicketkeeper and he wasn't a great batsman,' said his team-mate Phil Carrick, 'but he was a great cricketer.' In 1980 he was playing an ODI at the SCG: England needed 35 to win in six overs and Graham Stevenson walked out to bat. 'Evening, lad,' said Bairstow. 'We can piss this.' And they did.

Mark Ramprakash *(September 5)*

In scoring 50,651 career runs – as Barney Ronay noted on his retirement – Mark Ramprakash ran at least 380 miles, or the entire length of England, with a bat in his hand.

Norman 'Mandy' Mitchell-Innes *(September 7)*

There's so much luck involved in this game, as the career of Norman Mitchell-Innes bears out. (Why was he nicknamed Mandy? It's probably best not to ask.) In four seasons at Oxford University (1934–7), Mandy scored 3319 runs at 47.41. No one has ever scored more. In May 1935 he hit a magnificent 168 against the touring South Africans, and was immediately picked for the first Test at Trent Bridge. The England batting order read Sutcliffe, Wyatt, Hammond, Mitchell-Innes, Leyland, Ames. Unfortunately Mandy played back when he should have played forward and was lbw for 5. He was retained for the next Test at Lord's, but dropped out because he was suffering from hay fever. 'I might be sneezing just as a catch came in the slips,' he wrote to Plum Warner. He was replaced by his friend Errol Holmes, and never played Test cricket again.

Siegfried Sassoon *(September 8)*

In his second volume of autobiography, *The Weald of Youth* (1942): 'The Blue Mantles averages in my old scrap-book show that in the years 1910 and 1911 I had 51 innings, with 10 not-outs, and an average of 19. This I consider quite a creditable record for a poet.'

Jos Buttler *(September 8)*

Every bat he has used since early adolescence has had the words 'FUCK IT' written on the top of the handle. He looks down, thinks 'fuck it' and hits the next ball for six.

Fred Spofforth *(September 9)*

'The Demon' was 'a tall, wiry man, 6 feet 3 inches in height, with a high delivery, good length, a deceptive break and a deadly yorker' (F. S. Ashley-Cooper).

In 1882, Australia toured England for a second time and played a single Test at the Oval. The pitch was tricky, scores were low and W. G. Grace set the tone for more than a century of ill feeling and mutual resentment when Australia were 110 for 6 in their second innings. The number eight batsman, Sammy Jones, left his crease to pat down a divot. Grace immediately whipped off the bails and appealed. The umpire gave him out. Australia were all out for 122; England needed 85 to win. The Demon thundered into England's dressing room between innings and called Grace a cheat. 'This will lose you the match!' he yelled. And to his team-mates, he said, 'This thing can be done!' England looked comfortable enough at 51 for 2, but Grace hit an uppish drive straight to mid-off and Spofforth blew away the rest with 7 for 44. Australia won by seven runs. The tension was so extreme that a spectator bit through the handle of his umbrella. Spofforth later described this session as 'the most exciting cricket I ever witnessed'.

K. S. Ranjitsinhji *(September 10)*

'He was blest with supreme natural gifts,' wrote H. S. Altham in 1926, 'and an alert and receptive mind, physique that was at once strong, supple, and perfectly co-ordinated, and, as a result, a lightning quickness of conception and execution that no man, not even Victor Trumper, has ever quite equalled. But it was by unremitting application that he trained himself to make the utmost of these innate advantages.'

Robin Smith *(September 13)*

Halfway through his England career, Smith was asked to choose his favourite innings so far. He had already scored seven Test centuries, but instead went for a pre-tea mini-session in Antigua in 1990, during which Ian Bishop and Courtney Walsh bowled bouncer after bouncer at him on a lively pitch. Smith made 0 from 14 balls and had his jaw broken. 'It's the only one of my innings I've ever wanted to keep on video,' he said. 'It was unbelievably exhilarating.'

Shane Warne *(September 13)*

In 2006, the lads' mag *Zoo* nominated Warne as the pre-eminent role model for male Australian youth. Explained the editor, 'He's supposedly shagged a thousand women, he's fat, he smokes and he drinks beer.'

As Amol Rajan wrote in *Twirlymen*, 'Before every single one of his four tours of England, Warne put it about that he'd invented a new delivery. He never had.'

Colin Ingleby-Mackenzie *(September 15)*

Astoundingly posh captain of Hampshire between 1958 and 1965, whose image as a bit of a roué became fixed in the public view after a TV interview he gave on a long-forgotten programme called *Junior Sportsview*.

'Mr Ingleby-Mackenzie,' asked the interviewer, 'to what do you attribute Hampshire's success?'

'Oh, wine, women and song, I should say.'

'But don't you have certain rules, discipline, helpful hints for the younger viewer?'

'Well, everyone in bed in time for breakfast.'

'Yes, thank you. Perhaps we could take a look in the dressing room.'

'Certainly, if you don't mind me wandering around in the nude.'

The only time I ever encountered him, not long before his death in 2006, he had the ruby red nose and cheeks of a life well lived. 'Golf,' he once said, 'is a game to be played between cricket and death.'

Abdul Qadir *(September 15)*

According to Barney Ronay in the *Guardian*, Abdul Qadir had three googlies: 'the one he let you see; the other one he let you see; and the one that got you out'.

Derek Pringle *(September 18)*

Enormous not-very-fast bowler and not-particularly-destructive batsman who everyone agrees was extraordinarily lucky to play thirty Tests for England in the 1980s and early 1990s. And yet Pringle is the only Englishman ever to take three wickets in a World Cup final. He opened the bowling in the 1992 final against Pakistan, and took an astounding 3 for 22 in his ten overs. Unfortunately, everyone else bowled like drains and England lost by twenty-two runs.

Pringle's 'always popular warm-up routine before coming on to bowl,' says Wikipedia, 'involved him lying on his back and apparently wrestling with an invisible octopus'. While at Cambridge University he was an extra on the film *Chariots of Fire*. He ended his first class career with a batting average of 28.26 and a bowling average of 28.26.

Darren Gough *(September 18)*

Yorkshire and England fast bowler of the 1990s, shorter than most of his kind at 5 foot 8 inches, who nonetheless had the nickname Rhino. Asked by a team-mate why he was called this, he said, 'Cos I'm strong as an ox.'

In 2003 Gough became the first England cricketer ever to appear in a comic strip, when he made a brief cameo in 'Billy Whizz' in the *Beano*. He had one word to say: 'Chortle!'

Learie Constantine *(September 21)*

Played eighteen Tests between 1928 and 1939, and took the West Indies' first-ever wicket in Test matches. 'I never wanted to make a hundred,' he once said. 'Who wants to make a hundred anyway? When I first went in, my immediate objective was to hit the ball to each of the four corners of the field. After that, I tried not to be repetitive.' Constantine qualified as a barrister in 1954, became well known as a journalist and broadcaster, and was eventually made a life peer in 1969, two years before his death. For public service, though, not for services to cricket. Lord Constantine was the first black man ever to sit in the House of Lords.

After several years at Nelson in Lancashire, in 1939 Learie signed for the Yorkshire village Windhill as their overseas pro. He was paid twenty-five pounds a game, three times what first-division footballers were then earning.

Chris Gayle *(September 21)*

Charming ladies' man of the old school, who always opens doors for women and walks on the outside on pavements. In May 2016 he was being interviewed by Charlotte Edwardes of *The Times*, and claimed to have 'a very, very big bat, the biggest in the wooooorld,' before asking, 'You think you could lift it? You'd need two hands.' On his Instagram account, the West Indies opener uploaded photographs of his new house, complete with purpose-built strip club. 'From the pool to the strip club,' he posted. 'If U don't have a strip club at home, U ain't a cricket "Player" ... I always make sure my guests are well entertained and feel like they are at home.' Which of course they will do, if their home also has a pole-dancing pole in its front room.

Martin Crowe *(September 22)*

Possibly New Zealand's greatest-ever batsman, the younger Crowe brother became an unusually thoughtful and emotionally articulate writer on the game in his last few years, before dying outrageously young of cancer in March 2016, aged fifty-three. I would love to read a book of his collected writings, and to be honest I am shocked and appalled that there hasn't been one. Here are just a few of his utterances:

'I found a mask, and I began to fake it until I made it. Part of the mask was to copy great players to hide my own inadequacies.'

'I learnt to remove emotion by forcing my body language so strongly as to bluff the opposition that I was "on" on any given day, in the zone ... The mindwork I did proved exhausting – having to disguise a contaminated flow of thoughts. Not surprisingly, the lack of natural positive thinking, of authenticity, got me in the end.'

'Ross [Taylor] called me ... I asked him to slowly explain a typical night before an important match. I repeated it back to him. He realised he had stopped living a normal life.'

'I loved batting. But I grew to hate myself and the mask I wore. Off the field I was totally lost.'

And these are the words of a man who was not just talented, but extraordinarily gifted. What chance do the rest of us have?

Henry Blofeld *(September 23)*

In the two-hundred-year history of the Eton v Harrow match, there has only ever been one hat-trick. Its third victim was the commentator Henry Blofeld. After his last Test behind the microphone in September 2017, Blofeld paraded around Lord's wearing a lime green jacket, a pale pink shirt, and matching crimson trousers and cravat.

Pat Pocock *(September 24)*

Off-spinner who once took six wickets in nine balls, and seven wickets in eleven balls, for Surrey against Sussex in 1972. Yet he always felt he had bowled better in a Test match in Jamaica in February 1974, when his figures were 57–14–152–0.

Hansie Cronje *(September 25)*

Good-looking, upright South African captain of deeply held Christian beliefs, or so we thought. He had a tattoo that read 'WWJD', meaning What Would Jesus Do? 'Possibly Jesus would not have fixed matches and corrupted young cricketers in exchange for a few rands and a leather jacket' (Simon Barnes). Banned from cricket for life, Cronje seemed to escape justice when he died in a suspiciously convenient plane crash in 2002. A few years later he was voted the eleventh-greatest South African of all time.

Adam Lyth *(September 25)*

Yorkshire's cue-ball-headed opener made his Test debut for England in May 2015 against New Zealand, the 666th man to play for England. He played seven Tests and averaged only 20.45, so if Beelzebub wasn't bowling, he was almost certainly umpiring.

Ian Chappell *(September 26)*

Nuggety batsman, aggressive Australian captain and owner of the second-most ferocious moustache in world cricket (after Dennis Lillee's), Chappell was once asked what spin bowlers were for. His answer: 'To get you from sixty to a hundred as quickly as possible.'

Brendon McCullum *(September 27)*

Originally a swashbuckling wicketkeeper and one-day hitter of no little power, McCullum is one of a few players who visibly grew as a Test captain. 'I loved playing cricket as a kid,' he explained. 'Just because there's more at stake now, it doesn't mean you should lose the innocence of why you got into the game in the first place. For a long time I had lost that, and I think the team had lost that, but it's one thing we've tried to recapture. It sounds corny, but we talk about the little boy who fell in love with the game, and that's what we've tried to do as a group.' As well as becoming the first New Zealander to score a triple hundred in Tests (302 against India in 2014), he hit the fastest-ever Test century (fifty-four balls) in 2016, and promptly retired. Oddly enough he never scored a century against England in any international match, which is probably why we like him so much.

Trevor Howard *(September 29)*

Actor and cricket tragic who insisted on having a clause inserted in his contracts to allow him to leave filming to attend Test matches. In 1960 he agreed to appear in a charity match at Buxton. He got up at five o'clock in the morning, drove the 180 miles up to Derbyshire and was caught behind first ball.

David Steele *(September 29)*

Grey-haired, bespectacled saviour of English cricket in 1975, when Lillee and Thomson were running riot and batsmen of suitably phlegmatic temperament were conspicuous by their absence. Although he looked like your dad, he was actually only thirty-three at the time. Steele recalled the scene as he walked out at Lord's:

'People were looking at me. I could hear them muttering, "Who's this grey old bugger?" as I walked past. Tommo stood with his hands on his hips. I said, "Good morning, Tommo." He said, 'Bloody hell, who've we got here, Groucho Marx?"'*

Steele scored 50, 45, 73, 92, 39 and 66 against the Australians that summer and became only the second cricketer to win BBC

---

* According to other sources, Thommo's first words were 'Who's this then? Father bloody Christmas?' Get your stories straight, fellows.

Sports Personality of the Year. His mild manner concealed a strong competitive streak. 'I'd have played Mitchell Johnson off the front foot,' he said in 2015.

Mark Nicholas *(September 29)*

Hugely confident former Hampshire batsman and captain who, after retirement, turned his good looks, Melvyn Bragg hair and tendency to say 'crikey!' at odd moments into a lucrative television career, presenting cricket shows from all over the globe. And not just cricket, either. In 2002, he hosted the second season of the godawful reality show *Survivor*, and between 2007 and 2010 he helmed ITV's *Britain's Best Dish*. Did you know this? Nor did I. But for a TV sports presenter there can't be a safer gig than hosting a daytime cookery show. Your core audience will never know, and so will never have to forgive you.

In 2016 Nicholas published *A Beautiful Game: My Love Affair With Cricket*, a very odd book indeed, in that about half of it is self-indulgent celebrity waffle, and the other half is some of the most insightful and incisive writing about cricket you'll find outside Mike Brearley. But that does seem to be the man. You don't get one without the other. Would he have made a good captain of England, as was much mooted in the late 1980s? I suspect so: sheer charm and ebullience would surely have prevailed, as they often do.

Quiz 3

1. Who was chosen as one of *Wisden*'s five Cricketers of the Year in 2013, seventy-four years after his grandfather?
2. In his twenties he worked for a bank and played cricket at the weekend. In his thirties his leg spin got him a

place in the Victorian state team, and in 2009 he played
a Test for Australia at the age of thirty-five. He bowled
eighteen overs, conceded 149 runs without taking a
wicket and was never picked again. His name?

3. The lowest total to contain a century in all first-class
   cricket was recorded in 1981, when Nottinghamshire
   scored 143 against Hampshire. Which Notts batsman hit
   105 that day? He died in 2015.

4. Shane Warne, famously, has scored most runs in Test
   cricket without making a hundred. Which Englishman
   has scored most runs in Test cricket without making a
   double hundred?

5. Of all the countries that play Test cricket, which is the
   only one that won its first Test match?

6. What names – first name and surname – were shared by
   a Zimbabwean batsman who played for Leicestershire
   and Gloucestershire in the 1970s and 1980s, and
   the drummer for The Nice, Keith Emerson's first
   commercially successful band?

7. Which Middlesex fast bowler, who was picked for
   England's 1989–90 tour of the West Indies but did not
   play, was forced to retire because of injury two years
   later, retrained as a pilot and eventually became Virgin
   Atlantic's first black captain?

8. In cricket's County Championship, which Midlands
   county failed to win a match between May 14 1935
   and May 29 1939, a run of ninety-nine matches, before
   overcoming Leicestershire by an innings and 93 runs?

9. In 1999, while playing for England vs New Zealand
   at Edgbaston, the Surrey bowler Alex Tudor set the
   England record for the highest score in an innings by a
   nightwatchman, with 99 not out. Whose record did he
   break? It had stood for more than sixty-six years.

10. At the Oval in 1948, in his last Test innings, Don
    Bradman was famously bowled by Eric Hollies second
    ball for 0, four runs short of finishing his career with an
    average of a hundred. Who was the batsman at the other
    end? He was on his way to making 196, although no one
    seems to remember that now.

Answers next month.

Favourite Tests

The Oval, September 7, 8, 9, 10, 11 2018

ENGLAND vs INDIA: Fifth Test

England

A N Cook	b Bumrah	71	—	c Pant b Vihari	147
K K Jennings	c Rahul b Jadeja	23	—	b Mohammed Shami	10
M M Ali	c Pant b Sharma	50	—	b Jadeja	20
*J E Root	lbw b Bumrah	0	—	c sub b Vihari	125
†J M Bairstow	c Pant b Sharma	0	—	b Mohammed Shami	18
B A Stokes	lbw b Jadeja	11	—	c Rahul b Jadeja	37
J C Buttler	c Rahane b Jadeja	89	—	c Mohammed Shami b Jadeja	0
S M Curran	c Pant b Sharma	0	—	c Pant b Vihari	21
A U Rashid	lbw b Bumrah	15	—	not out	20
S C J Broad	c Rahul b Jadeja	38	—		
J M Anderson	not out	0	—		
	b 26, lb 9	35		b 14, lb 4, w 2, p 5	25
		332		(8 wkts dec)	423

1–60 (2), 2–133 (1), 3–133 (4), 4–134 (5), 5–171 (6), 6–177 (3), 7–181 (8), 8–214 (9), 9–312 (10), 10–332 (7)

1–27 (2), 2–62 (3), 3–321 (4), 4–321 (1), 5–355 (5), 6–356 (7), 7–397 (6), 8–423 (8)

Bumrah	30–9–83–3		Bumrah	23–4–61–0
Sharma	31–12–62–3		Sharma	8–3–13–0
Vihari	1–0–1–0		Mohammed Shami	25–3–110–2
Mohammed Shami	30–7–72–0		Jadeja	47–3–179–3
Jadeja	30–0–79–4		Vihari	9.3–1–37–3

India

S L Rahul	b Curran	37	—	b Rashid	149
S Dhawan	lbw b Broad	3	—	lbw b Anderson	1
C A Pujara	c Bairstow b Anderson	37	—	lbw b Anderson	0
*V Kohli	c Root b Stokes	49	—	c Bairstow b Broad	0
A M Rahane	c Cook b Anderson	0	—	c Jennings b Ali	37
G H Vihari	c Bairstow b Ali	56	—	c Bairstow b Stokes	0
†R R Pant	c Cook b Stokes	5	—	c Ali b Rashid	114
R A Jadeja	not out	86	—	c Bairstow b Curran	13
I Sharma	c Bairstow b Ali	4	—	c Bairstow b Curran	5
Mohammed Shami	c Broad b Rashid	1	—	b Anderson	0
J J Bumrah	run out	0	—	not out	0
	b 4, lb 10	14		b 10, lb 16	26
		292			345

1–6 (2), 2–70 (1), 3–101 (3), 4–103 (5), 5–154 (4), 6–160 (7), 7–237 (6), 8–249 (9), 9–260 (10), 10–292 (11)

1–1 (2), 2–1 (3), 3–2 (4), 4–120 (5), 5–121 (6), 6–325 (1), 7–328 (7), 8–336 (9), 9–345 (8), 10–345 (10)

Anderson	21–7–54–2		Anderson	22.3–11–45–3
Broad	20–6–50–1		Broad	12–1–43–1
Stokes	16–2–56–2		Ali	17–2–68–1
Curran	11–1–49–1		Curran	9–2–23–2
Ali	17–3–50–2		Stokes	13–1–60–1
Rashid	10–2–19–1		Rashid	15–2–63–2
			Root	6–1–17–0

Umpires: J S Wilson (WI) and H D P K Dharmasena (SL)
Third Umpire: B N J Oxenford (A)
Referee: A J Pycroft (Z)

Most of the Tests chosen for this book were played when the series was still alive. In 2018, England were 3–1 up with one to go, against (according to the ratings) the best team in the world. But India still have a problem playing away from home, and Jimmy Anderson's bowling had been extraordinary. The last Test of the summer was also the 162nd and last Test of Alastair Cook's career. The past couple of years had suggested that Cook was close to the finishing line: fifties were now rare and hundreds a distant memory. Had he ever had an opening partner who was any good, he might even have been dropped. But for once a great cricketer was allowed to go out at a time of his own choosing and in a manner of his own choosing. Could he reward the faithful with some runs?

On the first day, Cook was the only batsman who made batting look at all straightforward. He was out for 71, to widespread disappointment, and the pitch, previously thought to be placid and sluggish, became a snake pit as 133 for 1 became 134 for 4 and, by the close, 198 for 7. Mohammed Shami passed the outside edge so many times without a snick that Vic Marks nominated his bowling as the best 'nought-for' of the summer. The following day Jos Buttler played an innings of magnificent judgement and maturity, Stuart Broad stuck with him for an hour and a half, and the innings climbed to 332: unimagined riches. It was one of those matches you couldn't stop watching because something else was going to happen. India were 94 for 2 and cruising; Virat Kohli looked the best batsman and then some. Anderson and Broad came back into the attack, Anderson hit Kohli on the pad, it was given not out, they declined to review, and the DRS showed it would have hit the stumps. Argh! But wickets were falling at the other end, and on 49 Kohli pushed at Ben Stokes slightly harder than he would have done to Anderson and was snaffled at second slip. End of day's play: 174 for 6.

Again, the morning proved fruitful for the batting side. India managed 292, thanks to Hanuma Vihari, in his first Test innings, and the old hand Ravindra Jadeja. England were 114 for 2 by the end of another intriguing day's play, because Cook was still there again, on 46 not out. He had played with a freedom and a joy that had been absent from his batting for a long, long time. On the fourth day he moved serenely to his inevitable century, as spectators alternately wept, cheered and gave him three-minute standing ovations. Along the way he passed Kumar Sangakkara's Test runs and so became the highest-scoring left-hander in Test history. When he reached three figures, the fifth man to do that in his final Test, he passed Steve Waugh's centuries total. Theresa May and Mick Jagger tweeted congratulations. Joe Root also scored a century, K. L. Rahul broke the record for the number of catches taken by an outfielder in a Test series, and when England declared they led by an insurmountable 463.

India, though, are a decent side, led by a terrific batsman whose sculpted beard knows no surrender. There were moments on the final day when doubts crept in and you wondered whether they weren't going to do it after all. But 464 to win was just too many, and the equation boiled down to this: India had one wicket left, the batsman on strike was Mohammed Shami, not the best number ten in the world, and Jimmy Anderson needed one wicket to pass Glenn McGrath's total of 563 Test wickets. Result: splattered stumps, and moments later Anderson was on a microphone trying to talk to Wardy. The words wouldn't come, but the tears did. As did mine. 'Probably the most entertaining [series] in this country since 2005,' wrote Simon Burnton on the *Guardian*'s OBO service, wholly correctly.

JULIAN'S XIs

Metalworkers

1	B. Ironmonger	(Denbighshire)
2	A. Silverman	(Middleton Stoney)
3	J. Coppersmith	(Sunshine Coast Under-14s)
4	H. Arrowsmith	(Pontarddulais)
5	Goldsmith	(Jockeys and Racing Officials)
6	H. Shearsmith	(York and District Clergy)
7	H. Shoesmith	(Buckinghamshire Amateurs)
8	B. Sixsmith	(South Wales)
9	A. Smith	(Hodnet and Peplow)
10	Leadbeater	(Training Battalion Grenadier Guards)
11	F. Mercury	(St Helens Recreation)

The Village Year

I have written before about Simon, our most obsessive player, for whom cricket seems like a terrible curse rather than a source of lasting pleasure. What other team in the world can say that their longest-serving player (more than 250 games) is an opening batsman with a career average of 7? Simon is fluent and elegant in the nets, and he is in the nets a lot of the time. It's only when he plays in a match that he runs into trouble. Anxiety gets the better of him. Fear of failure bedevils him. In first-class cricket people talk about a batsman scoring a thousand runs before the end of May. In Rain Men, we have hushed conversations about Simon amassing twenty-five before the end of June.

So why does he still open? Because, in short, no one else wants to. It's a tough old job, batting at 1 or 2, especially if you are low on confidence, as many of my team usually are. Simon is a kind and thoughtful man, but in a cricketing context he tends to demonstrate the single-mindedness and self-centredness, if not the talent, of Geoffrey Boycott. In all these years he has scored only one fifty, and it was scored so slowly (almost every run a smear through third man) it lost us the game. Simon was thrilled to bits when he came off the field, and may not have noticed that all his team-mates wanted to murder him in cold blood. In early 2018 we played a game in Essex with a weak side even for us. Indeed, we had one decent batsman, Major Tom, who scores centuries at will. Simon ran him out for 12. Of course he did! Simon was out two balls later and spent the rest of the afternoon sitting in the pavilion apologising to random passers-by. We lost by miles.

Other, more ruthless teams would probably get rid of him, or just ask him to bat at number 9, his natural position. But Simon is one of us. He is ours, for better or for worse. Towards the end of 2018 he became increasingly disheartened by his constant failures and dropped out of the last half-dozen fixtures. We genuinely missed him. (Admittedly we did come closer to winning a few games without him, but that's neither here nor there.) In the close season, rumours abounded that he had sold all of his kit on eBay and bought a ukulele. Will we see him again on a cricket pitch? Watch this space.

October

October Birthdays

2: Sir Pelham Warner (1873), Tom Moody (1965)

3: Ray Lindwall (1921)

4: Don Mosey (1924), Basil D'Oliveira (1931), Rishabh Pant (1997)

6: Richie Benaud (1930), Tony Greig (1946), Morne Morkel (1984)

7: Graham Yallop (1952), Zaheer Khan (1978)

8: Neil Harvey (1928)

10: Lance Cairns (1949)

11: Keith Boyce (1943), Ryan Harris (1979)

12: Jack Crapp (1912)

13: B. J. T. Bosanquet (1877), John Snow (1941), Gareth Batty (1977)

14: Roland Butcher (1953), Tillakaratne Dilshan (1976)

15: P. G. Wodehouse (1881)

16: Jacques Kallis (1975)

17: Major Reginald Edwards (1881), Aravinda da Silva (1965),
    Anil Kumble (1970)

18: Gladstone Small (1961)

19: Harold Gimblett (1914)

20: Chris Cowdrey (1957), Allan Donald (1966), Virender
    Sehwag (1978)

21: Jim Parks (1931), Geoffrey Boycott (1940), Damien Martyn (1971)

22: Mike Hendrick (1948), Owais Shah (1978)

23: Douglas Jardine (1900), Colin Milburn (1941), Brad Haddin
    (1977), Steve Harmison (1978)

27: Chris Tavaré (1954), Mark Taylor (1964), Kumar Sangakkara
    (1977), David Warner (1986)

28: Evelyn Waugh (1903)

29: Wilfred Rhodes (1877), Matthew Hayden (1971),
    Michael Vaughan (1974)

30: Courtney Walsh (1962)

Sir Pelham Warner *(October 2)*

Former England captain, *éminence grise* at Lord's and hopelessly ineffectual, hand-wringing manager during the Bodyline crisis, Sir Pelham was famous in his family for his minimal appetite. His granddaughter, the no-less-eminent historian Marina Warner, told the *Guardian*, 'One evening at dinner, when he was asked if he would like a second helping, he replied, "One pea, please."'

Ray Lindwall *(October 3)*

According to his obituary in the *Daily Telegraph*, Lindwall was 'arguably the greatest of all fast bowlers. At once graceful and menacing, [he] was able to send down an over of six very different balls with perfect disguise.' He was temperamentally a fast bowler off the field, too. In the same obituary a story is told of the 1948 tour, in which Len Hutton asked Keith Miller to introduce him to Lindwall. Hutton had batted against him often enough but they had never met off the field. Miller told Hutton that Lindwall thought the world of him and encouraged him to go and talk to him. Hutton went off but returned moments later, looking crestfallen.

'What happened?' asked Miller.

'He said he was sick of the sight of me when I was batting against him and told me to bugger off,' said Hutton.

'Told you he admired you,' said Miller.

Basil D'Oliveira *(October 4)*

Film stars, models and Test cricketers are all wont to lie about their age. When Basil D'Oliveira first played Test cricket in 1966, the selectors thought he was thirty-one. Once he was established in the side he finally admitted to having been born in 1931. In his autobiography, D'Oliveira sheepishly admitted that even that figure might have not been entirely accurate. In 1979, however, the *Playfair Annual* was widely agreed to have gone too far by giving the year of his birth as 1031.

Peter Oborne's 2004 book about him is, to my mind, one of the best cricket books ever written. About one of the most important players, too. As Scyld Berry wrote, 'History may well decide that the lives of millions of non-white South Africans would have been made wretched for even longer but for Basil D'Oliveira.'

Rishabh Pant *(October 4)*

In his second Test in England in 2018, the young Indian wicket-keeper was scoring runs at a precipitate rate. 'Pant's on fire,' said Phil Tufnell on *TMS*.

Richie Benaud *(October 6)*

Steely, hard-as-nails Australian captain and leg-spinner who after retirement transformed himself into the best and most sagacious of all TV commentators on the sport. Benaud believed that if you had nothing to say, then you should say nothing – something that Ian Botham, to name but three, should be forcefully reminded of from time to time. Like every commentator, Benaud had his catchphrases. 'Morning, everyone' at the start of the day's play. 'Marvellous.' 'Four from the moment it left the bat.' Thanks to the joy of replays, some of his utterances will live for ever. For instance, at Headingley at 1981, of one of Ian Botham's sixes: 'It's gone into the confectionery stand and out again. Don't bother look-ing for that.' Who needs videotape? Close your eyes and there it is.

But his greatest commentary moment, for me, consisted of two words. Edgbaston, 2005, England vs Australia. Last pair at the crease. Harmison bowling. Three runs to win. No one has breathed for several minutes.

Harmison bangs in one short, Michael Kasprowicz edges the ball, Geraint Jones takes a tumbling catch down the leg side.

Benaud: 'Jones!'

Camera cuts to umpire Billy Bowden, who raises a crooked finger.

Benaud: 'Bowden!'

That really was all he said. This was genius at work.

Tony Greig *(October 6)*

Six-foot seven-inch South African all-rounder, England captain and main cheerleader and salesman for Kerry Packer's World Series Cricket revolution of the late 1970s. It's hard now to remember how angry people were with Greig for what they saw as, essentially, treason, and what he saw as a hard-headed business decision. In *The Times* John Woodcock wrote, 'What has to be remembered, of course, is that he is an Englishman not by birth or upbringing, but only by adoption. It is not the same thing as being an Englishman through and through.' Sir Derek Birley goes on: 'Greig's other disadvantages as an England captain – his games-manship, his mastery of the art of needling opponents, his violent mood swings, impetuosity and so forth – were presumably also attributable to his insufficient Englishness.' He was sacked from the national captaincy in disgrace in 1977, but the following year Sussex declined to follow England's lead and reappointed him their skipper. Nottinghamshire proposed a motion to expel Sussex from the County Championship, and Lancashire seconded it.

Greig's gravest error, of course, had come a year earlier when he was still captaining England. 'You must remember that the West Indians, these guys, if they get on top are magnificent cricketers,' he told a TV interviewer. 'But if they're down, they grovel, and I intend, with the help of Closey and a few others, to make them grovel.' In the final Test at the Oval, Greig was bowled middle and leg by Michael Holding. As he returned to the pavilion, one fan offered him a copy of 'Who's Grovelling Now?', a record that had recently been released by the reggae artist Ezeike. 'Everyone had a copy,' recalls the DJ Trevor Nelson. 'I remember learning all the words from my dad.' For some reason no England captain has ever used this verb again.

Keith Boyce *(October 11)*

A fine fast-medium bowler for Essex (1966–77) and the West Indies (for whom he played twenty-one Tests in the early 1970s), Keith Boyce was born on October 11 1943 and died aged just fifty-three on October 11 1996. Which makes him the first, and so far only, Test player of any country to die on his birthday.

Jack Crapp *(October 12)*

Gloucestershire batsman who played seven Tests for England on the 1948–49 tour of South Africa. It is said that on that tour he shared a room with one of the Bedser twins. One night, having enjoyed local hospitality to its fullest extent, he returned to the hotel and approached the reception desk. 'Bed, sir?' asked the receptionist. 'No, Crapp,' said Jack. The receptionist pointed him in the direction of the gentleman's lavatories.

Throughout a forty-three-year career as both player and umpire, Crapp always wore the same pair of cricket boots.

B. J. T. Bosanquet *(October 13)*

Bernard James Tindal Bosanquet, who played seven Tests for England in the early twentieth century, has three claims to fame. He invented the googly (still called the bosie in Australia as a tribute), the ball bowled by the leg spinner that appears from the action to spin away from the right-handed batsman as usual, but actually spins into him. 'It's not unfair,' said Bernard, 'only immoral.' He was also the father of Reginald Bosanquet, rug-wearing, bibulous linchpin of ITV's *News at Ten* in the 1970s and 1980s. And third, he is one of only six Test players to die the day before his birthday. The most recent to do so were England's David Sheppard (the reverend, not the umpire) in 2005 and New Zealand's Bev Congdon, lantern-jawed early 1970s skipper, in 2018. Bernard Bosanquet also represented Oxford University at billiards (1898 and 1900) and hammer throwing (1899 and 1900). In 1977 Reginald Bosanquet was the first person to tell a grieving nation that Elvis Presley had died.

John Snow *(October 13)*

Ferocious, wild-haired poet-cum-fast-bowler who rarely celebrated a wicket, but just walked back to his mark to bowl the next one. John Snow taught Dennis Lillee how to bowl a leg-cutter.

Tillakaratne Dilshan *(October 14)*

Aggressive Sri Lankan opening batsman who may or may not have invented the Dilscoop shot, but was undoubtedly best at playing the damn thing. He unveiled it during the Twenty20 World Cup in England in June 2009, and says he developed it in the nets during the IPL tournament a couple of months earlier. The basis of the stroke is to go on one knee to a ball of good length or slightly short of a length, and scoop it over the wicketkeeper for four. It looks amazing, it's extremely effective, and you're likely to get hurt if you get it wrong, especially if you aren't wearing a helmet. (Some of his team-mates called it the 'starfish shot', because you wouldn't play it if you had a brain.) Dilshan is now one of three judges on *Sri Lanka's Got Talent*, and markets a fashion line called Dil Scoop.

In New Zealand the shot is called the McScoop, after Brendon

McCullum, who also plays it rather well. (The shot was actually first played by Somerset captain Brian Langford in a county match in 1962, but it being a county match, no one noticed.)

P. G. Wodehouse *(October 15)*

Wodehouse's love of cricket was well known: he played for the Authors XI and Hollywood Cricket Club, and named Reginald Jeeves, the immortal valet, after Percy Jeeves of Warwickshire (*see* March 5). Less well known is that it was a cricket match that made his career. in 1902, P. G. was a twenty-one-year-old bank clerk who had written a few articles but not yet published a book. Bored insensible at work, he took a half-day off to go and see the last day of the Ashes Test at the Oval. England were set 263 to win, but with them at 48 for 5, he returned to the office, assuming the match was gone. He therefore missed Gilbert Jessop making a century in an hour and a quarter, and England putting on 76 for the last three wickets, to win by one wicket. Wodehouse later wrote that, on seeing the following day's papers, he decided that if banking made him miss things like that, he would be better off trying to be a writer. Over the next five years he published eight novels, and never looked back.*

Major Reginald Edwards *(October 17)*

Made only one first-class appearance, for the Rest of England in 1921, but was a great lover of cricket. His obituary in *Wisden* records that he 'spent a considerable time in Africa, and ... found solace during solitary days up country reading *Wisden*' and that 'in a later expedition to Southern Russia he lost all his baggage except for his set of *Wisden*, which accompanied him on all his travels'.

---

* Thanks to Patrick Kidd for this wonderful story.

Virender Sehwag *(October 20)*

A lot of bowlers over the years, including our own beloved James Anderson, have been nicknamed Daisy: some days 'e does, some days 'e doesn't. It all seems terribly unfair, as it is surely batsmen who are the ultimate daisies. Take Virender Sehwag. If he was out of form he looked as though he didn't know which end of the bat to hold. And when he was in form, well, good grief.

Sehwag scored twenty-three hundreds in Tests for India, of which only nine were below 150. He hit four double centuries and two triple centuries. The first of those triples, 309 against Pakistan in Multan in 2004, was the fastest of all time in Test matches, until he scored the second, 319 against South Africa in Chennai in 2008. The second three hundred came off just 278 balls, and is the highest score to have a strike rate over a hundred. This is more than seeing it like a football; this is seeing it like a basketball. Maybe his most impressive performance, though, came against Sri Lanka in 2008, on a turning pitch with Muralitharan and Mendis wreaking havoc. Sehwag, who was now seeing it like a very large spherical boulder, promised his team-mates he would score a double century. His 201 not out came from a score of 329. Off the spinners alone, he hit fifteen fours and four sixes. Asked about his approach in a press conference, he gave a four-word reply: 'See ball, hit ball.'

Geoffrey Boycott *(October 21)*

In 1985, Boycott launched an illustrated coaching series called *Brighter Cricket with Geoff Boycott*. Number one was called the Backward Defensive Stroke.

In 1999, at the age of fifty-nine, Boycott wrote, 'I miss playing to such an extent that I can honestly say I would exchange the rest of my life for five more years of playing for England at the height of my form.'

A horse chestnut he practised against as a schoolboy was short-listed in 2000 for the title the Greatest Tree in Yorkshire.

'I play best when I'm surrounded by people who appreciate me,' he once said. But how would he know?

Douglas Jardine *(October 23)*

According to Bill Bowes, 'To me and every member of the 1932–33 MCC side to Australia, Douglas Jardine was the greatest captain England ever had. A great fighter, a grand friend and an unforgiving enemy.'

In the Second World War, Jardine was commissioned into the Royal Berkshire Regiment and went with the British Expeditionary Force to France, where he served with distinction. In 1982, this story appeared in the *Observer*: 'He was sent by headquarters in Dunkirk into Belgium to discover why troops there had not made contact. Jardine found them all dead, commandeered a troop carrier and drove himself back through enemy lines.' His biographer Christopher Douglas was not able to verify this story but believed that 'such an act of cold courage would have been quite in keeping with Jardine's character'. In his later years he became interested in Hindu philosophy, and according to a friend of his, 'had a speculative mind, intent on ethical and religious problems'. Cricket he regarded as 'only a game'.

In the execrable 1984 Australian mini-series *Bodyline* – one of the worst drama series ever made – Jardine was played as the most panto of villains by the young Hugo Weaving, who has since gone on to a successful Hollywood career. Presumably he has bought all prints of that programme and burned them in a giant bonfire, and if he hasn't, he probably should.

David Warner *(October 27)*

There are a few stereotypes about short men. Every one of them applies to David Warner. As Martin Crowe put it in 2015: 'Watching from the luxury of my couch and after hearing numerous accounts from respected cricket people, there is a growing concern that David Warner's thuggish behaviour has gone too far. Soon one day it will lead to an incident that will sully the game for good.'

Evelyn Waugh *(October 28)*

The great English novelist is known to have played, and written about, village cricket only once, as an undergraduate at Oxford in 1923. Michael Davie, while compiling *The Faber Book of Cricket*, tracked this one down. It was first published in the *Cherwell* under Waugh's customary pseudonym there, Scaramel:

'When I returned home, I reasoned thus with myself: today I have wearied myself utterly; I have seen nothing and no one of any interest; I have suffered discomfort of every sense and in every limb; I have suffered acute pain in my great toe; I have walked several miles; I have stood about for several hours; I have drunken several pints of indifferently good beer; I have spent nearly two pounds; I might have spent that sum in dining very well and going to a theatre; I might have made that sum by spending the morning, pleasantly, in writing or drawing.

'But my brother maintained that it had been a great day. Village cricket, he said, was always like that.' (*See also* July 8.)

Wilfred Rhodes *(October 29)*

Played his first Test at the age of just twenty-one and his last, against the West Indies in 1930, when he was fifty-two years and

165 days old. Not only was he therefore the world's oldest Test cricketer, but he could also boast the longest Test career: thirty years and 315 days. In all first-class cricket he took 4187 wickets (the most by anyone) and scored 39,802 runs (the eighteenth-highest aggregate). 'We don't play this game for fun,' he once said, in true grim Yorkshire style.

Michael Vaughan *(October 29)*

As Rob Smyth wrote in *The Nightwatchman*, 'The greatest trick Michael Vaughan ever pulled was convincing England they could beat Australia. As brilliant as England's 2005 side were, they had no real place beating one of the greatest teams of all time. Yet by convincing them they could win the Ashes, Vaughan kickstarted a series of events that enabled them to do just that. You can see why Steve Harmison called Vaughan "the best liar I've ever played with".'

Courtney Walsh *(October 30)*

Bowled uphill, into the wind and first change for the first nine years and fifty-eight Tests of his career, before he finally got his hands on the new ball. And eventually took more wickets (519 at 24.44) than any of his countrymen.

Quiz 3 Answers

1. Nick Compton.
2. Bryce McGain.
3. Clive Rice.
4. Alec Stewart.
5. Australia. (By winning the first-ever Test match, in Melbourne in 1877.)

6. Brian Davison.
7. Ricardo Ellcock.
8. Northamptonshire.
9. Harold Larwood. (98 at Sydney in the 1932–33 Bodyline
   Test series.)
10. Arthur Morris.

Terms and Conditions

Cricket's lexicon is huge and, apparently, growing every day, as people think up ever dafter terms for ever dafter things. Ten years ago we had the reverse sweep but not, possibly, the ramp shot, the switch hit or the Dilscoop. Bowlers now have reverse swing and cross-seamers to master, and must always now bowl in the right 'areas'. All this terminology must be mystifying to the neophyte, and it's pretty tough for the cricket tragic too. There's a crucial gap between thinking you know what you're talking about and actually knowing what you're talking about, and that gap gets larger, I find, as the day's play progresses. Here, then, is a brief glossary of cricketing terms, some of them so old no one knows where they came from, and some so new even Nasser Hussain hasn't started using them yet. Keep it with you at all times for easy reference.

1. Quack

Duck. A score of nought for the batsman, short for duck's egg, which resembles the digit 0. Literally anyone can get out for 0. Michael Atherton could score 185 not out against South Africa in 1995, in 643 minutes, facing 492 balls. He also made twenty ducks at Test level, which is roughly twenty more than he would have preferred.

Failing to trouble the scorers. Quasi-humorous, but in fact deeply depressing, euphemism for duck.

Golden duck. Out first ball. Silver duck is out second ball, and bronze duck (for some reason a phrase rarely used) is out third ball. I was often out for a paper duck – twenty-seventh ball – having never at any time looked like scoring a run.

Diamond duck. Out for 0 without facing a single ball. This can happen in one of three ways: when you're the non-striker and you're run out without facing a ball; when you're batting and you're out first ball, but it's a no ball or a wide so it doesn't count as a ball in the scorebook; or when you're timed out.

Royal duck. Out first ball of the team's innings. It's getting worse, isn't it?

Golden goose. Out first ball of the team's first innings in the first match of the season. Strangely, not a duck.

Platinum duck. Invented by the radio producer Jon Harvey, because it happened to him: out to the first ball you have ever faced.

Pair. Two innings, two ducks, two broken bats, two holes punched in the dressing-room wall.

On a pair. When a batsman scored a duck in the first innings, he is said to be 'on a pair' before he has scored a run in the second innings.

King pair. Two innings, two golden ducks.

Emperor pair. This is being out to the first ball of each innings, so two royal ducks. We are in the realms of fantasy here, or possibly nightmare.

2. Out

There are nine methods of dismissal in cricket, each of them utterly dispiriting. (There were ten, but one was withdrawn. *See below*.)

Bowled. The bowler bowls, you miss, the ball hits the stumps. If you hit the ball and it is deflected onto the stumps, you are said to have 'played on'. For some reason this is considered slightly less sad than being bowled in the normal fashion, and people will say 'unlucky' to you on your return to the pavilion, but you're still in the pavilion, aren't you? (Incidentally, it is not considered polite, when told you have been 'unlucky', to growl, seethe or scream invective at the top of your voice. It is satisfying, though.)

Caught. The ball hits the bat, it doesn't hit the ground and a fielder catches it, often brilliantly, one-handed, inches off the deck. Fifteen minutes ago another batsman popped up a dolly to him and he dropped it. This is not a coincidence; it is the grim inevitability of fate. If the bowler catches you, you are 'caught and bowled'.

Run out. Your job is to run between the wickets and therefore score runs. (Run: verb first use, noun second use.) If you don't quite make it into the crease and the fielder knocks down the stumps with the ball, you are run out. This is also considered 'unlucky'. Alternatively, one batsman may run and the other may not, and you may both end up in the middle of the pitch shouting at each other and hitting each other with your bats. This is not considered 'unlucky'.

Stumped. One of several ways a spin bowler will try to get you out. As he teases you with the flight of his bowling, which is so slow it seems to be a trick, you lose all patience and you run up the pitch, aiming to smack the ball for six somewhere over his head. But he is better than you, and he knows he is better than you. You miss the ball completely and the wicketkeeper removes the bails. Because you are outside the crease you are out. Our regular wicketkeeper, who was widely known as the Human Sieve, has managed to stump four or five people in his long career. All of them were halfway back to the pavilion by the time he completed the feat, having assumed they were out and not bothered trying to get back into the crease. The fools.

Leg before wicket. If the ball was going to hit the stumps and you get your leg in the way first, you should be out leg before wicket, or lbw. But not if you hit it first with the bat. And not if it pitched (i.e. bounced) outside the line of leg stump. And not if the ball hit the pad outside the line of off-stump and the batsman was playing a stroke. And not if the umpire doesn't know what he's doing, which he won't, approximately 83 per cent of the time.

Hit wicket. Generally in cricket you play forward, or you play back. If you play too far forward, you might get stumped. If you play too far back, you might hit your wicket. And not just with the bat. I have seen caps fall on the bails and, in one notable incident, glasses. No false teeth yet, but it can't be long.

Handled the ball. Hit the ball with your bat, or failing that, your pad. If it's going to hit your stumps, try not to knock it away with your hand. Graham Gooch, Steve Waugh and Michael Vaughan all did this in Tests. In 2017, for no reason, this method of dismissal was removed from the laws. You still can't do it, though, and if you do you'll be out obstructing the field (q.v.).

Hit the ball twice. Intentionally, that is. This is to stop people hitting the ball up and then biffing it out of the ground, like a tennis serve. It works, too. No one has ever been out this way in Tests.

Obstructing the field. As a batsman, you have to get out of the fielding side's way. They can stand there and call you a fat c*** until the cows come home, but should your bat accidentally collide with their testicles on the way through, it'll be you who is off to the pavilion.

Timed out. The baby of these dismissals, as it was only added to the laws of cricket in 1980, which is the day before yesterday in cricket's mind. If it takes more than three minutes (raised from two in 2000) for you to put your box on and fiddle with your gloves on the way to the crease, the umpire can give you out. When the West Indian fast bowler Vasbert Drakes was given out timed out, he was actually on a plane. But they still gave him the full three minutes out on the pitch.

3. Pitch

Crease. You won't be surprised to learn that this was originally an actual crease, a furrow in the surface. This was how pitches were marked until 1865, when someone came up with the bright idea of using paint.

Popping crease. In cricket's earliest days, when a batsman completed a run he had to place his bat in a 'popping hole' that was cut into the turf. And in order to get the batsman out, the wicketkeeper had to put the ball in this hole before the batsman could get there with his bat. Result: serious hand injuries. In time the popping hole came to be represented symbolically by the popping crease, to signify the completion of a run.

Wicket. One of so many words in cricket's lexicon that has different meanings in different contexts, thus confusing any Estonians, Hungarians or Basques trying to pick up the game. The wicket (definite article) is a strip of ground between two sets of stumps. The wickets (plural) are the stumps. A wicket (indefinite article) is something a bowler takes, and what a batsman becomes when a bowler has taken it. The fact that wicket rhymes with cricket has led to some very bad poetry indeed.

Stumps. They're stumps of wood. Obvs.

Bails. From the Latin *baculum*, meaning stick. Bails are the two little bits of wood that lie across the top of the stumps, and often get lost in an umpire's pocket, where also reside six stones (for counting the six balls in each over), a cloth (for wiping the ball if it gets wet), possibly a spare ball if there's room and certainly an emergency pack of Cheesy Wotsits for that all-important pre-tea snack.

Heavy roller. Captains can theoretically choose whether to have the heavy roller (a roller that is heavy) applied to the pitch before they bat, or the light roller (a roller that isn't so heavy). Whether it makes the slightest difference to the pitch is debatable. Groundsmen, though, love rollers. The Edgbaston groundsman Steve Rouse rolled his Test pitch so enthusiastically that he became known as Rawhide, because he was always rollin', rollin', rollin'. At the level I play at, very few grounds have one roller, let alone two, but if you do happen to have access to one of those motorised rollers, you will already know that driving the thing is one of the greatest pleasures a man can have with his trousers on. Or off, if you prefer driving it in shorts.

4. Balls

Over. A word that has twenty-seven different meanings in my dictionary, the twenty-seventh of which is six balls all bowled from the same end by a single bowler. The over is the SI unit of cricketing exhaustion.

Maiden over. An over during which no runs are scored. The word 'maiden', of course, originally meant virgin, and thus also came to be used as a synonym for unproductive, for if you haven't engaged in sexual relations with a man, you are unlikely to have had many children by him. In any other sport this would be considered a strangely old-fashioned term, but then in any other sport you wouldn't talk about 'the new lbw law' when it was introduced in 1972.

Wicket maiden. A maiden over in which a wicket falls, i.e. a batsman is dismissed.

Double and *triple wicket maiden.* We've been on the wrong end of a few of these.

Hat-trick. This term, wonderfully, comes from the mid-nineteenth-century custom that any bowler who took three wickets in three balls was presented with a hat. H. H. Stephenson of Surrey was the first player to be thus awarded, after doing the business for the All England XI against Hallam in 1858.

Swing. If you keep one side of the ball polished and let the other side deteriorate naturally, the ball will start to swing through the air, either away from the batsman or into him, depending on how you hold it. There are so many factors here to consider, such as the bowler's action, his speed and what he had for dinner last night. In exhaustive testing, scientists have repeatedly demonstrated that balls do not swing, which suggests a catastrophic failure of imagination, among other things. When a spin bowler swings the ball, it's called drift. No one knows why.

Reverse swing. Invented by Sarfraz Nawaz and perfected by other Pakistani bowlers of the 1980s and 1990s, reverse swing is the process that makes old balls swing in the opposite direction to newer balls. Sometimes. In certain conditions. People keep trying to explain reverse swing to me, but as the years pass and my incomprehension increases, I have found it easier just to work on the assumption that it is a form of magic.

Dobber. Medium-pace bowler of little threat and less penetration. When Simon Hughes called Alec Bedser a dobber in a newspaper article, there was an almighty stink. Bedser took 236 wickets in fifty-one Tests. Hughes took none in none.

Dibbly-dobblies. Balls bowled by dobbers. If you're lucky, they 'do a little' in the air. So called because the word takes even longer to say than the ball takes to arrive.

Fast-medium and medium-fast. Fast-medium is more medium than fast, but it's faster than medium-fast, which itself is faster than medium. Hope that's clear.

Yorker. The evil toe-crunching ball that, ideally, slips beneath the toe of your bat to bowl you. Slightly disappointingly, it's named after a Yorkshireman who was rather good at them.

Full toss. Ball that doesn't bounce before it reaches the batsman, usually at a nice unthreatening height to hit for four. Underconfident batsmen often get out to this ball, because, in the split-second before the ball arrives, they realise that they are *supposed* to hit it for four, but they lack the talent or the timing or the placement to do so, so they change their minds and decide to defend it, but it's too late because the ball has already gone through and bowled them.

Beamer. High full toss that is deeply illegal and frowned upon, because when bowled at speed can cause terrible harm. Bowler then holds up hand to indicate that it was a mistake, whether it was a mistake or not. No one ever bowls a beamer deliberately, other than those who do.

5. Shots

Forward defensive. The first shot you'll learn and the last you'll forget. Often played to best effect in front of a mirror with a ruler in November.

Backward defensive. Once, and only once, have I played a backward defensive so perfect that the ball went vertically down onto the pitch and bounced on the spot. For a moment I knew how Rahul Dravid must feel every day of his life.

Drive. Song by The Cars.

Cut. For many years this was my shot. Short, outside off-stump, bang. Then I found myself less and less able to control it. It kept going in the air, straight to a fielder, who caught it. Four times in a row I was out in the same way, for 0. I went off for intensive batting therapy with qualified coaches, practised it incessantly, and did the shot come back? No, of course it bloody didn't.

Sweep. Friend of Sooty.

Nurdle. Like batting but can't hit it off the square? Become a nudger and nurdler, scoring all your runs with annoying deflections that look accidental and probably are, but let's not worry about that now. The weird thing about nudging and nurdling is that if you time one, it'll probably go straight to a fielder for no run, but if you don't, there's an easy single. There's no justice in this game, and there never has been.

Smear. Whatever this shot started out as, and wherever you aimed it, a smear will always go down to third man for one. They don't have third men in Test cricket, but at village level there's no position more crucial.

Edge. When someone edges the ball and knows that they have done so (roughly 99 per cent of the time), they always look straight behind to see whether the wicketkeeper has caught it. Whereas if they have missed it, they don't. Umpires should be taught this in the first week of umpiring school.

6. Places

Long leg. Fielding position behind square on the leg side at about 45° on the boundary. But for some reason 'long leg' has gone out of fashion. Some captains will say 'fine leg' (which is actually further around towards long stop) and others will say 'deep backward square' (which is further around towards deep square leg), but for some reason it is regarded as *infra dig* to use the traditional term. Why is that?

Long stop. Wicketkeepers used to have a long stop directly behind them, but this condom of a fielding position fell out of fashion long ago. Even the Human Sieve forswears one.

Slips. An early description of long stop says he was 'required to cover many slips from the bat'. So slips mean mistakes. There used to be two slip positions: short-slip, where first and second slip now stand, and long-slip, now renamed fly slip or short third man.

Gully. Again, means what it says. A gully is a narrow channel, and on the cricket field it's the narrow channel between point and the slips.

Point. Used to be much closer to the bat, and originally called 'point of the bat', because you were standing close to the bat's end.

Cover. According to John Nyren, writing in 1832, this was 'the man who covers the point and middle wicket', but that was too long to be much use. Does anyone actually know the difference between cover, cover point and point? No, me neither.

Silly mid-on and silly mid-off. Not, as I and everyone else always thought, a reference to the clear folly of fielding so close to the batsman. The *Oxford English Dictionary* lists a rare use of the word to mean 'defenceless', which given all the padding they usually wear is more than slightly ironic.

Julian's XIs

Canine

1	H. Basset	(Lewes Priory)
2	J. Beagle	(Cambridge University Colleges XI)
3	J. Russell	(Willoughby-on-the-Wolds Second XI)
4	A. German	(Somerset County Colts, Weston-super-Mare)
5	Shepherd	(Guernsey Island Cricket Club)
6	A. Terriere	(Surrey Women)
7	G. Dane	(Easterns Under-15s)
8	A. R. Border	(Australia, Essex, Gloucestershire, New South Wales, Queensland)
9	Collie	(Royal Air Force)
10	A. Boxer	(Winchmore Hill)
11	H. Fetch	(South Bedfordshire)
12th man	V. E. Puplett	(Canterbury Clergy)

The Village Year

So where do I fit in in all this? It's a good question, not easily answered. I used to be able to do two things on a cricket pitch to some degree of competence. I took catches, not necessarily elegantly, but usually cleanly. And while I rarely scored runs in any number, I could stay in for ages. The gritty, hour-long 4 not out to save a game was my speciality. Then, about three or four years ago, the catches stopped sticking, and I started to get out for 0 with worrying regularity. Confidence is a fragile thing on a cricket field, and my confidence has always been a Ming vase, held by someone with a serious tremor in both hands and at least one shoelace undone. It happened slowly, over three or four seasons, but I gradually came to hate and fear the playing of cricket. I liked the team, I liked meeting in the pub for lunch, I absolutely loved tea, and I didn't mind arranging all the games and updating the sad stats every Monday, but the bit on the field was becoming more and more painful. I started playing less often. Still going to the matches, scoring, umpiring, going off for long walks in the undergrowth, but not taking part. It all came to a head in early 2017 at a game against our old rivals the White Hunters, whose mainstays Richard and Roger insisted I played, because they'd never had a chance to bowl at me and wanted desperately to get me out for 0. Nothing particularly awful happened in the game – I didn't drop anything and I managed to avoid batting for the umpteenth time – but I was so miserable all day that in the car on the way home, I said, 'Right, that's it. I've retired.'

And I have. It's been wonderful. The odd thing about it is that since I stopped playing, my enthusiasm for the game has come back in great bursts and rushes. I hadn't realised it had gone. But I had stopped writing about cricket, reading about cricket, watching cricket, even. Now the pressure is off, the joy has returned, and this book is one happy consequence. Never again will I drill a twelve-year-old's slow half-volley through extra cover for four, the ball hitting the boundary before I'd even taken two steps up the field. But I only ever did it once, against Tusmore Park in 1997, so I think I can live with that, somehow.

'It's the batting order!'

November

November Birthdays

1: V. V. S. Laxman (1974)

2: Victor Trumper (1877), Mitchell Johnson (1981)

4: Rodney Marsh (1947)

5: Eddie Paynter (1901), Virat Kohli (1988)

6: Graeme Wood (1956)

7: Lionel Tennyson (1889)

8: Brett Lee (1976)

9: David Constant (1941)

11: Roy Fredericks (1942)

12: Dudley Nourse (1910)

14: Harold Larwood (1904), Adam Gilchrist (1971)

16: James Southerton (1827), Waqar Younis (1971)

20: Nathan Lyon (1987)

21: Sir F. S. Jackson (1870), Betty Wilson (1921), Andrew Caddick (1968), Justin Langer (1970)

22: Mushtaq Mohammad (1943), Wayne Larkins (1953), Marvan Atapattu (1970), Gary Ballance (1989)

23: Merv Hughes (1961), Gary Kirsten (1967)

24: Herbert Sutcliffe (1894), Ken Barrington (1930), Fred Titmus (1932), Sir Ian Botham (1955)

25: Imran Khan (1952), Peter Siddle (1984)

26: Ridley Jacobs (1967)

28: E. M. Grace (1841), Keith Miller (1919), Nick Knight (1969)

29: Younis Khan (1977)

Victor Trumper *(November 2)*

No film of Trumper batting survives, only an extraordinary photograph, taken by George Beldam in or around 1905:

This image is so famous, Gideon Haigh wrote an entire book about it.

Trumper was not a worldly man. He ran a sporting goods firm in Sydney but, according to Jack Fingleton, 'he was too generous with his gifts to accumulate money'. Once, on the morning of a Test match, he was working in the shop and allowed time to get away from him. Realising he was late, he put on his coat, took down a new bat from the rack, caught a taxi to the SCG, and made 185 not out. Fingleton continues:

An admirer of Trumper came into his shop after the match and asked whether he could buy a bat Trumper had used.

Yes, he was told. There was the bat used in the recent Test.

The admirer's eyes sparkled. How much it would be?

'Well,' said the impractical Victor, 'it was a 45s bat but it is now second-hand. You can have it for a pound.'

Rodney Marsh *(November 4)*

Ferociously competitive Australian wicketkeeper-batsman, another from the terrifying heyday of the cricketing moustache, and the first Australian wicketkeeper ever to score a century in a Test match. At Headingley in 1981, England had followed on and were already 0 for 1 in their second innings. Ladbrokes offered 500 to 1 against an England victory.* Marsh and his team-mate Dennis Lillee, serious punters both, could not resist. As David Gower told Rob Steen, 'Marsh and Lillee would have a punt on the Martians landing if they had got [those] odds. They've had a few bets on horses that barely answered to the description.'

You know what happened next. Botham scored 149 not out, Willis took 8 for 43 and England won by nineteen runs. Lillee won £5000 and Marsh £2500. As Steen points out, Marsh could have bought a new Ford Fiesta Popular with his winnings, while Lillee could have upgraded to the latest Ford Capri. In Australia, he could have bought a house.

No one genuinely believes that they threw the game in order to win the money. They, and their team-mates, just played like muppets. But that's not to say it's not tremendous fun to *pretend* that this was the most appalling example of match-fixing ever, worse than Salim Malik, more disgraceful than Mohammad Azharuddin,

---

* The bookmaker had recently offered an American woman the same odds against aliens landing on Earth.

more shocking and corrupt even than Hansie Cronje. Rob Steen, in the spirit of Gideon Haigh, wrote an entire book about the bet; presumably he's not a regular guest in either the Lillee or the Marsh homesteads.

Eddie Paynter *(November 5)*

Attacking Lancashire and England batsman of the 1930s who played twenty Tests for England and averaged 59.23, the fifth-highest Test average of all time. At Brisbane in 1932–33, Paynter wasn't feeling too well, so after the second day's play he went off to hospital, where he was diagnosed with tonsillitis. Back at the ground, England had started well in reply to Australia's 340, but then collapsed to 216 for 6. Send for Paynter! The poor man checked himself out of hospital, consumed a swift luncheon of eggs, brandy and champagne, and went out to bat in a sunhat. 'I'll never forget his face,' said Harold Larwood, who was batting with him. 'He looked white and ill. At no time a great talker, he had even less to say that day than usual.' At the end of the day's play Paynter was 24 not out and back in hospital. The following day he returned to the crease and was eventually dismissed for a battling, stoical 83. England acquired a valuable first-innings lead and eventually won the Test. Paynter himself hit the winning runs, a six off McCabe. 'It were nowt but a sore throat,' he said afterwards.

The Hon Lionel Tennyson *(November 7)*

Grandson of prominent versifier Alfred, Lord Tennyson, the Hon Lionel became the third Baron Tennyson in 1928. Before that, he was better known as a first-class cricketer, having captained both Hampshire (between 1919 and 1932) and England (for three Tests in 1921). Lionel was unusual even for the day in that he employed his manservant, Walter Livsey, as the county's wicketkeeper.

On the field he was a buccaneering captain and a hard-hitting batsman who knew no fear. He was in charge for the extraordinary game against Warwickshire in 1922, when Hampshire were bowled out for 15 in their first innings, followed on, scored 521 in their second innings and won the game by 155 runs. In another game, one of his players was at the crease and struggling to score runs. To the batsman's surprise, a small boy in a blue uniform walked out, holding a small envelope. He took the envelope and opened it. Inside was a telegram from his captain in the pavilion, asking him what he thought his bat was for.

Tennyson published his autobiography, *From Verse to Worse*, in 1933.

Roy Fredericks *(November 11)*

Not all cricketers have been huge. Roy Fredericks, the West Indian batsman who put international attacks to the sword for several happy years in the 1970s, admitted to five foot six, and *Wisden* put him at five foot four. Lindsay Hassett, great Australian captain of the 1940s, was five foot six, as was Hanif Mohammad. Gundappa Viswanath, who had wrists of iron, was five foot three. Alvin Kallicharran, who once scored 35 off ten balls from Dennis Lillee (4444414604), was five foot four. Sunil Gavaskar and Sachin Tendulkar were only five foot five. 'Tich' Freeman, who in 1928 took 304 first-class wickets, was five foot two. You could put one of them in your kitbag and no one would ever know.

Fredericks played one of the great Test innings against Australia on a lightning-fast wicket at Perth in December 1975. The West Indies had been heavily criticised for irresponsible batting in the previous Test, but how are you supposed to deal with the might of Dennis Lillee and Jeff Thomson at their peak? Fredericks came in and promptly dispatched Lillee's second ball for six (hooked off a top edge). After fourteen overs he was 81 not out. His century came in 118 minutes off seventy-three balls. He raced on to 169 out of 258 in 217 minutes, off 145 balls. As his *Telegraph* obituary said, 'It was a moment of imperishable glory.'

Harold Larwood *(November 14)*

When he died in 1995, aged ninety, Michael Parkinson wrote a wonderful, passionate obituary in the *Daily Telegraph*. 'Harold Larwood was a giant in my imagination, a legendary figure whose bowling frightened the greatest batsman there has ever been (and a few more besides) and in doing so created a political brouhaha of such resonance it echoes still, sixty years on.

'When I first saw him standing outside a Sydney restaurant in 1979, he looked like one of the miners who would loiter around the pubs on Sunday mornings waiting for the doors to open at mid-day ... He was medium height with good shoulders and the strong, square hands of someone who had done some shovelling in his life as well as bowling.'

The great irony of Larwood's life, of course, that he was summarily abandoned by the English cricketing establishment who had ordered him to bowl bodyline at Donald Bradman (and a few more besides), and that he was embraced and welcomed by the Australians he had so terrorised. After retirement he ran a sweet shop in Blackpool, before Jack Fingleton persuaded him to emigrate down under. The only man on the quayside when Larwood and his family left these shores for the last time was John Arlott. When Parky was in Sydney, his meeting with Larwood was arranged by Fingleton and Keith Miller, and attended by Bill O'Reilly, Arthur Morris and Ray Lindwall, cricketing royalty all of them. They all drank wine; Larwood said he was a beer man.

'Always had a pint when I was bowling,' he said. 'We used to sneak it on with the soft drinks. A pint for me and one for Bill Voce. You must put back what you sweat out.'

'I hope you weren't drunk when you bowled at me,' said Fingleton.

'I didn't need any inspiration to get you out,' replied Larwood.

He was awarded an MBE in 1993. 'Sixty years overdue,' said Parkinson. 'I will never see a greater fast bowler than Larwood,' said Fingleton. 'He was the master.'

Adam Gilchrist *(November 14)*

Formidably talented Australian wicketkeeper-batsman who repeatedly broke English hearts when coming in at (say) 90 for 5 and then scoring an unbeaten century. For years we just waited for him to retire. Gilchrist always walked when he thought he was out, and against India in 2000–01 he was out for a king pair – first ball each time. Other victims of king pairs in Tests, and there haven't been many, include several known rabbits (Bhagwat Chandrasekhar, James Anderson) and one very good batsman indeed: Virender Sehwag.

Only in one Ashes series did Gilchrist not score runs at will against flagging England bowlers: 2005. Indeed, he didn't reach fifty in ten completed innings. This was primarily due to Andrew Flintoff, who bowled round the wicket with speed and hostility, firing it in short, looking for the outside edge. Flintoff only got him four times out of those ten, but Gilchrist referred afterwards to the 'intense and personal' humiliation of his failures in that series. Sadly, it was a one-off. Eighteen months later, at Perth, he hit a fifty-seven-ball hundred: business as usual.

James Southerton *(November 16)*

Southerton has two records that will surely never be broken: he was the oldest player ever to make his Test debut, playing for England in the very first Test against Australia in Melbourne in 1877 at the age of forty-nine years and 119 days; and he was the first Test player to die, when he succumbed to pleurisy three years later.

Southerton represented Sussex, Hampshire and Surrey, sometimes during the same season. He started out as a batsman but became a bowler of great skill, and was the leading wicket-taker in the country in 1868. Batting for Surrey against the MCC in 1870, he cut a delivery hard into the ground, from where it bounced up into the hands of W. G. Grace. The bounce was so obvious that Grace didn't claim the catch, but Southerton walked anyway, and wouldn't be called back. The scorer, mystified, recorded him as 'retired, thinking he was out'.

Sir F. S. Jackson *(November 21)*

Stanley Jackson played twenty Tests, all of them in England, and captained five of them, against Australia in 1905. In that series he won the toss in all five matches and finished top of the batting and the bowling averages for both sides.

As a batsman he was renowned for his on-side play. The Suffragan Bishop of Knaresborough, who attended Jackson's funeral in 1947, wrote, 'As I gazed down on the rapt faces of that vast congregation, I could see how they revered him as though he were the Almighty, though, of course, infinitely stronger on the leg side.' That Bishop of Knaresborough was J. N. Bateman-Champain, who played a couple of times for Gloucestershire in 1899. Nine members of his immediate family also played first-class cricket: his three brothers C. E., H. F. and F. H., his brother-in-law F. A. Currie, four of his uncles – the Curries F., the Rev Sir F. L., R. G. and W. C. – and his cousin C. E. Currie, youngest son of the Rev Sir F. L.

It was the Rev Canon F. H. Gillingham who actually conducted Stanley Jackson's funeral. Gillingham played over two hundred first-class matches, mainly for Essex, and in 1927 was the first person to deliver ball-by-ball commentary on a cricket match for the BBC, on a match between Essex and the New Zealanders at Chelmsford (a game presumably chosen because of its proximity to the Marconi research centre at nearby Writtle). The *Daily Telegraph*'s wireless correspondent wrote, 'It is obviously impossible to broadcast anything but short periods of description of a three-day cricket match. The problem will be exactly how to anticipate the most exciting parts.'

Andrew Caddick *(November 21)*

After retiring from cricket, Andrew Caddick became a helicopter salesman.

Justin Langer *(November 21)*

Smaller half (or maybe about 45 per cent) of the mighty Hayden-and-Langer combo that scored more than five thousand runs for Australia, opening in Tests and very rarely getting out. Matthew Hoggard once called him a 'brown-nosed gnome'.

Marvan Atapattu *(November 22)*

Graham Gooch was out for 0 in his first two Test innings and went on to score 8900 runs. Marvan Atapattu went one better. In his first three Tests he scored 0, 0, 0, 1, 0 and 0. Worse, these innings were spread over four years. He had to wait nearly seven years after his debut to score his second Test run. In the end he played ninety Tests and scored 5502 runs, with six double centuries. But, like Donald Bradman and one or two others, he was a poor starter, notching up twenty-two ducks in Tests and four pairs, both of them records for top-order batsmen. He was also a good strong captain of Sri

Lanka for a couple of years in the mid-2000s, possibly because he had known suffering himself.

Marvan was actually his second name. His third was Samson.

Gary Ballance *(November 22)*

In July 2014 England drew the first Test against India at Trent Bridge. Later that night, Gary Ballance could be found in a Nottingham night club dancing topless, swirling his shirt above his head, shouting, 'I'm not a cricketer tonight! I'm just a drunken bastard!'

Merv Hughes *(November 23)*

When England played Australia in 1989, Hughes saw the young England batsman Michael Atherton as a natural victim. As Atherton later wrote, 'He snarled at me constantly through his ludicrous moustache. He was all bristle and bullshit and I couldn't make out what he was saying, except that every sledge ended with "arsewipe".' They're probably best of friends now.

In 2013, after Australia had been humiliated in Tests at Chennai and Hyderabad, Merv Hughes advised the Australian team to grow some facial hair. Beards and moustaches brought out the best in players, he explained, and also protected them from the sun.

Herbert Sutcliffe *(November 24)*

Here's R. C. Robertson-Glasgow: 'Herbert Sutcliffe is the serenest batsman I have known. Whatever may have passed under that calm brow – anger, joy, disagreement, surprise, relief, triumph – no outward sign was betrayed on the field of play. He was understood, over two thousand years in advance, by the Greek philosophers. They called this character megalo-psychic. It is the sort of man who would rather miss a train than run for it, and so be seen in disorder and heard breathing heavily.' In the fifty-four Tests he played, Sutcliffe's average never once fell below 60.

Fred Titmus *(November 24)*

The Middlesex and England off-spinner lost four toes in a speed-boat accident in Barbados in 1968. For many bowlers that would have been the end of a long and distinguished career, but Fred was back bowling for Middlesex the following summer, with a slightly remodelled approach to the wicket but no diminution in talent. The speedboat, incidentally, was driven by Colin Cowdrey's wife Penny.

Once, Titmus was batting with Ken Barrington in a Test match, and the two met up for a mid-wicket conference. 'Let's cut out some of the quick singles,' said Ken. 'OK,' said Fred, 'we'll cut out yours, Ken.'

Ian Botham *(November 24)*

Here's Harry Pearson in *Wisden*: 'Like a number of other top sportsmen ... Botham is a man filled with restless energy and an almost pathological fear of loneliness. Aware of this characteristic, Viv Richards instructed his international team-mates never to engage with Botham the batsman. It was the silence as much as the pace that contributed to his poor record against the West Indies.'

Botham retired in 1993, his body wrecked by fast bowling, long charity walks and, very possibly, buckets of red wine. His last game was for Durham against the Australian touring team. Before his final delivery, he paused at the top of his run, unzipped his flies and ran in with the 'old man dangling free'.

Simon Barnes has described him as 'then as now ... a man who had escaped the tyranny of abstract thought'.

E. M. Grace *(November 28)*

Elder brother of W. G., Edward Mills Grace was every bit as wilful and eccentric as his legendary sibling. W. S. Medlicott of Hawick wrote this in a letter to the *Daily Telegraph* in June 1961:

I was at a preparatory school at Clifton about 1890. The Australians came to play against Gloucestershire on the county ground at Bristol and we were taken to see the match.

During the game, 'E. M.' was batting to Jones, the fast bowler, who was bumping them a great deal, and 'E. M.' did not like it; after each ball of the five in one over he flung his bat down the pitch and wrung his hands as if he had been rapped on the fingers.

After the last ball a man in the crowd shouted out some remark (I forget what it was) which pricked 'E. M.'; he left the wicket and ran off to get at the man, who when he saw him bowed out of the ground through the entrance gate, 'E. M.' after him.

'E. M.' was away about ten minutes and it was said that he chased the man a long way down into the town. He then returned and continued to bat. We boys were much annoyed at losing ten minutes' cricket.

A week later, a letter was printed from S. T. Freeman of Worcester:

I saw [E. M.] many times captain the Thornbury side against Gloucester City on the 'Spa' ground.

Arthur Winterbottom, the Gloucester skipper, usually bet him £1 that he would not take five wickets (solely with the object of keeping him on).

On one occasion with the Gloucester score 210 for three, a

member of his side ventured a suggestion of a change at his end (he had bowled since the opening).

His reply was: 'A very good idea. I'll try the other end!'

He usually stored a large whisky and soda between the square leg umpire's legs and refreshed himself regularly between overs.

Keith Miller *(November 28)*

'To young eyes, quickest to perceive the things that make cricket, Miller is an Olympian god among mortals. He brings boys' dreams to life. He is the cricketer they would all like to be, the one who can hit more gloriously and bowl faster than anybody on earth' (Ray Robinson).

With what they used to call film-star good looks and a devil-may-care nonchalance, Keith Miller was the only Australian Test player 'rumoured to have been friendly' with Princess Margaret. John Arlott once wrote that he was 'busy living life in case he ran out of it'. Richie Benaud thought him the best captain never to have captained his country. Once, when he was captaining New South Wales, someone pointed out that there were twelve men on the field. 'It seems we have too many men out here,' Miller said. 'Will one of you blokes piss off?' In fifty-five Tests between 1946 and 1956, he took 170 wickets at 22.97 and scored 2958 runs at 36.97. David Frith says these figures 'barely do him justice'. He played cricket hard, but for fun. He once took the field straight from a party, wearing black patent leather dancing shoes. In Donald Bradman's testimonial game, the great man took guard, expecting one off the mark. Miller bowled a bouncer and nearly took his head off. Presenting the prizes at a greyhound derby in England, he turned up in full morning dress, picked up the victorious animal and kissed it on the nose. Michael Parkinson, in his *Telegraph* obituary, described him as 'a romantic warrior ... a proper hero and a singular man'. His portrait hangs in the Lord's pavilion: he is one of only three Australians (with Bradman and Victor Trumper) to be so honoured.

Quiz 4

1. Geoffrey Boycott famously scored his hundredth first-class century in 1977, in a Test match against Australia at his home ground, Headingley. But he was the second person to make a hundred hundreds that year. Who had done it earlier that season in a county match?

2. There were two centenary Test matches between England and Australia, one in Melbourne in 1977 and the other at Lord's in 1980. Who was the only Englishman who played in both?

3. Two England cricketers have played in five Ashes-winning series. One was Ian Botham. Who is the other?

4. Which West Indian cricketer, who started as a wicketkeeper and later bowled serviceable medium pace, is the only man to have taken ten or more wickets in Tests, and also make ten or more stumpings in Tests? He died in 2006, aged eighty.

5. In the 2010–11 Ashes series, who became the first man ever to take a hat-trick in a Test on his birthday?

6. Which England batsman was Shane Warne's 150th, 250th and 400th victim in Test matches?

7. Who is the only Australian batsman to score more first-class runs than Sir Donald Bradman? He accumulated 28,382 of them at an average of 50.23 before retiring in 2009.

8. Which minor county, when it applied for first-class cricket status in 1948, did not even receive the courtesy of a reply from Lord's?

9. In 1971, QPR gave trials to two fourteen-year-old goalkeepers. One was Phil Parkes, who went on to play for them with distinction for many years. The other was rejected as 'too short and too fat', and became a cricketer instead. What was his name?

10. In 1940 a seven-year-old batsman scored ninety-three in a prep school match. His headmaster wrote to Jack Hobbs, who in return sent the young shaver a new bat, and wrote in a letter, 'I hear you are very keen on the game so I feel sure you will score many centuries in the years to come.' He did: 107 of them at first-class level. Who?

If teams are tied at this stage, you'll need a numerical tie-break. Each team guesses the answer and the nearest one wins. The question is this:

How many Test cricketers, of all nations, were killed fighting in the Second World War?

Answers next month.

The Only Man

The only bowlers ...
to consistently get the better of Sir Viv Richards were Dennis Lillee (no surprises there) and the little Indian leg-spinner with the withered arm, Bhagwat Chandrasekhar. He only got him out four times in Tests, but as *All Out Cricket* put it, 'his variations reduced Richards to mere competence'. Sir Viv actually admitted that Chandrasekhar had given him the most problems in his Test career.

The only member of the British Royal Family ...

to have played first-class cricket was Prince Christian Victor, a grandson of Queen Victoria, who played once for I Zingari against the Gentlemen of England in August 1887. (This match was elevated to first-class status by sheer poshness.) He scored 35 and 0, and was bowled in the second innings by A. E. Stoddart.

There have always been rumblings of interest in cricket in the Royal Family. In *Wisden* 1969, there's a photo of Prince Charles, the Prince of Wales playing a sweep shot, rather well as it happens. His younger brother Prince Andrew was captain of Gordonstoun's first XI in 1979. Before you start wondering whether deference acquired him that post beyond the claims of better-qualified players, he averaged 23.55 with the bat and a mere 4.54 with the ball, having taken eleven wickets for just fifty runs. *Wisden* 1980 noted that 'Gordonstoun had an average team and report a difficulty in obtaining good school fixtures'. The presence of a royal teenager at the coin-toss might help with that.

The greatest of all royal cricketing achievements, though, must be that of King George VI, who is surely unique in regal history by taking a hat-trick when all three of his victims were present or future kings. This miracle took place on the private ground at Windsor Castle. First up was Edward VII, his grandfather: bowled. Second was his father, George V: bowled. Third was his brother David, later Edward VIII: bowled. Can King Juan Carlos of Spain say that he has done this? King Bhumibol the Great of Thailand? In *Wisden* 2001, Jonathan Rice pointed out that George VI was only fifteen when Edward VII died, which suggests that this was a young boy bowling in the back garden to people who had no aptitude for the game. Only in *Wisden* can you say such things. Here we shall be much more careful.

The only winner of the Academy Award for Best Director ...

to play at Lord's (as far as we know) is Sam Mendes, who won an Oscar in 1999 for *American Beauty*. Mendes was an exceptional schoolboy cricketer in the early 1980s, who, in two seasons at Magdalen College School, scored 1153 runs at an average of 46 and took eighty-three wickets at under 16. In 1997 he reached the final of the Village Cricket Cup with his Oxfordshire team, Shipton-under-Wychwood. He had played a match-winning innings in the semi-final but only managed 8 at Lord's. The *Independent* reported it thus: 'Mendes, whose latest production *Othello* is set for an ambitious world tour, fell not to excessive pride and jealousy, but Peter Urwin, a senior software engineer.' Number 24 of Mendes's 25 Rules for Directors is 'Always have an alternative career planned out. Mine is a cricket commentator.'

The only man ...

who played cricket for the MCC and was also suspected of being Jack the Ripper was Montague John Druitt, a fast bowler who played for Winchester College, the Butterflies and Blackheath, among other teams. In December 1888 he was found drowned in the Thames with stones in his pocket, aged just thirty-one. The last of the Ripper murders had been carried out only a month before. In 1894, Sir Melville Macnaghten, Assistant Chief Constable at Scotland Yard, named Druitt as a suspect in a private memorandum. But there wasn't a lot of evidence. Specifically, on September 1, the day after Mary Ann Nichols's murder, Druitt was playing cricket in Dorset. Also, Sir Melville appears to have been an idiot. He described Druitt as a forty-one-year-old doctor when he was a thirty-one-year-old barrister, and said he was 'sexually insane', without justifying those words in any way. And Druitt was a cricketer, for God's sake. No self-respecting cricketer has ever been a blood-hungry, gore-crazed serial killer, other than one or two Australian captains one could name. The number of Jack the Ripper suspects continues to grow: there are now more than a hundred different theories about his identity.

The only man ...

not to concede a single run in a List A one-day match was Brian Langford, Somerset off-spinner of the 1950s and 1960s and their captain between 1969 and 1971. In 1969 he was playing against Essex at Yeovil in the forty-over John Player League, and he recorded the following extraordinary analysis: eight overs, eight maidens, no wicket for no runs. Were they trying to hit him and failing? My guess is that very few reverse sweeps, switch hits or Dilscoops were played that day. Langford died in 2013 aged seventy-seven, but he could have lived another hundred years and not seen such a thing happen again. Live dragons landing on the strip at Old Trafford seem statistically likelier, or men being allowed into the Lord's pavilion without a tie.

The only living Test cricketer ...

to have seen active military service is Tony Dell, who played two Tests for Australia as a seam bowler in the early 1970s, having fought in Vietnam between May 1967 and May 1968. After his military service Dell suffered from Post Traumatic Stress Disorder (PTSD), which wasn't diagnosed until 2008. But how did he know it was that? Playing two Tests, three years apart, taking six wickets at 26.66 and never being picked again would mess with any man's fragile psyche.

The only man (until recently) ...

to score exactly the same number of runs as his age in a Test match *on his birthday* was Geoff Pullar, who hit 26 for England against Australia at Old Trafford in 1961 on the twenty-sixth anniversary of his first breath.

Until 2018, when Sam Curran scored 20 for England against Pakistan at Headingley on his twentieth birthday.

These facts are both tragic in their fatuity and utterly life-enhancing at the same time.

Curran was only the seventh teenager to play in a Test for England, following Jack Crawford (1905–06), Ian Peebles (1927–28), Denis Compton (1937), Brian Close (1949), Ben Hollioake (1997) and Haseeb Hameed (2016–17).

The only man ...

to score two hundreds in any first-class match at Headingley is the young West Indian batsman Shai Hope, who did so in a Test match in 2017, hitting 147 out of 427 in the first innings and an unbeaten 118 out of 322 for five in the second. (They won, damn them.)

It's worth remembering, though, that not too long ago Headingley was only one of more than a dozen grounds Yorkshire used each year. In a twenty-five-year career, Geoffrey Boycott played there only fifty-nine times.

The only man ...

to be dismissed in a Test match by two men who have the same initials as he has is Matt Renshaw, who was caught by Mushfiqur Rahim off the bowling of Mustafizur Rahman in September 2017, playing for Australia against Bangladesh.

Unless you count Rusi Surti, who was caught by Rex Sellers off the bowling of Robert (Bobby) Simpson for India against Australia in 1964–65. And I can see from the expression on your face that you do.

The only two batsmen ...

ever dismissed by the bowling of Alan Knott in first-class matches were Majid Khan and Alan Butcher. As a wicketkeeper, Knott caught or stumped a batsman on a mere 1344 occasions. As a bowler he only ever bowled 104 balls in eight matches. Maybe he should have bowled more. Majid Khan was c Pocock b Knott for Pakistan Under-25s against MCC Under-25s in Lahore in 1967, while Butcher was st Woolmer b Knott for Surrey against Kent at the Oval in 1980.

Before his back injuries took hold, Michael Atherton bowled leg-spinners of a sort and, in Tests, dismissed two batsmen with them. Dilip Vengsarkar was caught and bowled at the Oval in 1991, and Wasim Akram was lbw at Headingley in 1996.

The only cat ...

to be given an obituary in *Wisden* was Peter, the Lord's feline, who was thus honoured in the 1965 edition:

Cat, Peter, whose ninth life ended on November 5, 1964, was a well-known cricket-watcher at Lord's, where he spent twelve of his fourteen years. He preferred a close-up view of the proceedings, and his sleek brown form could often be seen prowling on the field of play when crowds were biggest. He frequently appeared on the television screen. Mr S. C. Griffith, Secretary of MCC, said of him: 'He was a cat of great character and loved publicity.'

The only wicketkeeper ...

ever to stump Sachin Tendulkar in a Test match was England's James Foster, arguably the most talented gloveman of his generation. Inevitably he played just seven Tests and eleven ODIs for England, all in 2002.

The only member of the 1966 World Cup-winning football team ...

to play first-class cricket was Geoff Hurst, who played one match for Essex against Lancashire at Liverpool in 1962. He made 0 and

0 not out, but took two catches in Essex's twenty-eight-run victory. Bobby Moore wasn't a bad cricketer, either. The first time Hurst and Moore played on the same side in any sport was for the Essex schools cricket team.

The only man ...

who ever replaced Donald Bradman in the Australian Test team after he had been dropped was Otto Nothling, a right-arm fast-medium bowler of German extraction. Bradman had made his debut in the first Test of the Ashes series of 1928–29, batted at number seven and scored 18 and 1. But Australia lost the match by 675 runs. For the second Test, at the SCG, the selectors decided they needed another bowler. Otto came in, opened the bowling and, in forty-six overs, took no wicket for 72. Although he scored 44 in the second innings before being run out, he too was dropped. Bradman returned at the MCG, scored 79 and 112, and twenty years of mayhem ensued.

Otto Nothling thus became a footnote in cricketing history, although he swore till his dying day that he should have been retained for that third Test. (He was a wet-wicket specialist, and the MCG was soaking.) Nonetheless, he was a fine all-round athlete. While at Sydney University, he played nineteen matches for the Australian rugby union team. As an athlete, he could do pretty much what he wanted: he could run the hundred yards in even time, and, according to Peter Roebuck, jump like a kangaroo. At the University Games one year, he was asked, out of the blue, to throw the javelin. He had never seen one thrown before, and on hearing that practice throws were not allowed asked if he could go last so he could observe the others. With his first three throws he broke the New South Wales, Australian and Australasian records. He never threw the javelin again because it was too dull. Later in life he played golf off scratch, became a prominent Queensland dermatologist and drove around in a Second World

War jeep, wearing a fedora. Eventually he became President of the Queensland Cricket Association, where he played billiards with touring players until dawn. He died in 1965 of a heart attack while mowing the lawn.

Canine 2nd XI

1	S. Wolf	(L. N. Constantine's XI)
2	G. Setter	(Stokeinteignhead)
3	S. Springer	(Barbados, Barbados Tridents, West Indies Under-19s)
4	A. E. Huskie	(Gordon Highlanders)
5	S. Bernard	(Stowmarket)
6	W. Pugsley	(Honourable Artillery Company)
7	G. Pointer	(I Zingari Australia)
8	Heel	(Sefton Third XI)
9	Hoose	(Royal Artillery Officers)
10	A. Good	(Sevenoaks Vine Fourth XI)
11	Boy	(Transvaal Country Districts)
12th men	S. Sitz	(Cosmos)
	Down	(Surrey Optimists)
	H. S. Walkey	(Royal Naval College Dartmouth)

The Village Year

The 2018 season was a season like any other, except slightly worse. We played eighteen games, but every village team knows that there's more to the game than merely turning up. Of those eighteen we won one, and lost a terrifying ten, several of them by quite a few. We're not quite Northamptonshire of the late 1930s, but we're not far off.

Still, we do have a couple of new players. Jonathan, who writes about sport for a living, said he was a bowler who batted a little. Well, he did bat a little. Not quite as much as we would have liked him to, but there's always next year. There may not be a next year for his bowling. He bowled 29.5 overs, with one maiden, and took two wickets for 231.

Adam is another writer, with an enormous beard and a very small baby. Can you hide the baby in the beard, we asked. He couldn't, quite: one leg kept sticking out. Adam is a wicketkeeper-batsman, who scores runs in droves for other teams: indeed, his only fifty of the season came when playing against us. He did score 49 for us, but that was in early May. After that he fell away a touch. He ended with six ducks, including three first-ballers. The last one was a vicious inswinging yorker by a bowler who may have bowled it by mistake. At our level, good balls are often accidents, but that doesn't make getting out to them any easier.

I can sympathise. One year, long ago, I opened the batting for a spell, and scored one run in seven innings. That's an average of 0.142857143. That run came in an innings of an hour, out of 40 for 4. I gave up opening after that.

What fascinated me about Jonathan and Adam's trials is that we, as a team, have an extraordinary power to nullify talent and bring people down to our own level. Steve Smith, Virat Kohli, Kane Williamson and Joe Root could come and play for us and they'd all be out for 0. Three of them would be run out by Simon and the fourth would smash it through cover to be caught one-handed on the dive by someone who had dropped everything for ten years. It's what we cricketers call the Grim Inevitability of Fate, as we walk off the pitch, staring at the bat furiously, as though it's the bat's fault.

December

December Birthdays

1: A. C. MacLaren (1871), Mike Denness (1940), Sarfraz Nawaz (1948), Arjuna Ranatunga (1963)

3: Les Ames (1905), Trevor Bailey (1923), Mark Boucher (1976), Mithali Raj (1982)

6: Cyril Washbrook (1914), Peter Willey (1949), Andrew Flintoff (1977)

7: Geoff Lawson (1957), Anya Shrubsole (1991)

10: Chris Martin (1974)

11: Sylvester Clarke (1954), Murray Goodwin (1972), Tim Southee (1988)

12: Wilf Slack (1954), Yuvraj Singh (1981)

14: Charlie Griffith (1938)

15: Carl Hooper (1966)

16: Sir Jack Hobbs (1882), Enid Bakewell (1940), Joel Garner (1952), Craig White (1969), Danish Kaneria (1980)

17: Kerry Packer (1937), Charlotte Edwards (1979)

18: Peter Moores (1962), Usman Khawaja (1986)

19: Ricky Ponting (1974)

20: Bill O'Reilly (1905), Simon Hughes (1959), Mohammad Asif (1982)

21: Hanif Mohammad (1934), Doug Walters (1945), Brian Davison (1946)

22: Dilip Doshi (1947), Chris Old (1948)

24: Colin Cowdrey (1932)

25: Clarrie Grimmett (1891), Marcus Trescothick (1975), Simon Jones (1978), Alastair Cook (1984)

26: Rohan Kanhai (1935), Barry Wood (1942)

27: David Shepherd (1940)

28: Donald Carr (1926), Intikhab Alam (1941)

29: Syed Kirmani (1949), David Boon (1960), Saqlain Mushtaq (1976)

30: Joe Root (1990)

31: Peter May (1929), Matthew Hoggard (1976), Ebony-Jewel Rainford-Brent (1983)

Trevor Bailey *(December 3)*

Essex and England all-rounder of the 1950s and, later, very slightly pompous summariser on *Test Match Special*, for which of course we loved him deeply. What's less well known about Bailey was his dark footballing past. He played as a half-back for Walthamstow Avenue, the amateur champions of their day, and in 1952–53 his club reached the third round of the FA Cup, in which they were drawn against Manchester United, away. Astoundingly, Walthamstow held them to a 1–1 draw, which meant a replay. Walthamstow's Green Pond Road stadium had a capacity of just 12,500, so the match was relocated to Highbury, where the plucky part-timers eventually succumbed 5–2.

Cyril Washbrook *(December 6)*

Took over from easy-going Nigel Howard as Lancashire captain in 1954 and instituted a Stalinist reign of terror. Chief among his victims was the wicketkeeper Frank Parr, whose immersion in jazz music he took vigorous exception to. Parr also made the disastrous error of turning up to a House of Commons reception in a blue shirt. In his next game Parr was a little untidy behind the stumps, and that was the excuse Washbrook had been looking for. 'Frank, you're going home,' he said. Parr was playing for the Seconds, and better than ever, leading to discussions about a move to Worcestershire. But Washbrook put paid to that with a letter to New Road, calling him a 'grave social risk'. Parr was devastated. 'It's probably when I took up serious drinking,' he said.

Washbrook scored 2569 runs in thirty-seven Tests at 42.81, but what is that compared to the destruction of a team-mate's career? Little Harry Pilling called him 'an arrogant professional who wished he was an amateur'.

Parr moved to London and joined the Mick Mulligan Band, for whom he played trombone.

Peter Willey *(December 6)*

According to legend, England were playing the West Indies, and Michael Holding was bowling, when in the *Test Match Special* box, Brian Johnston said, 'The bowler's Holding, the batsman's Willey.' Tireless researchers have listened to thousands of hours of tapes of the show without ever managing to verify this, although Henry Blofeld says it happened at the Oval in 1976, and he should know, as he was there. To those of us of a more sceptical turn of mind, belief in this happening seems to have become a matter of faith. It can't be proved, it can't be disproved, it can only be believed or disbelieved. Cathedrals have been built on less.*

Andrew Flintoff *(December 6)*

On his first-class debut for Lancashire against Hampshire in August 1995, Andrew Flintoff scored 7 and 0 and dropped five catches. After the 2005 Ashes, Ricky Ponting had this to say about him: 'We knew he was a very good player, but the way he has performed has been exceptional. Any side in the world would want him.'

Some years later, Simon Barnes and Michael Atherton agreed to disagree about Flintoff in the pages of *The Times*. Barnes said Flintoff was a great cricketer, because he was great for a single summer that changed English cricket. Atherton said that wasn't good enough. I find myself persuaded of both arguments, as I'm sure does Flintoff. In his more bullish moments he probably sides with Barnes. But at four o'clock in the morning, as he lies sleepless in bed, listening to cats fight and owls tu-whit-tu-whoo, I bet he sees the unanswerable correctness of Atherton's position.

---

* In his 2003 biography of his father, *Johnners: The Life of Brian*, Barry Johnston admits, 'I think Brian made it up.'

Flintoff retired from Tests at just thirty-one, his huge body racked by injury. Three years later, he took up a brief second career as a professional boxer. His first and so far only fight was a points victory against Richard Dawson (an American, not the former Yorkshire off-spinner). The bout, according to the *Guardian*, looked 'more like two burly farmhands trying to fend off a swarm of invisible bees than a boxing match'.

Flintoff is not entirely unconvinced that the earth might be flat.

Sylvester Clarke *(December 11)*

The only fast bowler Viv Richards ever admitted to feeling 'uncomfortable' facing. Graham Gooch had his helmet split down the middle by a Clarke bouncer. Zaheer Abbas was hit so hard that his helmet had a dent as deep as half the ball. David Gower had the padding and thumbguard torn from his glove, along with most of his thumbnail. They ended up 'near third slip'. When Steve Waugh played for Somerset in 1986, he felt the will of his team-mates 'disintegrating' a full week before they were due to face him. When Waugh himself came in to bat against Clarke, he faced 'the most awkward and nastiest spell' he could ever remember. It was 'something you can't prepare for. It's an assault both physically and mentally and the moment you weaken and think about what might happen, you're either out or injured ... '*

Simon Hughes was hit on the helmet by the third ball he ever faced from Clarke. As he later wrote, 'Of all [fast] bowlers, Malcolm Marshall might have been the most gifted, Richard Hadlee the most clinical, and Curtly Ambrose the most economical. But Sylvester Clarke was certainly the most frightening.'

---

* Thanks to Jon Hotten's *The Meaning of Cricket* for this magnificent list.

Sir Jack Hobbs *(December 16)*

As J. L. Carr wrote, 'this shrewd, lean Surrey player, a man of great natural dignity and forceful elegance of stroke, was the bridge between the Classic and Modern periods. He made 61,237 runs (average 50.65) and his knighthood was joyfully acclaimed by the nation.' Jack Fingleton adds, 'It is well to note Hobbs's claim that he never had an hour's coaching in his life. He was a self-made cricketer – observing, thinking and executing for himself.' His first-class record will never be beaten, or even threatened, and one Test record of his that remains is his twelve centuries against Australia in forty-one Tests. David Gower and Walter Hammond each hit nine and Herbert Sutcliffe scored eight; no other Englishman has come close.

As 'Evoe' wrote in *Punch* in 1925, in his poem 'Can Nothing Be Done?':

> Can nothing be done for J. B. Hobbs
> To make him sometimes get out for blobs?
> Or is he doomed for some dreadful crime
> To make centuries till the end of time?*

Kerry Packer *(December 17)*

Australian media mogul with a face like a bloater, who instituted World Series Cricket in the late 1970s after the Australian Cricket Board refused to give him exclusive TV rights to the international game. At the time we all hated him, for his wealth, arrogance and astonishing ugliness, but he was proved right

---

* 'Evoe' was the pen-name of E. V. Knox, who wrote light verse (usually to a deadline) for *Punch* for many years, and edited the magazine between 1932 and 1949. His daughter was the distinguished novelist Penelope Fitzgerald.

in the end. 'Cricket is the easiest sport in the world to take over,' he said. 'Nobody bothered to pay the players what they were worth.'*

Mike Selvey tells a story of Packer going one day to play golf at a course he happened to own. To his consternation, the course was full of other people.

'What's going on?' he demanded.

'It's a corporate day,' the manager explained. 'We make a lot of money from corporate days.'

'How much money?'

'A quarter of a million bucks a year.'

Packer took out his cheque book and wrote one for precisely that amount.

'Now, you go and tell them to piss off so I can get a game.'

Hanif Mohammad *(December 19)*

Fun-size Pakistani opener of the 1950s, younger brother of Wazir and Raees and older brother of Mushtaq and Sadiq. In 1957–58, against the West Indies in Bridgetown, Hanif played one of the greatest of all defensive innings. His 337 was spread over 970 minutes of playing time. Ramachandra Guha tells a wonderful story about this in *The Picador Book of Cricket*:

'Watching Hanif bat from a palm tree high above square leg were a group of Bajan boys. As the afternoon sun rose higher, one of them could no longer stand it. Delirious from the heat, from Hanif's relentless *thook thook* and doubtless from a steady intake of palm wine, the boy fell off the tree and landed on his head some forty feet below. He was taken to hospital, recovering

---

* When Donald Bradman retired in 1948, the home Test fee in Australia was seven times the average weekly wage. A quarter of a century later it was twice the average weekly wage.

consciousness twenty-four hours later. Inevitably his first words were "Is Hanif still batting?" The answer, alas, was in the affirmative.'

Bill O'Reilly *(December 20)*

Described by *All Out Cricket* as 'the greatest Australian spinner never to have gone out with Liz Hurley', O'Reilly is now chiefly remembered for hating Donald Bradman nearly as much as Jack Fingleton did. When Bradman was out for 0 in his final Test innings, Fingleton and O'Reilly were both in the press box, laughing like drains.

O'Reilly was one of four Catholics of Irish descent summoned to a meeting by the Australian Board of Control in the late 1930s to discuss an apparent schism in the national team. By the end of the war, all four had been dropped. Years later, Bradman wrote, 'With these fellows out of the way, the loyalty of my 1948 side was a big joy and made a big contribution to the outstanding success of that tour.' Gideon Haigh and David Frith described O'Reilly as 'a man of embedded prejudices'. But throughout his life, O'Reilly tended to keep his strongest feelings about Bradman to himself. He even suppressed them from his autobiography. 'You don't piss on statues,' he explained.

Doug Walters *(December 21)*

Attacking middle-order Australian batsman of the 1970s who averaged 48.26 in seventy-four Tests despite rarely making much of an impression in England, where the moving ball usually got him. E. W. Swanton wrote, 'Doug has made eleven hundreds for Australia [he eventually made fifteen], some of extreme brilliance, and if he ever played a dull innings I never saw it.' In 1969–70, Australia toured India and played a five-Test series. During the fourth Test at Calcutta, a ten-thousand-strong crowd picketed the Australian hotel and broke every window. They were objecting to Walters, who they thought had fought in the Vietnam War and killed women and children there. Except that he hadn't. They had mistaken him for someone else.

Walters was known to like a drop and his autobiography, published in 1988, was entitled *One for the Road*. There's a bar named after him in the Victor Trumper Stand at the SCG. Before he gave up smoking in 2010, he is believed to have smoked 785,300 cigarettes. In the words of the Australian *Telegraph*, 'if smoking was a sport, Doug Walters would have been a dual international'.

Chris Old *(December 22)*

One of the very few former England fast bowlers to own and run a fish and chip shop in Cornwall, and certainly the only one whose shop was visited by my cricket team on a Cornish tour. (We made a substantial detour. It seemed only appropriate.)

Despite being a fine natural athlete, and possessing a good sideways-on action, Old was constantly hampered by injury and would have played more than his forty-six Tests if he hadn't been. The first bowling machine installed at Lord's was nicknamed Chris Old because it broke down so often.

Colin Cowdrey *(December 24)*

Alan Ross wrote: 'I cannot think of a great player harder to coax into awareness of his reserves, not one who, in the mood, made the art of batsmanship seem more artless, more a mere extension of his own geniality. At his best he was a dolphin among minnows, gambolling between the green and the blue as if cares were not invented, almost patronising. At his less good he seemed imprisoned by some interior gaoler, feet chained, arms pinioned, shuffling away a long sentence.'

Here's a slightly less poetic view from Michael Henderson, writing in the *Telegraph*: 'Cowdrey used the reputation he had carefully established for fair play to serve him when it suited his purpose ... He wasn't a cheat, but within cricket he was not universally admired. When Chris Cowdrey, his son, was batting for Kent at Leicester, he received an introductory bouncer from Ken Higgs, the former England seamer, who told him, "That's for you." The next ball also went past the young man's nose. "And that," said the glowering Higgs, "is for your dad." Bowlers have long memories.'

Simon Jones *(December 25)*

England fast bowler of brief renown and many injuries, who reckoned that he was at his fastest before the age of twenty. In 2005 readers of *New Woman* magazine voted Simon Jones the ninth-sexiest man in the world. Andrew Flintoff came fifty-fourth.

Alastair Cook *(December 25)*

One of only five cricketers, and the only Englishman, to score a century in both his first Test and his last. Just before he retired from Tests in 2018, after 161 matches, thirty-three centuries and 12,472 runs, Barney Ronay wrote this in the *Guardian*: 'There are very few things as reassuringly English as this, Cook on a nibbly, breezy day that could go either way, the long-form drama of leave and edge and nurdle, as English as muggy weather and shiny bedspreads and weekend rail replacement services.' I can't tell you how much I admire the use of the phrase 'weekend rail replacement services' in that sentence.

Cook played 291 innings in Test matches, second only to Sachin Tendulkar (329). He faced 20,038 dot balls, and batted for

621 hours and forty-eight minutes, which is longer than it takes for a layer of human skin to regenerate. So Cook literally batted out of his skin. Graham Gooch, his cricketing mentor for many years, scored 57.9 per cent of his Test runs after the age at which Cook retired.

David Shepherd *(December 27)*

Well-padded Gloucestershire batsman who became a much-loved and even more roly-poly Test umpire. According to Derek Pringle, 'he played in an age when boundary hitting was popular simply because running between the wickets wasn't'.

David Boon *(December 29)*

Stocky, pugnacious, generously moustached Australian opening batsman of the 1980s and 1990s whose many splendid innings have been somewhat overshadowed by the fifty-two tinnies he is said to have consumed flying from Australia to England in 1989. Everyone knows Bradman's 99.94 Test average, Willis's 8 for 43 at Headingley, and Boon's fifty-two cans of lager on a single flight, when presumably there was a limited number of lavatories. Why does this story stick in the group memory so? According to Jonathan Liew in *The Nightwatchman*, 'Perhaps because it ticks so many of the different boxes of male prestige: measurement, competitiveness, alcohol consumption and meaningless statistics.' It's just a hunch, but I'm not sure he entirely approves.

Quiz 4 Answers

1. John Edrich.
2. Chris Old.

3. Ian Bell.
4. Sir Clyde Walcott.
5. Peter Siddle.
6. Alec Stewart.
7. Justin Langer.
8. Devon.
9. Mike Gatting.
10. Colin Cowdrey.

And the tie-break. The number of Test cricketers, of all nations, who were killed fighting in the Second World War was nine.

Favourite Tests

Adelaide, December 1, 2, 3, 4, 5 2006

AUSTRALIA vs ENGLAND: Second Test

England

A J Strauss	c Martyn b Clark	14	—	c Hussey b Warne	34
A N Cook	c Gilchrist b Clark	27	—	c Gilchrist b Clark	9
I R Bell	c & b Lee	60	—	run out	26
P D Collingwood	c Gilchrist b Clark	206	—	not out	22
K P Pietersen	run out	158	—	b Warne	2
*A Flintoff	not out	38	—	c Gilchrist b Lee	2
†G O Jones	c Martyn b Warne	1	—	c Hayden b Lee	10
A F Giles	not out	27	—	c Hayden b Warne	0
M J Hoggard			—	b Warne	4
S J Harmison			—	lbw b McGrath	8
J M Anderson			—	lbw b McGrath	1
	lb 10, w 2, nb 8	20		b 3, lb 5, w 1, nb 2	11
	(6 wkts dec)	551			129

1–32 (1), 2–45 (2), 3–158 (3), 4–468 (4), 5–489 (5), 6–491 (7)

1–31 (2), 2–69 (1), 3–70 (3), 4–73 (5), 5–77 (6), 6–94 (7), 7–97 (8), 8–105 (9), 9–119 (10), 10–129 (11)

Lee	34–1–139–1		Lee	18–3–35–2
McGrath	30–5–107–0		McGrath	10–6–15–2
Clark	34–6–75–3		Warne	32–12–49–4
Warne	53–9–167–1		Clark	13–4–22–1
Clarke	17–2–53–0			

Australia

J L Langer	c Pietersen b Flintoff	4	—	c Bell b Hoggard	7
M L Hayden	c Jones b Hoggard	12	—	c Collingwood b Flintoff	18
*R T Ponting	c Jones b Hoggard	142	—	c Strauss b Giles	49
D R Martyn	c Bell b Hoggard	11	—	(5) c Strauss b Flintoff	5
M E K Hussey	b Hoggard	91	—	(4) not out	61
M J Clarke	c Giles b Hoggard	124	—	not out	21
† A C Gilchrist	c Bell b Giles	64	—		
S K Warne	lbw b Hoggard	43	—		
B Lee	not out	7	—		
S R Clark	b Hoggard	0	—		
G D McGrath	c Jones b Anderson	1	—		
	b 4, lb 2, w 1, nb 7	14		b 2, lb 2, w 1, nb 2	7
		513		(4 wkts)	168

1–8 (1), 2–35 (2), 3–65 (4), 4–257 (3), 5–286 (5), 6–384 (7), 7–502 (8), 8–505 (6), 9–507 (10), 10–513 (11)

1–14 (1), 2–33 (2), 3–116 (3), 4–121 (5)

Hoggard	42–6–109–7		Hoggard	4–0–29–1
Flintoff	26–5–82–1		Flintoff	9–0–44–2
Harmison	25–5–96–0		Giles	10–0–46–1
Anderson	21.3–3–85–1		Harmison	4–0–15–0
Giles	42–7–103–1		Anderson	3.5–0–23–0
Pietersen	9–0–32–0		Pietersen	2–0–7–0

Umpires: S A Bucknor (WI) and R E Koertzen (SA)
Third Umpire: S J Davis (A)
Referee: J J Crowe (NZ)

If you were reading these pages and knew nothing else about cricket, you might come to assume that in Test matches England have a habit of coming from behind to squeeze narrow victories out of nothing, and that Australia lose pretty much constantly. Ah well, we can dream. In truth, to have been an England fan this past quarter-century has been to experience a life of almost constant suffering. At least when we go to the matches in England we can drink to forget. But when Australia are at home, they play while we sleep. This gives you a choice. You can either stay up and listen or watch until you drift off, or you can get up early and listen to or watch the last couple of hours' play. Either way, you are constantly prepared for the worst. Sometimes, as in early December 2006, it's even worse than that.

Adelaide was a road. England players thought it was the slowest batting pitch they had seen all year, and for bowlers it meant hours and hours of thankless toil. After Andrew Flintoff had won the toss, England batted and Paul Collingwood and Kevin Pietersen put on 310 for the fourth wicket. It wasn't the prettiest batting we had ever seen – Shane Warne bowling negatively round the wicket and batsmen kicking the ball away saw to that – but it was mighty effective. 'England batted like turtles with chronic fatigue syndrome,' wrote Robert Craddock in the Sydney *Daily Telegraph*. When they're insulting you, you must be doing something right. England's final score of 551 for 6 declared seemed impregnable. With hindsight one wonders: why on earth did they declare?

In return, Australia were briefly in trouble at 65 for 3. Ricky Ponting was looking a little scratchy and, on 35, mishooked Matthew Hoggard to Ashley Giles, who misjudged it and shelled it. Ponting made 142 and Australia ended on 513. At the end of the fourth day England were 59 for 1, and a tedious draw beckoned. The pitch was beginning to turn for Warne, but only slowly. Glenn McGrath seemed neutered. Nothing was doing.

I think I actually had a good night's sleep. There seemed no point in staying up to listen, and even less point rising early the next morning. There is no sleep sounder than that of the wrongly complacent.

Meanwhile, in Adelaide, England had collapsed to Warne and

their own hard-wired character flaws. Confident and disciplined in their first innings, their batting now was at best tentative, at worst agonisingly poor: in four hours they hit just three boundaries. Only Collingwood stood firm, but in the intervening couple of days he had forgotten how to score runs. All out at 3.42 on the final day, they left Australia needing 167 to win. With Ponting, Hussey and Clarke all now in top form, it was a foregone conclusion.

England didn't just lose a Test match; they lost heart; they lost the plot. From 1–0 down, and contemplating the delicious possibility of 1–1 with three to play, they swiftly went 5–0 down, only the second whitewash in Ashes history. Flintoff's captaincy proved so abject that many people managed to forget that he had ever actually been captain: we airbrushed it from our conscious memories. Gideon Haigh wrote this in the *Guardian*: 'Adelaide '06 deserves to haunt this generation of English cricketers as Headingley '81 once haunted Australians. Having waited fifteen years to recapture the Ashes, they donated them back in an hour.' That Adelaide Test was the last I watched or listened to that winter. When asked how I felt the cricket was going, my stock answer was, what cricket might that be?

Favourite Tests

Brisbane, December 9, 10, 12, 13, 14 1960

AUSTRALIA vs WEST INDIES: First Test

West Indies

C C Hunte	c Benaud b Davidson	24	—	c Simpson b Mackay	39
C W Smith	c Grout b Davidson	7	—	c O'Neill b Davidson	6
R B Kanhai	c Grout b Davidson	15	—	c Grout b Davidson	54
G St A Sobers	c Kline b Meckiff	132	—	b Davidson	14
*F M M Worrell	c Grout b Davidson	65	—	c Grout b Davidson	65
J S Solomon	hit wkt b Simpson	65	—	lbw b Simpson	47
P D Lashley	c Grout b Kline	19	—	b Davidson	0
†F C M Alexander	c Davidson b Kline	60	—	b Benaud	5
S Ramadhin	c Harvey b Davidson	12	—	c Harvey b Simpson	6
W W Hall	st Grout b Kline	50	—	b Davidson	18
A L Valentine	not out	0	—	not out	7
	lb 3, w 1	4		b 14, lb 7, w 2	23
		453			**284**

1–23, 2–42, 3–65, 4–239, 5–243,
6–283, 7–347, 8–366, 9–452, 10–453

1–13, 2–88, 3–114, 4–127,
5–210, 6–210, 7–241,
8–250, 9–253, 10–284

Davidson	30–2–135–5		Davidson	24.6–4–87–6
Meckiff	18–0–129–1		Meckiff	4–1–19–0
Mackay	3–0–15–0		Mackay	21–7–52–1
Benaud	24–3–93–0		Benaud	31–6–69–1
Simpson	8–0–25–1		Simpson	7–2–18–2
Kline	17.6–6–52–3		Kline	4–0–14–0
			O'Neill	1–0–2–0

Australia

C C McDonald	c Hunte b Sobers	57	—	b Worrell	16
R B Simpson	b Ramadhin	92	—	c sub b Hall	0
R N Harvey	b Valentine	15	—	c Sobers b Hall	5
N C L O'Neill	c Valentine b Hall	181	—	c Alexander b Hall	26
L E Favell	run out	45	—	c Solomon b Hall	7
K D Mackay	b Sobers	35	—	b Ramadhin	28
A K Davidson	c Alexander b Hall	44	—	run out	80
*R Benaud	lbw b Hall	10	—	c Alexander b Hall	52
†A T W Grout	lbw b Hall	4	—	run out	2
I Meckiff	run out	4	—	run out	2
L F Kline	not out	3	—	not out	0
	b 2, lb 8, w1, nb 4	15		b 2, lb 9, nb 3	14
		505			232

1–84, 2–138, 3–194, 4–278, 5–381, 6–469, 7–484, 8–489, 9–496, 10–505

1–1, 2–7, 3–49, 4–49, 5–57, 6–92, 7–226, 8–228, 9–232, 10–232

Hall	29.3–1–140–4
Worrell	30–0–93–0
Sobers	32–0–115–2
Valentine	24–6–82–1
Ramadhin	15–1–60–1

Hall	17.7–3–63–5
Worrell	16–3–41–1
Sobers	8–0–30–0
Valentine	10–4–27–0
Ramadhin	17–3–57–1

Umpires: C J Egar (A) and C Hoy (A)

Test cricket is such a finely tuned animal that genuinely close matches aren't rare, they are blessedly, diamonds-on-the-soles-of-your-shoes rare. When, on the last day of a Test match, a commentator says, 'All four results are still possible,' it's with a sense of wonder that such a thing could be true. And one of those four is the rarest of all, to the extent that for the first eighty-three years (and 501 matches) of Test cricket, it didn't actually happen.

The West Indies, captained by Frank Worrell, scored 453 in

their first innings, during which Gary Sobers scored his first fifty in only fifty-seven minutes, reached his tenth century and passed three thousand in Tests. Australia, led by Richie Benaud, countered with 505. We had two well-matched sides, oozing with talent. Both Worrell and Benaud believed in attacking cricket, so much so, in fact, that they actually played it. The only other sign that this Test could be special was that, for the first time, both umpires were called Col. The West Indies notched up 284 in their second innings, so Australia needed 233 to win in 310 minutes. Wrote Benaud, 'in retrospect, surely the most nerve-racking 310 minutes of all time'.

His side started badly. Bobby Simpson ducked into a Wes Hall bouncer and popped the ball to short leg. Neil Harvey went to a brilliant catch by Sobers at slip. Benaud's advice to Norm O'Neill as he went out to bat: 'Have a look and then thrash them.' But Hall was calling the tune: in his autobiography he wrote, 'I was fresh, marvellously fresh. I hurtled into the attack with a vigour which even I found a little amazing.' In the hour before lunch Australia scored just 30. After lunch O'Neill and Colin McDonald went slightly mad and hit 28 off four Hall overs, but then they got out: 49 for 2 became 57 for 5. Ken Mackay and Alan Davidson added 35 before Mackay tried to drive Sunny Ramadhin's leg-break and was bowled. 92 for 6. Benaud strode to the crease to join Davidson. 'I hadn't made many runs lately,' said Benaud, 'but if they were to come along, today would be the best time I could possibly imagine.'

They survived until tea, when 123 runs were still needed. Benaud was sipping his rooibos when he was joined by the Chairman of Selectors, Sir Donald Bradman.

'What are you going for, Richie? A win or a draw?' asked Sir Donald.

'A win, of course,' said Richie.

'I'm very pleased to hear it.'

Davidson had taken eleven wickets in the match and scored 44 in the first innings. 'What will happen when he's not around to bat, bowl and field for Australia brings a furrow to my brow,' said Benaud. The captain thought the West Indies would crack before he did. 'Pressure and more and more pressure and they'll crack ... they've done it so often before.' But this time they had a leader, 'a great player in his own right, a shrewd tactician and a man who had the respect and liking of his side, and of the opposition too'. Benaud and Davidson added around 50 in even time. 'In the crowd there was a frenzy I hadn't seen before at a cricket ground.' At the centre, though, the players remained cool. The runs mounted. The new ball was taken but the batsmen survived. At ten to six, Australia needed nine runs to win, with four wickets still intact.

But with seven still needed, disaster. Benaud pushed one wide of Joe Solomon at short square leg, called one, Solomon swooped, threw down the stumps and Davidson was run out. 'It was a bad call,' admitted Benaud, 'a dangerous call.' Wally Grout, possibly the best-named wicketkeeper of all time, came in and took a quick single, and with one eight-ball over left, to be bowled by Wes Hall, Australia still needed six.

First ball, Grout was hit on the thigh. Benaud called for a single and they took a leg bye.

Second ball was a bouncer. Benaud tried to hook but edged it to the West Indian wicketkeeper, Gerry Alexander. 228 for 8. 'All yours, Wal,' said Benaud as he passed him on the way back to the pavilion. 'Thanks very much,' said Wal.

Third ball, the new batsman, Ian Meckiff, hit it to mid-off for no run.

Fourth ball, Wes bowled well down leg side, and Grout called Meckiff through for a bye. Four to win from four balls.

Fifth ball, Wes Hall bowled another bouncer, but Grout misjudged his shot and popped it up to Rohan Kanhai, waiting at backward square leg to take an easy catch. Unfortunately Hall, veering away from his follow-through, also wanted to take it. 'Next moment,' said Benaud, 'the ball was whisked away from Kanhai's steady hands and fell to the ground.' Grout took a single. Three required from three balls.

Sixth ball, Meckiff had a mow ('a five-iron,' said Benaud) and connected. The ball went to the mid-wicket boundary where Conrad Hunte was stationed and ran two runs. A third run would win the game, so the batsmen took it. Hunte was eighty yards away, but his throw was flat, true and straight into Alexander's gloves. The bails were whipped off before Grout could get home. Scores were tied. Australia were 239 for nine, with two balls left.

In the dressing room the last batsman, Lindsey Kline, had been desperately looking for his gloves, only to find he was sitting on them. Seventh ball, he hit the ball to square leg, where Joe Solomon was still fielding. 'They crossed as Solomon was just about to gather it in both hands,' wrote Benaud. 'He picked up as Meckiff got to within about six yards of the safety of the crease. Solomon the quiet one … good and dependable … the sort of man for a crisis.' For the second time in the over, he had one stump to aim at, and he hit it. Meckiff was run out by inches.

The batsmen thought they had lost. The fielders thought they might have won. It was Sir Donald Bradman who wandered over and told them they had tied. 'You've made history,' he said.

JULIAN'S XIs

Musical

1	Tuba Hassan	(Lahore Schools Under-17s Women)
2	A. Penny	(Stragglers of Asia)
3	Whistler	(Warwickshire Club and Ground)
4	S. Viola	(Finland)
5	E. Tempo	(United Services Portsmouth Second XI)
6	Forte	(Rydal School)
7	R. W. T. Key	(England, Kent, Marylebone Cricket Club)
8	C. Sharp	(Gentlemen of Leicestershire)
9	Major	(Niagara Falls)
10	A. Bass	(Leeward Islands)
11	C. Minor	(Rugby School)
12th men	A. Treble	(Australian Defence Force)
	A. Flatt	(Norfolk Under-13s Women)
	V. Drum	(Old Belvedere)
	D. Trill	(Brondesbury)

The Village Year

It's in December that the following year's fixtures begin to take shape, and you discover which of the various teams you play has decided to give you the boot. It's all done in a very civilised manner: someone who would have contacted you to offer you a game simply doesn't. In the dating world, they call it ghosting. You meet someone a few times, you appear to be getting on really well, but in fact they're utterly tired of you telling the same stories about your grandfather's Nazi past and your Aunt Jane's career in MI6. So they cut you adrift. They don't reply to your texts, they certainly don't reply to your phone calls, and they defriend you on Facebook. Something similar takes place in the fixture world, although there are problems if the two teams are villages just a few miles away from each other. Two villages I know very well had this problem. A had been playing B for years, but didn't want to any more because B were miserable cheating gits. So A pretended it had disbanded. Very clever, except that some of their other oppositions heard the rumour and didn't get in touch in the usual way. Within three seasons A's fixture list had declined to such an extent that they actually did have to disband. At least that's what they told me when I contacted them to arrange the usual fixture.

So far (and I write in December 2018), we have been sacked by two teams. One we were going to sack ourselves, so that's no problem. They were very good, and horrible, and regarded us with obvious contempt. The other, it's true, may have been a bit of a mismatch. We played them twice. Both times they batted first and scored (let's say) 223 for 3. Then we batted and scored (let's say, because this is exactly how many we got) 36 for 7. Then the rains fell, both times, and we got away with a squeaky-bum draw. My guess is that if they had beaten us fair and square on either occasion they would still want to play us, and thrash us within an inch of our lives. But two draws was two too many, and our delight in the result each time was obviously galling. Played two, drawn two. I'm not proud of much in my long and mainly ignoble cricketing career, but I'm pretty proud of that.

'... and once again we have interruption of play
caused by movement behind the bowler's arm ...'

Acknowledgements

A book like this rests on the broad backs of many previous writers, editors and snufflers of cricket trivia. But I owe a particular debt to four men – Julian Parker, Richard Corden, Mitchell Symons and Steven Lynch – who have helped me throughout the project with ideas, feedback, expertise and ridiculous lists of cricketers with the names of freshwater fish.

Thanks also to Richard Beswick, Zoe Gullen and everyone at Little, Brown for their support and enthusiasm;

to my agent Patrick Walsh;

to Caroline Kington, for permission to republish her late husband Miles's piece from *Punch*;

to Matt Thacker, for permission to reprint several bits and bobs from *The Nightwatchman*, including my own piece as the introduction;

to Edward McLachlan, Geoff Thompson, Cluff (John Longstaff) and Pak (Peter King) for their splendid cricketing cartoons;

to Sheila Molnar, Ian Hislop and *Private Eye* for permission to reprint those cartoons;

to Russell Taylor and Charles Peattie for permission to reprint the *Alex* strips;

to Christopher Lane, John Wisden & Co. Ltd and Bloomsbury Publishing plc for permission to reprint various contributions from *Wisden Cricketers' Almanack*;

and to the following for all the usual stuff: Tanya Aldred, Cliff Allen, Maxie Allen, James Berkmann, Martha Berkmann, Jean Berkmann-Barwis, Paula Bingham, Lawrence Booth, Lucy Brazier, Charlie Campbell, Simon Canter, Hugh Chevallier, Tim Cooper, Thomas Coops, Sam Craft, Amanda Craig, Tim de Lisle, Alan Doggett-Jones, Chris Douglas, Susie Dowdall, Sally Ann Fitt, Martin Griffiths, Mel Griffiths, Sarah Hesketh, Tom Holland, Jon Hotten, Sarah Jackson, David Jaques, Emma John, Bob Jones, Jarrod Kimber, Nick Lezard, Jim Lynch, Tom McIlwaine, Mark Mason, Lucy Maycock, Roger Morgan-Grenville, Sally Morris, Andrew Mueller, Nick Newman, Dan Norcross, Sammy Nourmand, Simon O'Hagan, David Owen, Georgia Pairtrie, Sandra Parsons, Francis Peckham, Richard Perkins, Neil Pool, Graham Pryke, Neal Ransome, Padraig Reidy, Andy Robson, Simon Rose, Patrick Routley, Tom Russell, Terence Russoff, Kate Saunders, Michael Simkins, Adam Smyth, Phil South, John Stern, Hilary Todd, Robin Welch, Alan White, Helen White, Adrian Williamson, Jonathan Wilson, Robert Wilson and Robert Winder.

Bibliography

Wisden Cricketers' Almanack (various)

The Nightwatchman: The Wisden Cricket Quarterly (various)

Jonathan Agnew (ed.), *Cricket: A Modern Anthology* (Blue Door, 2013)

John Barclay and Stephen Chalke (eds), *Team Mates* (Fairfield Books, 2016)

Simon Barnes, *Epic: A 30-Year Search for the Soul of Sport* (Simon & Schuster, 2018)

Marcus Berkmann, *Ashes to Ashes: 35 Years of Humiliation (and About 20 Minutes of Ecstasy) Watching England v Australia* (Abacus, 2009)

Derek Birley, *A Social History of English Cricket* (Aurum, 1999)

Geoffrey Boycott (with Terry Brindle), *Opening Up* (Sphere, 1980)

Geoffrey Boycott (with Terry Brindle), *In the Fast Lane: West Indies Tour, 1981* (Sphere, 1981)

Mike Brearley, *The Art of Captaincy* (Hodder & Stoughton, 1985)

Mike Brearley, *On Form* (Little, Brown, 2017)

J. L. Carr, *Carr's Illustrated Dictionary of Extra-Ordinary Cricketers* (Quartet, 1983)

Brian Close and Don Mosey, *I Don't Bruise Easily: The Autobiography of Brian Close* (Macdonald & Jane's, 1978)

Michael Davie and Simon Davie (eds), *The Faber Book of Cricket* (Faber & Faber, 1987)

Ted Dexter and Clifford Makins, *Testkill* (George Allen & Unwin, 1976)

Ted Dexter (with Ralph Dellor), *Ted Dexter's Little Cricket Book* (Bloomsbury, 1996)

Christopher Douglas, *Douglas Jardine: Spartan Cricketer* (Allen & Unwin, 1984)

Ramachandra Guha (ed.), *The Picador Book of Cricket* (Picador, 2001)

Duncan Hamilton, *The Kings of Summer: How Cricket's 2016 County Championship Came Down to the Very Last Match of the Season* (Safe Haven Books, 2017)

Jo Harman (ed.), *Cricketing Allsorts: The Good, The Bad, The Ugly (and the Downright Weird)* (John Wisden & Co., 2017)

Matthew Hayden, *Standing My Ground* (Aurum, 2011)

David Hopps, *A Century of Great Cricket Quotes* (Robson Books, 1998)

Rob Kelly, *Hobbsy: A Life in Cricket* (Von Krumm, 2018)

Aubrey Malone, *Wicket Wit: Quips and Quotes for the Cricket-Obsessed* (Summersdale, 2006)

Vic Marks, *Marks Out of XI: England's Winter Tour – India & Australia 1984–1985* (Allen & Unwin, 1985)

Mark Nicholas, *A Beautiful Game: My Love Affair with Cricket* (Allen & Unwin, 2016)

Michael Parkinson, *Cricket Mad* (Stanley Paul & Co., 1969)

Harry Pearson, *Slipless in Settle: A Slow Turn Around Northern Cricket* (Little, Brown, 2010)

Amol Rajan, *Twirlymen: The Unlikely History of Cricket's Greatest Spin Bowlers* (Yellow Jersey Press, 2011)

David Rayvern Allen (ed.), *The Punch Book of Cricket* (Granada, 1985)

Philip Rhys Evans, *A Country Doctor's Commonplace Book* (Slightly Foxed, 2018)

Alan Ross (ed.), *The Penguin Cricketer's Companion* (Penguin, 1979)

Rowland Ryder, *Cricket Calling* (Faber & Faber, 1995)

Martin Smith (ed.), *Not in My Day, Sir: Cricket Letters to* The Daily Telegraph (Aurum, 2011)

Martin Smith (ed.), *The Promise of Endless Summer: Cricket Lives from* The Daily Telegraph (Aurum, 2013)

Rob Smyth, *The Spirit of Cricket: What Makes Cricket the Greatest Game on Earth* (Elliott & Thompson, 2010)

Rob Steen and Alastair McLellan, *500–1: The Miracle of Headingley '81* (BBC, 2001)

Geoff Tibballs, *No-Balls and Googlies: A Cricket Companion* (Michael O'Mara, 2013)

Phil Tufnell (with Peter Hayter), *The Autobiography: What Now?* (CollinsWillow, 1999)

Chris Waters, *Fred Trueman: The Authorised Biography* (Aurum, 2011)

John White, *The England Cricket Miscellany* (Carlton, 2006/8)

Notes

January

11 *'incorrigible romantic'*: Neville Cardus, 'The Millionaire of Spin', reprinted in Guha (ed.), *The Picador Book of Cricket*.
    'He has always, I fancy . . . ': R. C. Robertson-Glasgow, 'A king without a crown', *The Cricketer* (March 1964).
    'There was no triumph in me . . . ': Arthur Mailey, *10 for 66 and All That* (Phoenix Sports Books, 1958).
13 *'poetic, with flowing follow-throughs . . . '*: Steve Waugh, *Out of My Comfort Zone: The Autobiography* (Michael Joseph, 2006).
    'the historian in Waugh . . . ': Smyth, *The Spirit of Cricket*.
14 *'Only once did I see him flummoxed . . . '*: Mike Selvey, 'Flowing conversation', *Wisden* 2013.
15 *'Harrow men object strongly . . . '*: F. S. Ashley-Cooper, *Eton v Harrow at the Wicket* (St James's Press, 1922).
    'Byron played in that match . . . ': John Arthur Lloyd, quoted in Robert Harregar, 'Byron and Cricket', *The Byron Journal*, 14:1 (1986).
    'We have played the Eton . . . ': Letter to Charles O. Gordon, quoted in Ashley-Cooper, *Eton v Harrow at the Wicket*.
19 *'I can't remember exactly the first time . . .*: Quoted in 'Rahul Dravid reveals who first coined his nickname "The Wall"', zeenews.india.com, 20 July 2016.
20 *'Who wouldn't want to be me?'*: Chris Gayle, *Six Machine: I Don't Like Cricket . . . I Love It* (Viking, 2016).
22 *'When I first came to Adelaide . . . '*: Ashley Mallett, 'Of Scarlet, Fitteran, Cho, and others', ESPNcricinfo, 21 March 2014.
23 *'"Romney" might have been slightly more original'*: Frank Keating, 'Down Under and Out', reprinted in Guha (ed.), *The Picador Book of Cricket*.
    'There was nothing secret to it . . . ': Selvey, 'Flowing conversation'.
24 *'Sometimes they call me The Badger . . . '*: David Hopps, 'Badger revels in his role as England head pest', *Guardian*, 22 January 2007.
    'the most abrasive and irritating . . . ': Andy Bull, 'Why I love The Badger', *Guardian*, 7 February 2007.

25   *'Sausages were my favourite ... '*: Marcus Trescothick, *Coming Back To Me* (HarperSport, 2008).

February

33   *'On and off the pitch ... '*: 'Obituary: Bill Alley', *Telegraph*, 30 November 2004.
       'a gesture tantamount to tickling ... ': Quoted in ibid.
34   *'as good a player as anyone'*: Quoted in *Wisden* obituary, 1963.
       once rhymed his surname with 'rhododendron': John Betjeman, 'Pot Pourri from a Surrey Garden'.
35   *'He argued with authority ... '*: Quoted in Chris Waters, '"He could be harsh and gentle; witty and crude; selfish and kind. And he was, when the fire burned, as fine a fast bowler as any"', *Yorkshire Post*, 3 July 2006.
       'To say that it was one of the most ... ', Chris Waters, 'What's Goin' Off Out There', *The Nighwatchman*, 19 (autumn 2017).
36   *'A craftsman in a great tradition ... '*: Neville Cardus, 'Five stalwarts retire', *Wisden* 1960.
       'I think I was saying 3–0 or 4–0 ... ': Quoted in 'The Ashes: Days to go', *Telegraph*, 20 November 2006.
37   *'The doyen of English cricket writers ... '*: Reprinted in Smith (ed.), *The Promise of Endless Summer*.
38–9   *'It is a trick familiar ... '*: Quoted in Gordon Ross, 'Arrested in New Zealand', *Wisden* 1976.
39   *'Holding's feet hardly touched the ground ... '*: Bob Woolmer, 'The pain was incredible', ESPNcricinfo, 7 May 2009.
39–40 *'The first delivery was short of a length ... '*: Boycott, *Opening Up*.
40   *'He is the most complete batsman ... '*: Simon Hughes, 'A team player, freakish hitter and inventive shot-maker ... AB is cricket's Superman', *The Cricketer*, 23 May 2018.
41   *'A cricket ball can't hurt you'*: Quoted in Brearley, *On Form*.
       'Fielding in direct line of fire ... ': Brearley, *On Form*.
       'This champagne is all right ... ': In Hopps, *A Century of Great Cricket Quotes*.
42   *'I wonder if you see a ball very clearly ... '*: Quoted in Michael Billington, 'Eric Hollies', in John Stern (ed.), *My Favourite Cricketer* (A & C Black, 2010).
       'To catch a great sporting moment ... ': Simon Barnes, 'The conscience of cricket', *The Nightwatchman*, 19 (autumn 2017).
       'Come round. And bring your thirst': Quoted in ibid.
44   *'a novelist's fast bowler ... '*: Tanya Aldred, 'Tim Bresnan', *Wisden* 2012.
52   *'They couldn't complain ... '*: Quoted in Arunabha Sengupta, 'Cricketing Rifts 21: Holding's kick and Croft's shoulder charge', cricketcountry.com, 2 May 2012.
       'Clive Lloyd admits now ... ': Ibid.

March

59   *'Here, on the lovely ground at Hawes ... '*: 'The Unplayable Jeeves', in Ryder, *Cricket Calling*.

61   *'He's got a reputation for being awkward . . . '*: In Malone, *Wicket Wit*.
      'became introspective', 'In 1893 . . . ': Brian Halford, 'Agitator, Accumulator,
      Bore', *The Nightwatchman*, 9 (spring 2015).
64   *'To compound all his other frustrations . . . '*: Jon Hotten, *The Meaning of
      Cricket: Or, How to Waste Your Life on an Inconsequential Sport* (London:
      Yellow Jersey Press, 2016).
70   *'Their efforts not only dispelled . . . '*: Dicky Rutnagur, '2000–01 – India v
      Australia (Second Test): Very Very Special', *Wisden* 2002.
73   *'An indiscretion of youth'*: Quoted in Greg Baum, 'The Centenary Test 40
      years on – cricket with style', *Port Stephens Examiner*, 11 March 2017.
      'its concentration, soundness . . . ': David Rayvern Allen (ed.), *Arlott on
      Cricket: His Writings on the Game* (Willow Books, 1984).
74   *'This is not a f***ing tea party, Randall'*: Quoted in Berkmann, *Ashes to
      Ashes*.
      'a bit of a royalist': Quoted in Baum, 'The Centenary Test 40 years on'.

April

81   *'David Gower makes batting . . . '*: Quoted in David Gower, *David Gower's
      50 Greatest Cricketers of All Time* (Icon Books, 2015).
      'It's hard work making batting look effortless': In Malone, *Wicket Wit*.
      'Late in 2012 against Sri Lanka . .': Greg Baum, 'The leading cricketer in the
      world, 2012: Michael Clarke', *Wisden* 2013.
      'Batsmen faced with the problem of playing . . . ': H. Natarajan, 'Profile: Bapu
      Nadkarni', ESPNcricinfo.
82   *'Ultimately, it is difficult to avoid the conclusion . . . '*: 'Obituary: Les
      Jackson', *Telegraph*, 30 April 2007.
85   *'Bellringer asked me if I'd done any Morse'*: Andrew Lycett, 'Blowing the
      Cover on Cricket's Spies', *The Nightwatchman*, 20 (winter 2017).
      'He was the first umpire to combine . . . ': In Hopps, *A Century of Great
      Cricket Quotes*.
      'insufficiently violent', 'unmanly and unGerman': Oliver Locker-Lampson,
      'Adolf Hitler as I Know Him', *Daily Mirror*, 30 September 1930.
86   *'Sachin Tendulkar is, in my time, the best player . . . '*: Quoted in 'Sachin
      Tendulkar to retire after 200th Test', *The Australian*, 11 October 2013.
      'reserve hampers of hock and chicken sandwiches . . . ': Denzil Batchelor,
      C. B. Fry (Phoenix House, 1951).
86–7 *'Charles wrung me by the hand . . . '*: Denzil Batchelor, 'Fry', in Ross (ed.),
      The Penguin Cricketer's Companion.
87   *'Douglas Jardine, who saw many great batsmen . . . '*: Jack Fingleton,
      Masters of Cricket: From Trumper to May (Heinemann, 1958).
88   *As Lord Dunglass . . . according to* Wisden: 'Profile: Sir Alec Douglas-
      Home', ESPNcricinfo.
89   *'a left-hand opening batsman . . . '*: 'Obituary: Samuel Beckett', *Wisden* 1989.
      'I wouldn't go that far': Quoted in Mel Gussow, 'Samuel Beckett Is Dead
      at 83; His "Godot" Changed Theater', *New York Times*, 27 December
      1989.
90   *'tidy rather than terrifying'*: Lawrence Booth, 'Profile: Alan Mullally',
      ESPNcricinfo.

'Few players ... have carried the fortunes': Andrew Miller, 'Profile: Sir Richard Hadlee', ESPNcricinfo.

92   *'about to reshape the game in his image'*: Jon Hotten, 'The Oval's Soul', *The Nighwatchman*, 17 (spring 2017).

According to Sir John Major: Speech at the Pitch Perfect Cricket Diversity Dinner, 28 June 2010. Transcript at http://www.johnmajorarchive.org.uk/2010-2010/sir-john-majors-speech-at-the-pitch-perfect-cricket-diversity-dinner-28-june-2010/.

93   *'This was more impenetrable to the Germans ... '*: 'Obituary: Garland-Wells, Herbert Montandon', *Wisden* 1993.

'I would not have done ... ': Andy Sandham, 'A lifetime with Surrey', *Wisden* 1972.

94   *'To call him a run-getting machine ... '*: Quoted in Arunabha Sengupta, '21-year-old Don Bradman scores 309 in a day against England', cricketcountry.com, 25 June 2014.

'I tend to believe that cricket ... ': 'Pinter on Pinter', *Observer*, 5 October 1980.

95   *'How well I remember ... '*: Charles Collingwood, 'Anthony Ainley', in Barclay and Chalke (eds), *Team Mates*.

96   *'Getting Martin out'*: Brydon Coverdale, 'Profile: Chris Martin', ESPNcricinfo.

99   *'The Australians'*: Rob Craddock, 'West Indies v Australia: Third Test', *Wisden* 1996.

'It's Test cricket': Quoted in ibid.

100   *'To stand up to the best fast bowler ... '*: Quoted in Hotten, *The Meaning of Cricket*.

'had 17 fours, one six and six aching bruises ... ': Rob Craddock, 'West Indies v Australia: Fourth Test', *Wisden* 1996.

May

107   *'In the 2000s alone ... '*: Smyth, *The Spirit of Cricket*.

107–8   *'I went up to the changing room ... '*: Kelly, *Hobbsy*.

108   *'As a hitter, Jessop stands absolutely alone ... '*: H. S. Altham, 'The Golden Age of Batting: Ranji, Fry, Jessop', in H. S. Altham and E. W. Swanton, *A History of Cricket* (George Allen & Unwin, 1926; repr. 1949).

109   *'A shortish man ... '*: Carr, *Carr's Illustrated Dictionary of Extra-Ordinary Cricketers*.

'One afternoon Compton came in ... ': E. W. Swanton, 'Compton', in Ross (ed.), *The Penguin Cricketer's Companion*.

'hit sixes in accordance with his religious convictions': 'Obituary: T. C. "Dickie" Dodds', *Telegraph*, 20 September 2001.

110   *'You and I are amateurs'*, *'You've got to enjoy it ... '*, *'You know, Dickie ... '*: Quoted in ibid.

'Maurice Tate took 2783 wickets ... ': Carr, *Carr's Illustrated Dictionary of Extra-Ordinary Cricketers*.

111   *'So accomplished was his batsmanship ... '*: In Guha (ed.), *The Picador Book of Cricket*.

'Bradman's curious deficiency on wet wickets ... ': C. L. R. James, *Beyond a Boundary* (Hutchinson, 1963).

113   'I always found facing Devon Malcolm ... ': Quoted in *The Nightwatchman*, 18 (summer 2017).

114   'His personal example was outstanding ... ': Michael Atherton, 'Angus Fraser', in Barclay and Chalke (eds), *Team Mates*.

114   'Eeyore without the joie de vivre': Mike Selvey, 'Cricketer of the Year – Angus Fraser', *Wisden* 1996.

115   'We knew Richards was phenomenal ... ': Vic Marks, 'Viv Richards', in Barclay and Chalke (eds), *Team Mates*.
        'At county level Tavaré frequently belied ... ': Vic Marks, 'Chris Tavaré', in ibid.

116   'Warne owned the head-space of Cullinan ... ': Steve Waugh, *The Meaning of Luck* (Sams Marketing, 2013).

117   'Histrionics were not for him ... ': Mike Selvey, 'Wayne Daniel', in Barclay and Chalke (eds), *Team Mates*.

117–18 'Jack Simmons joined Lancashire very late in life ... ': David Lloyd, 'Jack Simmons', in ibid.

118   'On the field with him you sense ... ': Tony Lewis, 'Illingworth on a collision course with Atherton', *Telegraph*, 26 April 1994.
        'If I had my way, I would take him to the Traitor's Gate ... ': Quoted in Robert Winder, 'You'd be mad to do it, Beefy; PROFILE: Ian Botham', *Independent*, 6 April 1996.

119   'I loved the challenge of testing myself against Hansie ... ': Paul Nixon, *Keeping Quiet: The Autobiography* (History Press, 2012).

122   'A personable man, with a fondness for a pint and a fag ... ': Derek Pringle, 'Graham Dilley: Sultan of swing and Ashes hero', *Telegraph*, 5 October 2011, reprinted in Smith (ed.), *The Promise of Endless Summer*.

123   'I don't like you Reeve ... ': Dermot Reeve with Patrick Murphy, *Dermot Reeve's Winning Ways* (Boxtree, 1997).
        'His ability to be where the fast bowlers aren't ... ': *The Age*, 4 April 1978.
        'As I stood at the non-striker's end ... ': Mike Brearley and Dudley Doust, *The Ashes Retained* (Hodder & Stoughton, 1979).
        'Real officer class. Languid self-possession ... ': In Hopps, *A Century of Great Cricket Quotes*.
        'He was unstoppable. I'll be going to bed having nightmares ... ': As at 'Quotes of the Year', *Guardian*, 24 December 1998.

June

129   a poem called 'The Oval (1882)': Also known as 'Eighty-five to Win'. In John Masefield, *The Bluebells: and Other Verse* (Macmillan, 1961).
        'the most selfish cricketer I've ever played with': Ronny Lerner and Jesse Hogan, 'Shane Warne hits out at Steve Waugh, "the most selfish cricketer I've ever played with"', *Sydney Morning Herald*, 9 February 2016.

130   'A number six who comes out as all number sixes should ... ': Barney Ronay, 'Why England need to take a chance on talent and alter their top six', *Guardian*, 14 April 2018.

131   'I've heard it said that this game at Test level ... ': In Hopps, *A Century of Great Cricket Quotes*.
        'Ninety per cent of cricket is played in the mind': Ibid.

'If they want me to get down to that weight ... ': Angus Fraser, 'Giles' hip injury gives Blackwell his opportunity', *Independent*, 8 February 2006.

131–2 *'I definitely believe if any of our batsmen ... '*: 'Voyeurs, berets and Rip Van Winkle – the year in quotes', *Guardian*, 30 December 2005.

132 *'Theirs was one of the great rivalries of cricket ... '*: In Guha (ed.), *The Picador Book of Cricket*.

133 *'He has emerged from a hard school ... '*: Neville Cardus, 'Hutton, Hobbs and the Classical Style', in Nick Coleman and Nick Hornby (eds), *The Picador Book of Sportswriting* (Picador, 1996).

'Like probably all men who can do one thing better ... ': Alan Ross, *Cape Summer and the Australians in England* (Hamish Hamilton, 1957).

'I am Yorkshire bred and born ... ': Quoted in ibid.

134 *'What [can] metrics tell you ... '*: Andy Bull, 'You weigh Pietersen's achievements by the memories you are left with', *Guardian*, 20 March 2018.

135 *'Many of the most interesting pupils ... '*: Jonathan Smith, *The Learning Game: A Teacher's Inspirational Story* (Little, Brown, 2000).

136 *'Mason Crane has an unforgettable name ... '*: Vic Marks, 'County cricket returns with a curious buzz around the English game', *Observer*, 8 April 2017.

145 *in Mike Selvey's words*: Mike Selvey, 'Graham Gooch's finest hour', *Guardian*, 10 June 2011.

145–6 *'All I could do was to fight every ball ... '*: Quoted in Abhishek Mukherjee, 'Graham Gooch's 154 not out: One of the greatest innings of all time', cricketcountry.com, 9 June 2016.

148–9 *'While Walsh and Ambrose regularly honed in ... '*: Martin Johnson, 'First Cornhill Test: England v West Indies 2000', *Wisden* 2001.

July

157 *'It's a prized possession'*: Quoted in Derek Pringle, 'Sir Alec Bedser: A gentle giant whose timeless values still inspire', *Telegraph*, 5 April 2010.

158 *'Lockie would attack ... '*: Quoted in Rob Steen, 'Heroes and villains', *Guardian*, 30 July 2006.

158–9 *'In the early days, I was doing the experimental trials ... '*: Interview in Max Arthur, *Dambusters: A Landmark Oral History* (Virgin Books, 2008).

159 *'His lack of privacy surpasses anything ... '*: Marks, *Marks Out of XI*.

'the audacity and cunning of an ape ... ': 'Zero', *The Secret History of the Coningham Case* (Finn Brothers, 1901).

160 *'No monument, no portrait, no book ... '*: Lord Hawke, *The Memorial Biography of Dr W. G. Grace* (Constable & Co., 1919).

'He turned the old one-stringed instrument ... ': K. S. Ranjitsinhji, *The Jubilee Book of Cricket* (William Blackwood and Sons, 1897).

'W. G.'s batting had grandeur and not elegance': A. A. Thomson, 'The Great Cricketer', in Ross (ed.), *The Penguin Cricketer's Companion*.

'There is something monumental in his stance ... ': Andrew Lang, quoted in ibid.

'Leaving the ball alone never won matches': Quoted in ibid.

'He exists in our imagination ... ': Matthew Engel, quoted in Smyth, *The Spirit of Cricket*.

'beyond reasonable doubt': *Wisden* 2010.

161   *'He is one of the great fast bowlers . . . '*: David Frith, 'Dennis Lillee', in Ross (ed.), *The Penguin Cricketer's Companion*.

164   *'pale and determined by the midship rail aft of lifeboat 7 '*: 'Mr John Borland Thayer', encyclopedia-titanica.org.

165   *'The amount of time I spend away . . . '*: Andrew Baker, 'Taylor takes pleasure in double delivery', *Independent on Sunday*, 24 December 1995.

166–7   *[Bill Bradley's] first delivery I hardly saw . . . '*: Sir Arthur Conan Doyle, *Memories and Adventures: An Autobiography* (1905).

170   *'There will be nets tomorrow . . . '*: Quoted in Tibballs, *No Balls and Googlies*.

171   *the spy writer Andrew Lycett asked her*: In 'Blowing the Cover on Cricket's Spies', *The Nightwatchman*, 20 (winter 2017).

172   *'Those who cannot remember the past . . . '*: Santayana, *The Life of Reason: The Phases of Human Progress. Vol. 1: Reason in Common Sense* (1905).
        'Every television screen . . . ': 'Nuclear Test', *Telegraph*, 17 October 2000.

175   *'It was mid-July, but it felt like mid-April'*: Mike Brearley, *Phoenix from the Ashes: The Story of the England–Australia Series, 1981* (Willow, 1983).
        'One particular six . . . ': Gavin Ewart 'A Pindaric Ode on the Occasion of the Third Test Match Between England and Australia, Played at Headingley, 16–21 July, 1981', in *Selected Poems, 1933–1993* (Faber, 1996).

178   *'Some of the players made really terrible sandwiches'*: Quoted in Matthew Engel (ed.), *WHAT Did you Say Stopped Play? 25 Years of the* Wisden *Chronicle* (Bloomsbury, 2018).

August

183   *'His greatest contribution'*: Sir Learie Constantine, 'Destroyer of Myth', *Wisden* 1968.
        'We sat together in the back . . . ': Frank Keating, 'Down Under and Out', in Guha (ed.), *The Picador Book of Cricket*.

184   *'Angus Fraser deals in parsimony . . . '*: Mike Selvey, 'Cricketer of the Year – Angus Fraser', *Wisden* 1996.
        'I know from watching him bowl . . . ': Quoted in Michael Henderson, 'Raise a glass to Cook and all those men of grace', *Guardian*, 30 September 2008.

185   *'Tall, angular, beaky, balding . . . '*: Quoted in 'Passing – and failing – the cricket test', *Jewish Chronicle*, 15 July 2013.
        'Exactly fifty years ago (Saturday 27 August) . . . ': Reprinted in Smith (ed.), *Not in My Day, Sir*.

186   *'perhaps his most remarkable innings in a Test match . . . '*: Neville Cardus, *Cricket All the Year* (The Sportsman's Book Club, 1953).
        'Bradman will be batting tomorrow': Alan Eason, *The A–Z of Bradman* (ABC Books, 2004).
        'Is Don Bradman still alive?': Ibid.
        'It is strange, but I think true . . . ': Writing in *The Star*, 1938. Quoted in Charles Williams, *Bradman: An Australian Hero* (Phoenix, 2013).

188   *'I do not believe that brothers had ever before . . . '*: Quoted in Steven Lynch, 'Captain's hundreds, and a family dismissal', ESPNcricinfo, 5 June 2012.

189   *'A quick glance amongst the obvious candidates . . . '*: Quoted in Malcolm Watson, *The Wit and Wisdom of an Ordinary Subject* (Lulu.com, 2013).

189–90 *'Sir, Christopher Collins looks for the longest dismissal . . . '*: Ibid.

190   *the top ten, as compiled by criclife.com*: From H Natarajan, 'Top 25 long names in Sri Lankan cricket', criclife via cricketcountry.com, 23 December 2014.

192   *'I like the beauty of the game'*: Quoted in Richard Williams, 'Lily Allen's lyrical love of Test cricket is more than just flannel', *Guardian*, 25 August 2009.

193   *'one of the strangest sporting events . . . '*: Andrew Lownie, *Stalin's Englishman: The Lives of Guy Burgess* (Hodder & Stoughton, 2015).
         'the wives prepared a splendid tea . . . ': Andrew Lycett, 'Blowing the Cover on Cricket's Spies', *The Nightwatchman*, 20 (winter 2017).
         'a former American spy . . . ': Quoted in Lownie, *Stalin's Englishman*.
         'Honestly, if they send the key . . . ': Quoted in 'Ken Clarke loses red box key on Trent Bridge day off', BBC News, 30 July 2010.

194   *'A local umpire recalls having a chat with Chris . . . '*: Simon Turnbull, 'How Coldplay saved the sound of leather on willow', *Independent*, 2 June 2010.
         'Unexpectedly I suddenly identify . . . ': Hugh Cornwell, *A Multitude of Sins: The Autobiography* (HarperCollins*Entertainment*, 2004).
         'I might have more than five thousand . . . ': Quoted in 'Runs in the Family, *The Sun*, 22 March 2002.
         'secret gate-key to all [Pinter's] work': John Fowles, 'Afterword: Harold Pinter and Cricket', in Peter Raby (ed.), *The Cambridge Companion to Harold Pinter* (Cambridge University Press, 2001).

196   *'upper-class cricket commentator . . . '*: John le Carré, *The Tailor of Panama* (Hodder & Stoughton, 1996).
         'Oh Lord, if I must die today . . . ': Excerpt from 'Cricket Prayer', quoted in John Major, 'The Memories of the Oval', *The Times*, 7 September 2005.

196–7   *'Peter was bruised from head to foot . . . '*: Quoted in 'Obituary: Don Wilson', *Telegraph*, 2 October 2012.

197   *I saw Len Hutton in his prime*: Quoted in Michael Henderson, 'A cricketing Eden caught in no man's land', *Guardian*, 23 September 2008.
         'I am a geek': Matilda Battersby, 'Daniel Radcliffe: "I'm a geek, I'm obsessed with cricket. What a disappointment I must be to fans who meet me"', *Independent*, 5 November 2012.
         Keanu Reeves . . . mounted a stirring defence of the great game: Quoted in Matthew Engel (ed.), *WHAT Did you Say Stopped Play? 25 Years of the Wisden Chronicle* (Bloomsbury, 2018).

201   *'I must admit we were laughing a bit . . . '*: Quoted in Scott Oliver, '"I saw some of the so-called tough guys of world cricket tremble"', thecricketmonthly.com, 28 July 2017.
         'You guys are going to pay for this': Ted Corbett, '1994 – England v South Africa (Third Test): "You guys are history"', *Wisden* 1995.

202   *'the most devastating spell by an England bowler . . . '*: Ibid.
         'No one can honestly say they enjoy . . . ': Quoted in Oliver, '"I saw some of the so-called tough guys of world cricket tremble"'.
         'The South Africans, they crapped it a bit . . . ': Ibid.
         'absolutely murdered Allan [Donald] . . . ': Ibid.

September

213 *'perhaps the only unequivocally popular man in Yorkshire'*: 'Obituary: David Bairstow', *Wisden* 1998.
'He wasn't a great wicketkeeper ... ': Quoted in ibid.
'Evening, lad': Quoted in ibid.

213–14 *'I might be sneezing just as a catch came in the slips'*: Quoted in 'Obituary: Norman Mitchell-Innes', *Telegraph*, 30 December 2006.

214 *'The Blue Mantles averages ... '*: Siegfried Sassoon, *The Weald of Youth* (Faber & Faber, 1942).
'a tall, wiry man, 6 feet 3 inches in height ...': F. S. Ashley-Cooper, *Cricket Highways and Byways* (George Allen & Unwin, 1927).

215 *'He was blest with supreme natural gifts'*: H. S. Altham, 'The Golden Age of Batting: Ranji, Fry, Jessop', in H. S. Altham and E. W. Swanton, *A History of Cricket* (George Allen & Unwin, 1926; repr. 1949).
'It's the only one of my innings ... ': Quoted in Rob Smyth, 'Remembering the remarkable West Indies v England winter of 1989–90', *Guardian*, 10 May 2012.
'He's supposedly shagged a thousand women ... ': Quoted in Matthew Engel (ed.), *WHAT Did you Say Stopped Play? 25 Years of the* Wisden *Chronicle* (Bloomsbury, 2018).

216 *a TV interview*: Quoted in 'Obituary: Colin Ingleby-Mackenzie', *Telegraph*, 15 March 2006.
'Golf,' he once said: In Hopps, *A Century of Great Cricket Quotes*.
'the one he let you see ... ': Barney Ronay, 'Jimmy Anderson, the Elvis of Lord's, sparkles between downpours', *Guardian*, 10 August 2018.

217–18 *'I never wanted to make a hundred'*: In Malone, *Wicket Wit*.

218 *'a very, very big bat, the biggest in the wooooorld'*: Charlotte Edwardes, 'Chris Gayle: "You don't know me"', *The Times*, 21 May 2016.
'From the pool to the strip club': https://www.instagram.com/p/7jQ5NGoeSp/

219 *just a few of his utterances*: Quoted by Christian Ryan, *The Nightwatchman*.

220 *'Possibly Jesus would not have fixed matches ... '*: Barnes, *Epic*.
'To get you from sixty to a hundred as quickly as possible': Quoted in Brearley, *On Form*.

220–1 *'I loved playing cricket as a kid'*: Quoted in Richard Rae, 'Brendon McCullum: New Zealand cricket has got soul again', *Observer*, 7 June 2015.

221 *'People were looking at me ... '*: Quoted in Tony Francis, *The Zen of Cricket: Learning from Positive Thought* (Hutchinson, 1992).

222 *'I'd have played Mitchell Johnson off the front foot'*: Crispin Andrews, '"I'd have played Mitchell Johnson off the front foot!"', thecricketmonthly.com, 15 December 2015.

228 *'Probably the most entertaining [series] in this country since 2005'*: Simon in 'England beat India by 118 runs in fifth Test for 4–1 series win – as it happened', *Guardian*, 11 September 2018.

October

235 *'One evening at dinner ... '*: Marina Warner, 'My grandfather, Plum', *Guardian*, 11 June 2004.

'*arguably the greatest of all fast bowlers ...* ': Reprinted in Smith (ed.), *The Promise of Endless Summer.*

236   '*History may well decide ...* ': Scyld Berry, 'Basil D'Oliveira: the cricket star's extraordinary life', *Telegraph*, 19 November 2011.

237   '*What has to be remembered, of course...* ': Quoted in R. W. Apple, Jr, 'England's cricket world aflame as 50 players flout tradition', *New York Times*, 27 July 1977.

'*Greig's other disadvantages as an England captain ...* ': Birley, *A Social History of English Cricket.*

'*You must remember that the West Indians ...* ': Quoted in Joyce Greig and Mark Greig, *Tony Greig: Love, War and Cricket – A Family Memoir* (Pan Macmillan, 2013).

238   '*Everyone had a copy*': Quoted in David Tossell, *Grovel! The Story and Legacy of the Summer of 1976* (Pitch Publishing, 2007).

240   '*spent a considerable time in Africa, and ...* ': Quoted in Andrew Renshaw (ed.), *Wisden on the Great War: The Lives of Cricket's Fallen 1914–1918* (John Wisden & Co., 2014).

241   '*I miss playing to such an extent that I can honestly say ...* ': Geoffrey Boycott, *Geoffrey Boycott on Cricket* (Ebury Press, 1999).

242   '*I play best when I'm surrounded by people who appreciate me*': In Hopps, *A Century of Great Cricket Quotes.*

'*To me and every member of the 1932–33 MCC side ...* ': Quoted in 'Obituary: Douglas Jardine', *Wisden* 1959.

'*He was sent by headquarters in Dunkirk ...* ': In Donald Trelford (ed.), *Sunday Best 3* (Observer/Victor Gollancz, 1983).

'*such an act of cold courage ...* ': Christopher Douglas, *Jardine: Spartan Cricketer* (Methuen, 2003).

243   '*Watching from the luxury of my couch ...* ': Martin Crowe, 'Why cricket needs yellow and red cards', ESPNcricinfo, 18 January 2015.

244   '*The greatest trick Michael Vaughan ever pulled ...* ': *The Nightwatchman*, 10 (summer 2015).

255   '*required to cover many slips from the bat*': John Nyren, *The Young Cricketer's Tutor and The Cricketers of my Time* (1833).

256   '*the man who covers the point and middle wicket*': Ibid.

November

263–4   *according to Jack Fingleton*: Fingleton, *Masters of Cricket.*

264   '*Marsh and Lillee would have a punt on the Martians landing ...* ': Steen and McLellan, *500–1.*

265   '*I'll never forget his face*': Quoted in Martin Williamson, 'From hospital to hero', ESPNcricinfo, 25 November 2006.

'*It were nowt but a sore throat*': Quoted in Henry Cowen, 'The Ten: Irresistible Comebacks', wisden.com, 17 January 2014.

267   '*It was a moment of imperishable glory*': 'Obituary: Roy Fredericks', *Telegraph*, 8 September 2000.

a wonderful, passionate obituary: Reprinted in Smith (ed.), *The Promise of Endless Summer.*

'*Always had a pint when I was bowling*': Quoted in ibid.

268   *'I will never see a greater fast bowler than Larwood'*: Quoted in ibid.

270   *'brown-nosed gnome'*: Ed Kemp, 'The Definitive: Matthew Hoggard', wisden.com, 24 October 2013.

271   *'He snarled at me constantly ... '*: Quoted in Tibballs, *No-Balls and Googlies*.

271–2   *'Herbert Sutcliffe is the serenest batsman ... '*: R. C. Robertson Glasgow, 'Three English Batsmen', in Guha (ed.), *The Picador Book of Cricket*.

272   *'Like a number of other top sportsmen ... '*: Harry Pearson, 'Broad shoulders and a wide bottom', *Wisden* 2011.
        'old man dangling free': Ian Botham, *Head On: The Autobiography* (Ebury Press, 2007).
        'then as now ... a man who had escaped ... ': Barnes, *Epic*.

273   *'I was at a preparatory school at Clifton about 1890 ... '*: Reprinted in Smith (ed.), *Not in My Day, Sir*.

273–4   *'I saw [E. M.] many times captain the Thornbury side ... '*: Ibid.

274   *'To young eyes, quickest to perceive the things ... '*: Ray Robinson, *From the Boundary* (Collins, 1951).
        'barely do him justice': David Frith, 'Fault lines in a hero's tale', ESPNcricinfo.
        'a romantic warrior ... a proper hero and a singular man': Reprinted in Smith (ed.), *The Promise of Endless Summer*.

276   *'I hear you are very keen on the game ... '*: Quoted in Leo McKinstry, *Jack Hobbs: England's Greatest Cricketer* (Yellow Jersey Press, 2011).
        'his variations reduced Richards to mere competence': Phil Walker, 'The Ten: Bunnies', wisden.com, 8 November 2013.

278   *'Mendes, whose latest production Othello ... '*: Matthew Slater, 'Cricket: Caldy put Shipton to the sword', *Independent*, 1 September 1997.
        'Always have an alternative career planned out ... ': Bennett Marcus, 'Sam Mendes's 25 Rules for Directors', *Vanity Fair*, 11 March 2014.

December

289   *'grave social risk'*, *'It's probably when I ... '*: Quoted in 'Obituary: Frank Parr', *Telegraph*, 3 June 2012.
        'an arrogant professional ... ': Quoted in 'Obituary: Harry Pilling', *Wisden* 2013.

290   *'We knew he was a very good player ... '*: Quoted in Richard Hobson, 'New attack quick to put Ponting on the back foot', *The Times*, 13 September 2005.

291   *'more like two burly farmhands ... '*: Barry Glendenning, 'From Lord's to the Ring got the job done – just like Freddie, in fact', *Guardian*, 2 December 2012.
        'uncomfortable', *'near third slip'*, *'disintegrating'*: From Hotten, *The Meaning of Cricket*.
        'something you can't prepare for ... ': Waugh, *Out of My Comfort Zone*.
        'Of all [fast] bowlers, Malcolm Marshall ... ': Simon Hughes, 'Sylvester Clarke', in Smith (ed.), *The Promise of Endless Summer*.

292   *'this shrewd, lean Surrey player ... '*: Carr, *Carr's Illustrated Dictionary of Extra-Ordinary Cricketers*.
        'It is well to note Hobbs's claim ... ': Fingleton, *Masters of Cricket*.

'*Can nothing be done for J. B. Hobbs . . .* ': 'Evoe' (E. V. Knox), 'Can Nothing Be Done?', *Punch*, vol. CLXIX (July–December 1925).

293   '*Cricket is the easiest sport in the world to take over*': In Malone, *Wicket Wit*.

294   '*the greatest Australian spinner never to . . .* ': In Harman (ed.), *Cricketing Allsorts*.

'*With these fellows out of the way . . .* ': Quoted in Malcolm Knox, *Bradman's War* (Viking, 2012).

'*a man of embedded prejudices*': Gideon Haigh and David Frith, *Inside Story: Unlocking Australian Cricket's Archives* (The Herald and Weekly Times Ltd, 2007).

'*You don't piss on statues*': Quoted in Greg Baum, 'Swiftly fades the Don', *Sydney Morning Herald*, 30 October 2011.

'*Doug has made eleven hundreds for Australia . . .* ': E. W. Swanton, *Swanton in Australia with the MCC 1946–1975* (Fontana/Collins, 1975).

295   '*if smoking was a sport, Doug Walters . . .* ': Tony Vermeer, '785,300 ciggies later, Doug Walters finally declares', *Sunday Telegraph (Australia)*, 30 January 2010.

295–6 '*I cannot think of a great player harder to coax . . .* ': In Ross (ed.), *The Penguin Cricketer's Companion*.

296   '*Cowdrey used the reputation he had carefully established . . .* ': Michael Henderson, 'There's cheating – and then there's Australia', *Telegraph*, 25 March 2018.

'*There are very few things as reassuringly English . . .* ': Barney Ronay, 'Alastair Cook's long goodbye begins and underlines his ongoing value', *Guardian*, 7 September 2018.

297   '*he played in an age when boundary hitting was popular . . .* ': Derek Pringle, 'David Shepherd's loss mourned throughout cricket', *Telegraph*, 28 October 2009.

'*Perhaps because it ticks so many . . .* ': Jonathan Liew, 'War Minus the Shooting', *The Nightwatchman*, 20 (winter 2017).

301   '*England batted like turtles with chronic fatigue syndrome*': Robert Craddock, 'Take that Poms', *Daily Telegraph (Sydney)*, 6 December 2006.

302   '*Adelaide '06 deserves to haunt this generation . . .* ': Gideon Haigh, 'Adelaide '06 will haunt England as Headingley '81 did Australia', *Guardian*, 6 December 2006.

305   '*in retrospect, surely the most nerve-racking 310 minutes of all time*': Richie Benaud, *A Tale of Two Tests* (Hodder & Stoughton, 1962).

'*Have a look and then thrash them*': Ibid.

'*I was fresh, marvellously fresh . . .* ': Wes Hall, *Pace Like Fire* (Pelham, 1966).

'*I hadn't made many runs lately*': Benaud, *A Tale of Two Tests*.

'*What are you going for, Richie? A win or a draw?*': Ibid.

306   '*What will happen when he's not around . . .* ': Ibid.

'*It was a bad call*': Ibid.

306–7 '*Next moment . . . the ball was whisked away . . .* ': Ibid.

307   '*a five-iron*', '*They crossed as Solomon . . .* ', '*You've made history*': Ibid.

Credits

Favourite Tests

The scorecards are reproduced by kind permission of
www.cricketarchive.com.

Images

   6   www.harry-tates.org.uk

   6   © Paul M. Fenwick 'Images of Lincolnshire'

 53   Allsport UK/Allsport/Getty Images

263   George Beldam/Popperfoto/Getty Images